Training for Service Delivery to Minority Clients

Edited by Emelicia Mizio
and Anita J. Delaney

Family Service Association of America
New York

This publication was supported by the Shell Companies Foundation, Inc., Houston, Texas, and by ADAMHA Training Grant No. MH 15095 from the Division of Manpower and Training Programs of the National Institute of Mental Health.

Library of Congress Cataloging in Publication Data

Main entry title:

Training for service delivery to minority clients.

1. Social service and race relations—United States—Addresses, essays, lectures. 2. Social workers—Training of—United States—Addresses, essays, lectures. 3. Minorities—United States—Addresses, essays, lectures. I. Mizio, Emelicia. II. Delaney, Anita J. III. Family Service Association of America.
HV91.T69   362.8′4′0973   80-23468

ISBN 0-87304-180-1

Printed in the United States of America

Contents

Foreword

As part of its continuing efforts to relate meaningfully to ethnic minority concerns, Family Service Association of America secured funding from the National Institute of Mental Health (NIMH) for a two-year project for the development of model mental health service delivery systems to black and Puerto Rican communities. The project reflects the desire of FSAA and its membership to respond more appropriately to minority needs and issues and represents a major attempt by FSAA to refine and develop the knowledge, understanding, and skills needed for working in partnership with ethnic communities.

Although it was not possible to obtain funding to include other ethnic minority groups, many of the project findings are applicable to these communities as well because of the commonality of concerns related to racism and poverty. Service deliverers and other mental health workers with access to this knowledge would thus be in a better position to implement more relevant programs for the various groups.

With the support obtained from NIMH, the cooperation of FSAA membership, and the help of other experts outside of the family service field, it was possible for FSAA to establish an Advisory, Committee and both a black and a Puerto Rican task force. As a result of participants' deliberations, agency visits and consultations, and a strong service-focused literature base, the reports of the black and Puerto Rican task forces were published in 1979. These reports represent the culmination of the first phase of the project—the identification of the relevant content needed for the delivery of culturally sensitive, skilled, effective human services in black and Puerto Rican communities, and the development of a model for delivery of these services.

The second project phase included the development of materials that were used in a continuing education three-day workshop. Participants included member and nonmember agency staff and educators. The workshop and consultation activity were designed to assist in the implementation of the models contained in the Task Force reports. The materials developed were refined and supplemented for inclusion in this volume; it is hoped that they will be used in other continuing education programs and worshops for training to work effectively in partnership with minority communities. The publication of *Training for Service Delivery to Minority Clients* represents the completion of the FSAA Ethnicity Project but not the ending of FSAA's commitment to the development of quality services for ethnic minority communities.

It is hoped that the task force reports and this publication will be useful to human service trainers, students, practitioners, program planners, and all who are concerned with the quality of services addressed to minority communities. Although the materials discuss observed social conditions and cultural patterns, it should be clear that the needs of minority communities are not static; it is, therefore, anticipated that the users of the service models developed will be able to take advantage of their basic flexibility to meet changing needs. It should also be understood that, with the additional knowledge gained from the use of these models, there will inevitably be modifications made in the materials used for training.

FSAA and I are deeply indebted to the Advisory Committee for the Ethnicity Project, to the black and Puerto Rican task forces, and to other concerned individuals who gave of their time so willingly in order to make the ethnicity project a success.

We are also most appreciative of the efforts of the voluntary contributors to this volume, and of Anita J. Delaney, assistant project director, and Emelicia Mizio, project director. Their endeavors have made this volume one that will serve as an important reference work as well as a useful tool for the provision of relevant services to the minority communities.

W. Keith Daugherty
General Director
Family Service Association
of America

Introduction

Traditional service agencies have not been able, for the most part, to relate meaningfully to minorities. Often this has been due, in part, to a lack of commitment. However, even when commitment has been integral, gaps in understanding and information have precluded effective help. We are assuming that those interested in utilizing this volume share a common concern and are genuinely committed to improving the quality of services to minority communities.

The purpose of this book is to present materials that will contribute to an evolving body of knowledge useful for training for work with minority populations. Despite the fact that content focuses specifically on the black and Puerto Rican experiences, there are commonalities of concerns for all minorities. We wish to emphasize these commonalities because we believe that coalition efforts in relation to racism and poverty are imperative if a more humane society is ever to come into existence. There are, of course, individual cultural aspects that require essential and critical consideration in planning service development and delivery for a particular group, and this specific information would need to be acquired in order to work effectively.

Although we claim no expertise on the cultures of other ethnic minority groups, all appear to be generally humanistic and to value an extended family system so that commonalities with blacks and Puerto Ricans do exist. Thus, discussions dealing with the impact of external systems on black and Puerto Rican families and their culture and lifestyles in transaction with the wider American society will probably be useful to other ethnic groups affected in similar ways. Learning to individualize and respond to the needs of a particular community can only serve to sensitize us to the uniqueness of all people and the commonalities of all human needs.

The themes of service underutilization are frequently found in the literature with reference to ethnic minority groups. It is our expectation that utilizing the frameworks and information presented here can serve to enhance the quality of services to all these groups. The articles in this book represent a total package that can serve as a beginning point for thinking through service delivery needs and de-

1

veloping service programs. We do regret that research is not placed more prominently in this collection, as we recognize that theory and practice must be able to stand up to careful scrutiny and pass the test of efficacy. We hope, nevertheless, that we have at least succeeded in conveying the essential role of consumer feedback as one important form of research endeavor.

It has been our intent to reflect a practice perspective as well as to present a theoretical context for practice with the critical understanding that refinement of this knowledge base must be an ongoing process. This would not have been sufficient without making certain that readers appreciate that work with minority communities must be placed within the greater social work milieu. The body of knowledge and universal services already in existence serve as a foundation from which to build and from which modifications will stem.

The book is divided into three sections: theoretical, cultural, and practice considerations. The material in this book is unique, supplied by a group of overworked, dedicated practitioners who were willing to share with us their knowledge gained from years of direct service to minority communities. Each contribution brings to this volume a base of expertise with its own intrinsic worth, and together they support a common goal of enhanced service to minority communities.

We are not necessarily in accord with every position taken or statement made in this collection; nor do we see the material as a definitive work. We do wish to support the perspective that looks at the minority experience in this country from the vantage point of concern about a racist societal structure that requires incremental changes, and a mental health delivery system that must be restructured for social justice to prevail. Part of the restructuring of the mental health system must be a commitment to the training of minority professionals who will have open access to the power structure of this country. Currently, there are far from sufficient minority professionals and, therefore, it is also necessary to train committed Anglos to work with minority populations. Improved and increased training efforts in this direction should not, however, become a substitute for and ignoring of the essential nature of minority power in the service structure.

Although the organizing principle of this book was to present a collection that could be used for an ongoing workshop or course, it is expected to have value to all practitioners wishing to increase their understanding and improve their skills. Also, because our great concern is that the critical nature of minority input at all levels will not be recognized and racist practices will be unconsciously perpetuated, we stress its use for a minority trainer who, with a positive ethnic identification and a broad knowledge base, would prove invaluable in spotting pitfalls and in fostering quality services to minorities.

Section I brings together a cluster of learning that is basic to planners and practitioners who are determined to increase their skills and wish to design and deliver relevant services to minority communities. Sound practice must rest on a firm foundation made up of a theoretical structure and compatible philosophical orientation, and this section attempts to provide the required underpinning. Understanding of the interlocking and complex processes of racism are promoted and presented as critical knowledge. Working toward the eradication of racism is seen as a top priority. Acknowledgment of the significance of cultural patterns in establishing social policy, in developing service programs, and in supporting effective functioning is highlighted. The application of this appreciation is presented as necessary for the enhancement of minority survival and achievement of potential within the context of what must be recognized as a pluralistic society. An examination of the pluralistic nature of this society with reference to social policy considerations is presented.

The conceptual framework provides a way of perceiving both the form and function of the racism that permeates our society and the cultural adaptations that develop to combat its harmful consequences to the victim. Using ecological systems concepts, the operation of macro and micro systems are seen with greater clarity, appreciation for minority adaptive potential develops, and the implications for change strategies begin to emerge. Beyond these issues, the article on racism examines our total implication in racist processes and attempts to help practitioners come to terms with this involvement. The article on theory is of vital concern. It attempts to create a synthesis of diverse concepts that appear to have importance for work with minority populations; too little has been done in this area. It is our expectation that this article will stimulate further thought in this area and the importance of the refinements of these concepts will have been conveyed.

The concept of the dual perspective provides one of the most valuable tools in training for work with minorities. Although this concept should be an integral part of the skills repertoire for work with all people, its use is essential to the core of effective services to minorities. Use of this framework broadens the service giver's perspective to permit simultaneous assessments of the immediate environment, larger social systems, and the social worker's own values and attitudes toward the ethnic group being scrutinized. The change agent thus sensitized is prepared for more accurate assessment of minority clients within their specific sociocultural contexts and better able to offer help in areas of need and withdraw when it appears that cultural help systems are functioning adequately.

Training for work with minorities is shown to require both cognitive and attitudinal understanding if change agents are to be prepared to address the needs of minority client systems whose life chances are frequently limited by the negative impact of external systems. Also included in the first section is a review of the black and Puerto Rican task force reports, which represent the culmination of the first year's work of the Ethnicity Project.[1] Although it is recommended that both reports be read in total, this review offers a historical perspective and understanding on how the philosophical and theoretical framework emerged.

Section II presents specific content on the black and the Puerto Rican experiences in a format that should enhance the capacity for understanding the role of ethnicity in shaping the development and functioning of minority group members in this society. This material provides a body of knowledge essential to the accurate perception of cultural systems operations in transactions with the environment for survival and achievement. The articles addressed to the black experience are presented in a context that views racism in close linkage with the development of the capital-labor relationship system in America. This framework gives clarity to the persistent nature of racism and poverty in this society, and the coping strategies that have evolved over time in the black community. As trainees begin to recognize the form and substance of the shifting institutional barriers to black survival and achievement, greater appreciation develops for the natural support systems that can be used in the change or eradication of those elements interfering with the development of human potential. The study of the black experience can help in understanding the experience of other minorities.

Although the history and culture of black people has been widely studied and documented, the Puerto Rican experience has only in recent years begun to arouse the interest of researchers and human service planners. The articles addressing the history and cultural patterns of Puerto Ricans add a valuable body of knowledge to the social work literature base and are essential for training in the delivery of culture-specific mental health services to Puerto Rican communities. These materials provide a framework that enhances perception of Puerto Rican transactions with environmental systems and promotes the design of services to deal with the impact of external systems and internal stress, using culturally compatible and functional change strategies.

A comparison of black and Puerto Rican histories and cultures

4

reveals each group's unique qualities and highlights their similarities. The common experience of both groups, with institutional patterns of racism in larger systems and the resulting poverty, has produced commonalities in family structure and other coping mechanisms. Recognition of these commonalities provides a rationale for the development of coalitions. A service that succeeds in bringing these two groups together, as well as other oppressed minorities, would serve to enhance their understanding and respect for each other while strengthening the base of power required for the resolution of common issues.

Section III is designed primarily for service organizations and practitioners engaged in direct community practice, but nevertheless should be useful to others who also require a practice perspective. A practice perspective is essential to the policymaker as well as to the program designer. Although this material does not require the reading the task force reports, taken together they form a more comprehensive package.

It was the recommendation of both task forces that services provided by family service agencies should include at minimum advocacy, counseling, and preventive programs. Because societal conditions have a destructive impact on minority populations, advocacy is viewed as the core service. There are articles specifically dealing with these three services. These articles show how minority status enters into the provision of direct services and also reflect on techniques that cut across minority groups. There are specific details with reference to modifications in treatment related to cultural considerations that are necessary to engage the client successfully. It must be remembered that although modifications are stressed, the relationship factor is highly significant as in work with all clients.

The article that describes a model mental health program addressed to the needs of a Puerto Rican community delineates some of the most common errors made in offering services with limited knowledge of culturally different populations. The framework's applicability for blacks and other racially or linguistically different populations is readily seen as the model is well grounded in basic social work principles. Agencies committed to providing service to minority clients cannot afford to be one-service programs or psychoanalytic treatment centers. Low-income minority group members as well as poor white ethnics rarely, if ever, fit neatly into a predetermined structure; becoming clients of such predetermined structures means having needs go unserved. Even if this population may initially identify specific problem areas, it is essential that open access to other services be made available as needed. The critical nature of service

5

integration is examined and insight provided into how this can be achieved structurally and programatically. The differences in process and goals among these three prominent service components of family agencies are examined in depth. For their purposes to be achieved and linkages to be established, this understanding is essential. The critical nature of advocacy is again also highlighted in this article.

Because it will not be possible for practitioners to deny the responsibility to serve as advocates for their clients, the pieces on advocacy and its "how-tos" deal with the worker's role in this area. Although it takes expertise to be a specialist, all workers have an important role to play and one that flows naturally from their clinical practice.

In the final analysis, it is the worker-client encounter that will in greatest measure determine the validity of the service. The outcome may not be exactly what both consumer and worker envisioned, but there can be something positive in the experience for both if the worker cares and is skillful. It is important to know how white practitioners feel about their experiences in cross-cultural situations in order to assist them effectively in working with minority clients. The article dealing with a white worker's personal reflections provides such an insight. The author's belief that the power held by the Anglo must be transferred to the powerless is an important conviction for those working in this area. The role of the minority consumer and minority professional in determining their own destiny cannot be overstated. Nevertheless, there is great truth in the same author's profound belief that it is possible for thoroughly knowledgeable practitioners, who respect cultural differences, to work effectively with clients in cross-cultural, racial situations.

Notes

1. See Emelicia Mizio, ed., *Puerto Rican Task Force Report: Project on Ethnicity,* and Anita J. Delaney, ed., *Black Task Force Report: Project on Ethnicity* (New York: Family Service Association of America, 1979).

Training for Work with Minority Groups

Emelicia Mizio

Training for work with minority groups requires first and foremost
the recognition that there is a central core of values, knowledge, and
skill that undergirds work with all groups. As social workers we have
at minimum a general philosophical, theoretical, and practice base
from which we can build to work with minority populations. Without
this perspective the social work field has a built-in rationalization for
not assuming its educational and service responsibility for work with
minority populations and can ignore the struggle for attainment of
social justice.

A Common Knowledge Base

Few would quarrel that there are universal and interrelated needs of
a physical and emotional nature that all mankind share. Charlotte
Towle's *Common Human Needs*[1] is a social work classic that provides
a context for viewing the commonalities of our concerns and responses. It specifically examines the needs and feelings of the public
assistance recipient and succeeds in demonstrating lucidly the similarity of all human needs. However, rather than the public welfare
system, a guaranteed income and right-to-work legislation would
serve much better to preserve human dignity. Developing universal
strategies and interventions to respond appropriately to improve the
quality of life, alleviate suffering, and advocate for society to meet its
obligations to all its citizenry has always been social work's mission as
a profession. The National Association of Social Workers' code of
ethics specifies a professional commitment to respect the individual's
and group's integrity, in effect the right to self-determination, and
the obligation to work toward improving social conditions and supporting programs of human welfare.[2]

Social work must be careful not to give mere lip service to the philosophical tenets that are central to its practice. The following values require continual reaffirmation of belief and, as expressed through practice, in work with minority and majority clients:

1. The individual [and his or her community] is the primary concern of this society.
2. There is interdependence between individuals in this society.
3. Individuals have social responsibility for one another.
4. There are human needs common to each person, yet each person is essentially unique and different from any other.
5. An essential attribute of a democratic society is the realization of the full potential of each individual and the assumption of his or her social responsibility through active participation in society.
6. Society has a responsibility to provide ways in which obstacles to this self-realization (that is, disequilibrium between the individual and his or her environment) can be overcome or prevented.[3]

Training for work with minority populations will need to focus on professional values. The trainee will need to be alerted to role clashes that can be anticipated and will need preparation to make the adjustments to meet this. As Paul A. Abels states with reference to all of social work practice: "The social worker suffers role conflicts not only in terms of differing demands of the profession and the agency, but also in the clash between humanitarian values and agency and professional norms, and in terms of the discrepancies between agency and professional roles."[4] This conflict will be forever present for those in the profession who are truly committed to gaining equal access to resources for minorities.

In order to gain general acceptance, emergent knowledge or technology has had to show itself compatible with the explicated value system. Social work's body of knowledge and technology, although often taking detours and reflecting societal climate, has aimed to find ways to work with competence at the interface of mankind and the environment. Some practitioners have stressed working with the individual as the primary concern; others have viewed society as the basic target.[5] Although there are theorists at different ends of the continuum, the field as a whole always comes back to searching for ways to reconcile differences and establish equilibrium.

In terms of minorities it is essential that balance be maintained, particularly when we consider that:

A practitioner considering a theory that focuses only on the internal self would probably conclude that black and white psyches operate on the same color-blind principles. However, in a theory that attempts to link the internal self with the external world or social environment, it would be

8

difficult to conclude that color could be irrelevant in the practice of social work when it is highly significant in all other social activities. To deny or to ignore the oppressed status of minority groups clients is to ignore the reality of their external environment.[6]

Person-in-Transaction

Historically, the field early talked about person-in-situation with a heavy dependency on psychological and sociological constructs; it is important for minorities that workers continue to seek ways to integrate and apply this knowledge. Such theorists as Erik H. Erikson proved useful in placing human development in a sociocultural context. The attempt to use such frameworks as a social problem structure and to use an integrated methods approach represents the same attempt at working at both sides of the equation. With the incorporation of sophisticated systems terminology we now have better tools with which to work and we can speak of "the matching of people's coping patterns with the qualities of impinging environment for the purpose of producing growth-inducing and environment-ameliorating transactions."[7]

Person-in-situation has now become person-in-transaction-with-environment. Greater society, which is a much larger system than a minority individual, minority family, or minority community, furnishes these smaller social systems with the conditions necessary for their survival.[8] Systems theory "reflects a returning awareness of the interrelatedness of individual problems with larger social structure failures."[9] This is very compatible with a theoretical framework that looks at the minority experience from a structural and environmental determininistic perspective, such as presented by Frederico Souflee and Graciela Schmitt in describing the Chicano experience,[10] that most certainly has implications for all minority communities.

The trainer will need to convey the perspective that the validity and usefulness of theories will have to be measured against applicability to minority populations. The philosophical belief in the commonalities of human needs, the reaffirmation in belief and practice of professional values, and the open system for obtaining knowledge and technology related to the fit of man and milieu serve as a satisfactory underpinning for work with all people, majority and minority.

Differences in Service Delivery

Awareness of commonalities among people must not obscure the fact that, as opposed to white minorities, there are differences in some of the ways in which we should work with minority populations re-

9

gardless of class. These "differences appear only in the form comparable professional interventions assume with various client entities. To account for these differences and to provide principles that direct worker interventions, refinements to theory are developed."[11]

The required differences in interventive forms and necessary theoretical refinements translate into special service programs for minority clients. This does not point to inadequacies in minority clients or inherent differences from the majority. The need for special services stems from the racist and societal environment that has created the distinction of majority and minority populations. All of social work teaching must address racism to fulfill its commitment to the elimination of social injustice. Social work students and practitioners need a thorough grounding in its operation.

The trainer must stress that this is critical knowledge and skill for work with minority populations. Trainees must be provided with the information and technology for assessment and interventions that will work toward the eradication of racism. Because the elimination of racism will require basic structural changes in society that are not to be expected in our lifetime, we are talking about teaching the use of incremental approaches that partialize and prioritize strategies for intervention. Recognizing the limitations of our present repertoire of skills means that training must instill in each practitioner the responsibility of looking toward the refinement of skills in dealing with macro systems and the codification of these approaches.

Training will also encompass materials related to culture and lifestyles with reference to the impact of external systems on the minority group under study. This cultural and societal understanding would be examined from the perspective of how to deliver culturally attuned services. The concept of the importance of responding to an ethnic value system for relevant services should not be viewed as invented with the "discovery" of service irrelevancy to minority communities. Rereading Mary Richmond's *Social Diagnosis*, originally published in 1917, one finds the following: "One of the social worker's difficulties with foreigners is that he does not understand their conventions any more than they do his; a knowledge of their history and of their old world environment is indispensable to the most helpful relations with them." In another excerpt she describes a young social worker's difficulties: "whenever she visited a family in 'Little Italy', who were bred in the tradition that the courteous thing to do was whatever a guest seemed to desire . . . there was a clash of standards which finally brought about her assignment to a district less alien to her traditions." With reference to interpreters, Richmond states: "The use of interpreters also presents difficulties. When people who do not speak

10

English have to be interviewed through one, the results are the reverse of satisfactory. As one worker put it, if an interpreter can fulfill his part in a honest, unbiased, and intelligent way, he had better be turned into a social worker and do the casework needed himself."[12]

These excerpts reflect the field's early awareness of the potential for obstacles in the bicultural encounter even when color factors are not of concern. They also, by implication, raise the question of the criticalness of only bicultural and bilingual workers serving their own ethnic group. Whatever the answer, we do not have a sufficient pool of minority workers to draw from so that the nature of the training of Anglo professionals remains a vital concern. It is essential that the trainer be able to help the participants understand the critical nature of the role of self-help. Also, the trainer must help them to accept the philosophical tenet that minorities have the right to self-determination translated into power in decision-making processes.

Training Anglo Professionals

It can be anticipated that participants coming to a training program will have an elementary sociological background, either from undergraduate experience or early social work training. Certainly, some understanding can be expected of concepts such as community, class, race, color, culture, ethnicity, values, minority, majority, role, status, and so on. The trainee will probably have some knowledge of a culture other than the wider American one. Also, the trainer can have the expectation that social work training has stressed the development of self-awareness and the professional use of self.

With these assumptions, the trainer will need to forge ahead with providing information on culture and lifestyles and the societal conditions under which the group exists. For more than just intellectual understanding, the trainer will need to work at helping the trainee incorporate a dual prespective approach. Training can then include more than providing knowledge of the minority group's value system. The intent would be to help the trainee obtain "substantive knowledge and appreciation of both the majority societal system and the minority client system, as well as a conscious awareness of the social worker's own attitudes and values. Thus the dual perspective allows one to experience each system from the point of view of the other."[13]

Trainers must be careful to help the trainee recognize that it would be erroneous to assume that we have succeeded in looking at the situation through the eyes of another. There must be a continual check on our perceptions. Involvement of the consumer in decision making must be taught as a creed. Once there is an understanding of the culture and the situation in which minority clients find them-

11

selves, there will need to be training content related to the manner in which this enters service delivery at all levels. It is true that trainees will be skilled and interested in different methods. Coming out of different practice settings, they will need more specific content with reference to different types of service programs. It is essential, however, that all trainees understand changes that are necessary for appropriate service delivery. Training must aim at encouraging participants to improve on an advocacy stance to obtain required services.

Change Strategy

There is no doubt that social work has the core base on which to build and from which to deliver culturally sensitive and relevant service programs to work with minority populations. There is specialized content that must be taught to practitioners, but this information base is compatible with social work's theoretical structure. What is unique, however, about the minority situation is that despite the usefulness of the field's body of knowledge, although admittedly imperfect in all areas for all clients, we have a situation where social work is under attack for its irrelevancy and its lack of service to minority clients. "This is not an indictment of the profession in the abstract—it is an indictment of the profession in the concrete . . . . Our argument, therefore, is not with the ideals of the profession, but with the persistent incongruity between vows and vocation, evidenced by the profession's reluctance in aggressively adopting and implementing change strategies designed to make its offerings more palatable to the barrio."[14] Is Mary Richond, then, ahead of *our* time?

Change strategies will have to effect an educational and training system that must be prepared to meet its obligation to use its resourses to develop a specialization for work with minority populations. Changes would also need to come about in developing bicultural service delivery models that would allow for power and authority realignments, with minorities assuming greater controls. To this last point there is really entrenched resistance.[15] We are dealing with a situation in which social work itself suffers from the societal affliction of racism. Training for work with minority groups will need to penetrate this all-pervasive barrier.

As part of this change strategy, the study of racism will need to be much more encompassing than originally implied in this presentation. It is not only a societal indictment that has been made, but also an indictment of the field and of ourselves that we must address in training. No matter what area of minority concerns is under discus-

12

sion, the factor of racism must be borne in mind or we will not have dealt with the concern.

The Experiental Component in Training

There is a growing body of knowledge, such as the data contained in this book, that is suitable for didactic purposes in training for work with minority groups. There are materials available from which the trainer can expand dealing with culture and lifestyles for the various groups (more information on some groups than others), ethnicity's place in service delivery, racism in its operation, and so on. The acquiring of such information in an open-minded individual should have experiental value in and of itself.

To deal more directly with the experiental component will be considerably more difficult. Great sensitivity and skill is called for on the teacher's part if the defensiveness of the participants is not to be stimulated. If the outcome of the training is unsuccessful there will need to be an exploration of the transactions between the trainer and trainees. Neither racism in the trainees nor ineptitude of the trainer should be assumed. If trainer and trainees are of different racial and ethnic backgrounds, each will come with a backlog of experiences and expectations of the interracial situation. Each may be to the other a symbolic representation of the interracial and intercultural experience. Affixing blame is not appropriate; rather, an examination to help find the most effective way of training for relevant services to the minority communities is necessary.

The experiental component begins with a minority person as the key trainer. The importance of a minority person in this central role cannot be overemphasized. This does not only relate to the special knowledge that comes from having a common heritage and identification as a minority person; the majority-minority relationship is not just an abstract to be talked about, but exists in the here and now of the training situation. It provides an opportunity for experiencing and obtaining some awareness of power considerations, whether or not the feelings aroused come under discussion. This role reversal may tend to cause discomfort for the trainee. The area of minority concerns seems to be one that tends to provoke anxiety. For many, having a minority person in a superior position will be a new experience. It is to be hoped that for all it will prove a positive experience and, as such, a chance to improve race relations.

The trainer must attempt to convey the uniqueness, pain, and strength of the minority experience so that it can be understood by the trainees. At the same time, this experience must not be made to

13

appear so different and so alien from the majority experience or human experience that the majority trainee will feel incapable of experiencing empathy for the minority client.[16] The trainee will need to be able to note the similarities as well as the differences in cultural patterns and lifestyles, dreams, and aspirations in order to minimize anxieties about working with a group that is different from the majority. The need for creating security in all types of learning experiences for the trainee to be able to risk self is well established theoretically.[17] This would appear especially necessary in terms of cross-cultural and interracial training situations.

Social work educators have also confirmed the importance of creating a climate of trust in such a situation.[18] Encounter-type activities such as confronting and raising guilt, blaming white participants for societal racist conditions, calling trainees racists, labeling attitudes and behaviors, making moral judgments, haranguing, manipulating, and so on are not recommended. In addition, it must be recognized that "white guilt" has subsided and, if anything, there is a regressive trend among whites that comes from a feeling of having already given up too much for minorities. Confrontation techniques in these times do not seem generally useful and are now, apparently, rarely employed. It is felt by some, however, that they may be necessary again in times of crisis.[19]

These techniques contain the seeds for explosiveness and destructiveness. If encounter techniques are still to be used, they call for a highly skilled trainer and require an ongoing time period for working through the feelings aroused—at least sufficient time to place the feelings in focus. If the encounter approach is to be used at all it seems more appropriate for programs that center exclusively on race-relations training. The participant has contracted for this in-depth look at racism and is prepared for self-exposure. Thus, training is an orderly systematized process in which the primary goal and focus is the development of racial awareness per se and a working through of prejudice. One university program in race relations involved the following steps: "Stage one required making participants aware of racial/cultural/sexual differences through information sharing. Stage two dealt with definitional analytical activities. Stage three required the use of and familiarization with measurement of racial attitudes in a personal assessment. Stage four involved looking at sources of racial attitudes. Stage five involved setting [personal] goals, and Stage six involved establishing [personal] goals for future behavior."[20] Although the development of racial awareness should be an important goal basically of all training for work with minority clients, it becomes

14

secondary to the primary goal of training to work effectively with minority populations.

Dispelling Myths and Stereotypes

There is enough evidence to conclude from clinical work and other sources that rooted in the unconscious of all humans there are myths and stereotypes that relate whiteness to purity and blackness to evil.[21] Segregating, scapegoating, denigrating minorities, and projecting unwanted ideas and feelings on minorities are not uncommon defense mechanisms. Encounter activities may hit against these processes without any opportunity to handle fully what has been provoked. It can increase defensiveness. It can leave the participant in a state of anxiety and promote rage or guilt. Ugly divisions can occur in the group as the group members become clashing factions. Accusations may be thrown around and there may be an aggravation of racial conflicts rather than race relations being positively cemented. The trainer may unwittingly become cast in the role of group therapist without the group's mandate or cooperation. Some members may become so frightened that they "drop out," in fact or feeling, making them inaccessible to further learning. They may protect themselves in the future by avoiding contact as much as possible with minority concerns.

The trainer should not wish to create a group therapy situation. Goals must be perceived realistically. Trainers must be clear on the line between helping trainees to develop an intellectual understanding of racism, its causes, its operation, and its manifestations in individuals, field, and society from working on the development of racial awareness. Racial awareness deals with (1) knowledge of how one perceives and feels about race and about members of other races; (2) movement from fixed to more flexible knowledge about different ethnic lifestyles.[22] The development of racial awareness, in turn, contrasts with the analytical process of working through of the unconscious determinants of racism. There is most certainly an overlap, but the trainer needs to be clear on purpose and aim.

It would be unfortunate to downplay the importance of intellectual understanding. By providing theoretical materials it should be possible to develop curiosity and concern in trainees regarding where they stand on the racist continuum. The trainer would attempt to stimulate in them the desire to delve further into self-knowledge for professional use of self and to seek increased knowledge and skill in working with minority people. This can only be done if the individuals do not feel threatened and have a sense of acquiring tools to cope with the societal illness of racism.

One way of approaching the experiential part is through the ex-

15

amination of the universality of racism as a phenomenon. Group discussions could be held in which members identify situations and provide examples of where they have seen racism in operation. Participants are then moved, gradually, into the more personal realm. G. Winifred Kagwa recommends using the examination of a term such as "nonwhite" as a possible beginning point and noting its implications. People are evaluated and measured against a standard of whiteness.[23]

Simulations

There are many useful games and exercises of simulation that encourage racial awareness and can allow for a selected and circumscribed focus on a particular issue with an anticipated experential outcome. These simulations have the important safeguard of being controlled, structured activities with definite procedural rules so that closure is built into the game or exercise. Both the trainer and trainees take comfort in knowing that there are clear expectations and limitations. Of special value are those experiential situations that tap into power issues and value clarification.[24]

Simulations are generally an important experiential method in the training of human service providers and also useful in training for work with minority clients. They have been described as involving "a smaller or miniature representation of a larger whole . . . of some greater or complex social system or process . . . in a form which can be manipulated and whose parts are dynamic or operating [as contrasted with static models such as pictures or diagrams]. The simulation duplicates selected features of the environment."[25] In addition, "the most significant advantage is that gaming-simulation rapidly enhances the sophistication of the players regarding the factors at work and the relationships between the key roles in the real world. Players come to the games with imperfect concepts of community, and they leave it with shattered myths. Usually, they achieve a sense of what kind of action, when coordinated, yields what kinds of outcomes."[26]

Role Playing

A specially useful form of simulation is role playing, which can lend itself to enacting in a laboratory situation any type of problem or situation that a social worker may need to handle. This could be in relation to an individual client, client group, institution, or community issue. Many human service professionals and agencies, because of their lack of experience or lack of success in minority communities, may feel inadequate to the task. They may then manage to practice avoidance and not be there to meet the needs for service in the minority community. Other professionals may be aware of their own prejudice, feel ashamed and, consequently, become immobilized. The trainer must be able to establish a climate that is permissive and protective. This would allow the trainees to experiment with various approaches. They would be able to test themselves without fearing ridicule in the laboratory situation or having to immediately test the possibility of hurting anyone or retaliation from client or organization.

Role playing can allow not only the experience of being the helper, but also allow for the experience of being the minority client. Being able to "get into the skin" of the client provides a significant experience and identification, as often the majority person has not been able to comprehend the minority experience in other than an intellectual way. The minority worker can also role play with the majority worker to see if he or she can understand a colleague better. Minority workers find themselves called on to serve as links between the minority community and the Anglo worker. This understanding could prove critical to this linking function.

An important element of simulations is the peer factor and its effect on the transactions between trainer and trainee. Because feedback from peers is credited as part of the essential learning and because they are encouraged to lend each other support, this will serve to mitigate the illusory perception of the trainer as the repository of all knowledge in terms of minority issues. This frequently occurs despite the seeming contradiction that often majority members assume minority faculty to be unqualified with reference to most areas of knowledge. In terms of minority concerns, the extent of the above perception greatly depends on the degree of social distance the trainee has maintained from minorities. The greater the distance the more likely are they to feel intimidated by the minority trainer. "A dilemma for Blacks [and other minorities] in becoming absorbed in white institutions is to overcome their suspicion of the delegation of power by whites."[27]

The trainer, by becoming part of the simulations, can serve as a role model and diminish for the trainees some of their fear of exposure. The trainees can be expected to recognize that the trainer is also seeing this as a learning opportunity and that they have something to offer that the trainer is willing to accept from whites. Trainees will be able to reconcile the trainer's power, by virtue of his or her role as trainer, human vulnerability, and by virtue of his or her allowing trainee access. Commonalities between trainer and trainees should emerge and social distance be lessened. The experience of

17

dealing with minorities at the peer level also serves as a learning experience for Anglos and can help to break down social distance.

Minority trainees may also need help in dealing with the minority-white transaction. For the minority participant it is often a source of pride to see one's own "making it" in the white establishment. Trainers will need to be cognizant of the needs of the minority attendees. They should be expected to have conflict about minority-majority relationships, and simulations are useful for arriving at an identification of this as a problem in working with clients. There may be a hatred of whites. There is also a possibility of identification with the aggressor. The trainer will need to help minority attendees become alert to potential pitfalls that they may have to come to terms with and that may make it difficult to assess the strengths and weaknesses of their clients both minority and white.

Simulations, even when in combination with solid didactic materials and the goodwill of trainer-trainees, should not be expected to resolve deep underlying conflicts of either the minority or white attendees. Where these are present, it is the trainer's responsibility to help trainees spot their need for assistance and to see if they can be helped to find resources to work them out. It is imperative that the participants not review the simulation activities or the total program as a cure for their prejudices. It should not be perceived by any as obtaining a prescription or formula.

Participants must remain focused on the need to individualize. The goals to be achieved are individual style, development, and coordination knowledge.[28] This points to the importance of simulation not being simply skill development or immediate practice concerns—broader issues should pertain. This should lead, in turn, to the development of new systematic professional knowledge, which, in turn, will become part of the body of knowledge used in the training and educational process.[29] The experiential component that ultimately will have the most significance will be the engagement with the minority client and community, especially if receiving support from a minority trainer, supervisor, or consultant.[30]

Conclusion

Delivery of relevant and effective bicultural services goes far beyond the delivery of relevant and effective training or programs. Committed trainees who have secured knowledge and an increased skills repertoire will require agency support. Without these supports, the trainees who have learned their lessons will have to dissipate their energies in working toward internal organizational changes. A successful program of service to minority communities requires more than a knowledgeable worker and more than a minority worker with a positive minority identification. It requires a total agency commitment and an investment by board, administration, and staff in a program of service to the minority communities.

Notes

1. Charlotte Towle, *Common Human Needs* (New York: National Association of Social Workers, 1945).

2. Code of Ethics contained in National Association of Social Workers standards for social work personnel practices: professional standards, rev. 1975. NASW Policy Statement 2, pp. 38-39.

3. Working definition of social work practice (reprinted from *Social Work* 3, no. 2 (April 1958) quoted by Harriet M. Bartlett, *The Common Base of Social Work Practice* (New York: National Association of Social Workers, 1970), p. 221.

4. Paul A. Abels, *The New Practice of Supervision and Staff Development: A Synergistic Approach* (New York: Association Press, 1977), p. 14.

5. Special Issue devoted to Conceptual Frameworks, *Social Work* 22, no. 5 (September 1977).

6. Harriet P. Trader, "Survival Strategies for Oppressed Minorities," *Social Work* 22, no. 1 (January 1977): 10-11.

7. Gordon Hearn, "Introduction," in *The General Systems Approach: Contributions Toward an Holistic Conception of Social Work*, ed. Gordon Hearn (New York: Council on Social Work Education, 1969), p. 10.

8. William J. Goode discusses this concept in relation to family (also applicable to the above systems), in *The Family* (Englewood Cliffs, N.J.: Prentice-Hall, 1964), pp. 51-52.

9. Robert D. Leighninger, Jr., "Systems Theory in Social Work: A Re-examination," *Journal of Education for Social Work* 13, no. 3 (Fall 1977): 45.

10. Federico Souflee and Graciela Schmitt, "Educating for Practice in the Chicano Community," *Journal of Education for Social Work* 10, no. 3 (Fall 1974): 76.

11. Carl M. Shafer, "Teaching Social Work Practice In An Integrated Course. A General Systems Approach," in *General Systems Approach*, ed. Hearn, p. 30.

12. Mary E. Richmond, *Social Diagnosis* (New York: Free Press, 1965), pp. 73-75.

13. Dolores G. Norton, ed., *The Dual Perspective* (New York: Council on Social Work Education, 1978), p. 3.

14. Souflee and Schmitt, "Educating for Practice," p. 77.

15. Ibid., p. 77.

16. See David Macarov, "Empathy: The Charismatic Chimera," *Journal of Education for Social Work* 14, no. 3 (Fall 1978): 86.

17. Mary Louise Somers, "Contributions of Learning and Teaching Theories to the Explication of the Role of the Teacher in Social Work Education," in *Teaching and*

Learning in Social Work Education, comp. Marguerite Pohek (New York: Council on Social Work Education, 1970), p. 176.

18. See, for example, Elaine B. Pinderhughes, "Teaching Empathy in Cross-Cultural Social Work," *Social Work* 24, no. 4 (July 1979); and G. Winifred Kagwa, "Utilizing of Racial Content in Developing Self-Awareness," *Journal of Education for Social Work* 12, no. 2 (Spring 1976).

19. John F. Coffey, "The State of the Art," *Race Education/Training*, Contract no. DADA 1576-M-P869 (Washington, D.C.: U.S. Goverment Printing Office, 1976), pp. 1-31.

20. Ibid, p. 23.

21. Hugh F. Butts, "Psycholoanalysis and Unconscious Racism," *Journal of Contemporary Psychotherapy* 3, no. 2, (Spring 1971): 71.

22. Susan B. Strober and Milton Grady, "Effects of Race Relations Training in Racial Awareness," *Social Work Research and Abstracts* 14, no. 2 (Summer 1978): 13.

23. Kagwa, "Utilizing Racial Content," p. 23.

24. For use in training, see Judy H. Katz, *White Awareness: Handbook for Anti-Racism Training* (Norman, Okla.: University of Oklahoma Press, 1978).

25. Jack Rothman and Wyatt Jones, "A New Look at Field Instruction: Education for Application of Practice Skills," in *Community Organization and Local Planning* (New York: Association Press, 1971), pp. 116.

26. Ibid., p. 111.

27. Louis H. Carter, "The Black Instructor: An Essential Dimension to the Content and Structure of the Social Work Curriculum," *Journal of Education for Social Work* 14, no. 1 (Winter 1978): 17.

28. Alan Gartner and Frank Reissman, "New Training for New Services," *Social Work* 17, no. 6 (November 1972): 59.

29. Ibid., p. 63.

30. George Anderson et al., "A Seminar on the Assessment and Treatment of Black Patients," *Professional Psychology* (August 1977): 345, reprinted. The authors state that "the opportunity for white trainees to work with black patients while receiving supervision from black consultants was one of the most significant features of this seminar. This experience seemed to enhance the trainees' abilities to interact efficiently with black families."

A Review of the Black and Puerto Rican Task Force Reports

Emelicia Mizio

This article examines the service models contained in the black and Puerto Rican task force reports[1] with some reference to their conceptual framework. Both reports are in two sections—a conceptual framework for the development of an appropriate service model or models and a presentation of the service models. This review does not pretend to do justice here to the models presented nor to the many issues raised and explored. It merely highlights some of the important areas and recommends the reading of both reports.

Examination of the black and Puerto Rican task force reports reveals a similarity that is not surprising. Poverty and racism affect all minority communities, are issues with which all ethnic minorities must be concerned, and require the development of strategies of eradication. Both reports describe the havoc that racism plays in terms of survival and self-esteem and pose ways to deal with these concerns.

Service Model

A theoretical service model was developed by both of the task forces, with advocacy as the core program. Counseling, family life education, and other group methods are also important components. In addition, program elements such as consultation, information and referral, research, and evaluation were also explored and seen as having service relevance.

Advocacy

Both the Puerto Rican and black models are similar in that advocacy is viewed as the most central program of service. When we speak of advocacy, we are talking about working toward the changing of dys-

21

functional systems, the filling of service gaps, and the meeting of unmet needs in innovative ways. We are also talking about internal advocacy within one's own self and one's own organization, as well as the organization dealing with outer systems. Further, we mean total agency participation in advocacy from the level of the consumer to the board structure.

If we are not to be continuously concerned with the same problems and "if prevention is to be a component of a unified and rational mental health system, then measures to improve the quality of life for special [minority] populations is a necessary corollary. Public policy and legislation directed toward eradicating racism, sexism should be recommended and supported."[2]

Advocacy, then, must be perceived as crucial. At the core of the advocacy component must be the concepts of empowerment and consumerism. We must sustain a partnership with the minority community. The paternalistic stance of *doing for* is abhorrent and *doing with* must become our creed. Clients *must* have power in the determination of service priorities and service programs.

Counseling

Counseling is another important component of both models. The need for counseling to be placed within a cultural framework that acknowledges the survival mechanisms and adaptations that clients have made in a racist society is of importance and is stressed for work with all minority groups. Counseling services must be more than psychotherapy because clients need a whole host of concrete services. The Puerto Rican task force report uses the concept of client or consumer as a "customer." The requests then are not viewed as unrealistic expectations and, thereby, are seen generally as legitimate. Thus, a negotiated consensus can be more readily arrived at between therapist and client.[3]

No treatment method is seen in either report as the treatment method of choice. The Puerto Rican task force report points out that there has been insufficient treatment experience with the Puerto Rican population to make any definitive treatment recommendation, and the black report highlights the need for differential diagnosis in making treatment choices and a need to avoid preconceived notions about so-called nonverbal clients. The Puerto Rican report points to the abuses of drug therapy with the Latino population, which of course holds true as well for black and other minority communities.

Although counseling is recognized by the Puerto Rican task force report as critical in providing service to the Puerto Rican community because of a high rate of mental illness, it is felt that this program component might have to wait for the agency to have established its credibility with the minority community. In addition, an agency might be able to help the minority community get counseling services elsewhere through its advocacy activities. The agency could then further use its resources to concentrate on securing other services to the community through the same advocacy activities. The maximization of resource use and priority setting emerge as strong themes in the report. Service multipliers must be a guiding principle of work with all minority communities.

Family Life Education

Another program component common to both reports is the group approach, with a particular stress on family life education programming. Family life education is basically an educational approach designed to serve a preventive purpose. "FLE helps group members to understand and anticipate the normal patterns and stresses of individual family and community living in order to prevent and reduce situational crises, to improve and expand the range of coping capacities, and to stimulate self-actualization and growth."[4]

Both reports deal with modifications that are necessary in group work in terms of the cultural value system and the environmental press. For example, because of the Puerto Rican value of *respeto* the deference and respect shown to authority figures, a family life education group on assertiveness training would need to make the distinctions between assertiveness and aggression very carefully, thereby helping to secure their rights. The black task force report points out that the group should be structured with tasks and goals established within the limits of the client's social reality. Specificity and focus would be of value in work with all clients. The importance of dealing with environmental factors in all areas of work cannot be overstated with ethnic minority populations. Both reports point to the need to help clients advocate for themselves, and family life education is an excellent vehicle for helping clients join together in common causes.

Research and Evaluation

Research and evaluation is another essential program component in working with minority communities. The Puerto Rican report points out that a research orientation is essential in providing service to the minority community to determine needs and priorities and to establish how best to meet these needs and make the knowledge gained transferable to others. As the black report indicates, it is important that service givers be sensitive to the different value orientations operative when evaluating service outcomes in the black community.

The black report recognizes that the assessment by the client, compared with the worker's evaluation, will tend to be more general and to relate more accurately to the client's social realities. A client's perception of what is desirable may differ from the professional's in terms of this very different value orientation.

Other Program Components

The Puerto Rican report includes other program components as important, particularly consultation. This component, including educational processes, is seen as an important service multiplier. Through the process of consultation with community caretakers, with grassroots organizations, and even with other professional and social work organizations, it is possible to expand the range of relevant services to minority communities. The consultant must, however, perceive his or her role as that of advocate—meeting the unmet needs of minority populations.

Another desirable component contained in the Puerto Rican report is that of an information and referral service, which works to deter service fragmentation and fulfills the essential role of social brokerage. Linkage with other organizations, attempts at facilitating access, and activities in other areas of advocacy are necessary as an everyday occurence for any worker in a minority community. The function that such a formal program could serve has been termed by Alfred Kahn as "unbiased case channeling." This service can mean that assessment, information, advice, and referral not only reflect the perspective of specialized services, but allow for the consideration of all possibilities.[5] An agency would work at establishing cooperation ties with other organizations within the service network that would be of mutual advantage in terms of appropriate referrals. One could even envision an intake that could serve a multiple function for the various organization, once confidentiality considerations were assured. Service duplication, which causes wastefulness of badly needed funds for other minority services, must be avoided.

Theoretical Base of Models

Both reports stress, therefore, that any model of service must flow from an ecological and systems perspective. As the black report indicates, solutions cannot be found to complex problems by thinking that changing the minority family system is the answer. It specifies concepts from role theory and speaks of Erikson's concept of developmental stages and White's concept of competence and mastery. Although not discussed per se in the Puerto Rican model, these certainly have usefulness in work with the Puerto Rican and other minority populations, because they recognize environmental factors as important to ego development and adequate functioning. Perspective on the need for environmental change must, however, be maintained and given priority.

Cultural Considerations

We also take note that, in terms of the black community, cultural aspects need to be considered in service delivery. The black task force report points to the fact that there is a view that many blacks are only impoverished versions of white, middle-class Americans. This perception has obscured the cultural aspects of the observed differences in behavior, attitudes, and thinking.

In the mental health professions there has been, generally speaking, a clearer understanding that there is a "Latino culture," even if understanding that one cannot put all Latinos in the same pot is lacking. There has been less understanding of the existence of a black culture as distinct from middle America. One needs, therefore, to be cognizant of the African cultural base of the black population, as well as the specifics of the culture of each particular Latino, Asian, or Indian population.

Self-help

The black report highlights the necessity for using the strengths of black families in service delivery. All minority communities have had to depend on kin relationships to help them survive in an often hostile environment. There are also other natural helping systems that support individuals and families in both meeting their expressive and instrumental needs. The black church is highlighted in the black report as a major sustaining element in the struggle to cope with social realities. Certainly, the church has played a significant and sustaining role in the Puerto Rican experience, but insofar as it has, for some, contributed to their resignation to fate and to their looking only to a reward in an afterlife it has not been helpful. Indigenous helpers, such as spiritualists, are emphasized in the Puerto Rican task force report. The significant help that traditional folk medicine and healers can provide is a view shared by many in the minority communities.

Both reports address the importance of grass-roots organizations—all existing social networks must be examined as potential helping networks. Natural helping networks are in a position to respond directly to consumer needs and preferences. They can serve a valuable information function for the professional in terms of the development of service programs because they are often composed of local, central figures. If the professional is successful in establishing constructive relationships with the central figures, the effective reach of professional efforts can be expanded enormously.[6]

Language

Language is another point of similarity and an important consideration in working with both populations. It is perhaps easier to accept that a practitioner would need to understand and speak Spanish, as well as the language of the various other groups, than it is for some practitioners to appreciate that the black *patois* has to be accorded the same respect.[7] As Dorcas D. Bowles points out, black English is a complex language that is highly organized. It serves the communicative function by its great usefulness and its understandability.[8] Language also serves a survival function in providing a sense of group solidarity. Practitioners must not only understand but also respect the language of all minority communities if they are to be of service.

Notes on Similarities in the Reports

The similarities in the two task force reports outweigh the differences. The main difference seems to be in the expectations of what the program components should be for any and all family agencies. The black task force report calls for agencies having advocacy, counseling, and preventive components. The Puerto Rican task force, although seeing these programs as essential ones for any agency providing service to the Puerto Rican population and agreeing that advocacy is the central program, believes, however, that timing and maximum resource utilization are of the essence in the development of these and other program components.

Limited funding means a stress on service multipliers. Consultation services to other resources providing counseling and family life education might be more efficient for the minority community. Also, the use of counseling services and other services often means a prior development of credibility, which may mean that the counseling component will have to wait until there is acceptance in the minority community of an organization, and an expression of desire for its service.

Notes on Common Themes

Some of the following themes of importance are contained in either or both reports. It must be clear that not all minority people require

26

special programming; nevertheless, no course of treatment will be complete without dealing with the identity issue because of the racist society in which we all live. It is critical that there be community input at all levels of service delivery that have an impact on decision-making processes. Also, it is important that the service program be set up in a way so that it is viewed by the community as its own program. Ties must be developed by the professional service with the community's indigenous helpers. Professional services are, nevertheless, essential in concert with the minority professional. Special training needs to be built in for the Anglo professionals. The staff development emphasis should be on awareness, sensitivity, appreciation of the culture, and an individual perspective on each client served by the agency.

The minority program also must be held accountable to function at the same level of standards that the total agency does. To do otherwise is to continue to practice racism. The Puerto Rican report proposes a set of well-thought-out standards for agencies that are applicable to other minority communities. Supports must be provided for by the agency for quality work. Care must be taken for the unit not to see itself as a second-class service because of how it is being perceived and treated by the organization.

Conclusion

Information, knowledge, skills, and tools are essential in the provision of appropriate service. Despite their importance, relevant service to minority communities can only come about when there is truly a commitment in the human services to the elimination of racism, and a restructuring of society to make the American dream a reality for all. The necessity for a partnership with minority communities cannot be overemphasized. It is critical to look for models that successfully integrate mutual aid and systems and connect them, in turn, with large social movements that are working toward institutional changes.[9] The task is awesome, the challenge great, but the opportunity is ours to demonstrate that just as minorities have shown inordinate strengths agains impossible odds, so can the helping professions succeed in working with an oppressive system.

Notes

1. See Anita J. Delaney, ed., *Black Task Force Report: Project on Ethnicity,* and Emelicia Mizio, ed., *Puerto Rican Task Force Report: Project on Ethnicity* (New York: Family Service Association of America, 1979).

2. Report of the Special Populations Subpanel on Mental Health of Minorities, Women,

27

Physically Handicapped, *Task Panel Reports Submitted to the President's Commission on Mental Health* (Washington, D.C.: U.S. Government Printing Office, 1978), p. 733.

3. This concept is proposed by Aaron Lazare et al., "The Walk-in Patient as a Customer," *American Journal of Orthopsychiatry* 42, no. 5 (October 1972).

4. From the definition proposed in "Overview of Findings of the Task Force on Family Life Education, Development and Enrichment" (New York: Family Service Association of America, 1976), p. 2.

5. Alfred J. Kahn et al., *Neighborhood Information Centers: A Study and Some Proposals* (New York: Columbia School of Social Work, 1966), pp. 35-45.

6. Alice Collins and Diane Pancoast, *Natural Helping Networks* (Washington, D.C.: National Association of Social Workers, 1977), p. 29.

7. "Black English has been accorded legal recognition as a language in a 12 July, 1979 decision in Detroit," *New York Times*, 13 July, 1979, p. A8.

8. Dorcas David Bowles, "Intervention Strategies for Black Families Suffering Multiple Trauma and Stress." Paper presented at the National Urban League Conference on Black Families, Chicago, Illinois, 2-4 November, 1977, p. 5.

9. For an examination of the self-help movement and a look at both the potentials and limitations of self-help, see Alan Gartner and Frank Riessman, *Self-Help in the Human Services* (San Francisco: Jossey-Bass, 1977).

The Conceptual Framework

Emelicia Mizio

This article presents a conceptual framework for the development of model mental health delivery systems to minority communities. The framework specifies the elements necessary for service relevance and is placed in the context of existing societal conditions. Discussion with experts from Asian American, American Indian, black, and Chicano communities confirm its usefulness to all groups.[1] The American Indian who has remained on the reservation is to some extent an exception, because territorial issues and a lifestyle that includes remaining apart from the mainstream of society make for greater differences. Racism and poverty are, however, a commonality that all Indians share with all minorities.[2]

Racism and the Service Delivery System

Any model of service to be developed must consider the issues of racism and its eradication. This means examining and dealing with racism in society, the racism that is present in the total health and welfare structure, the racism in a particular organization, and the racism that is in us, the service deliverers. Few in this field would quarrel that racism exists in society. We are all fairly knowledgable about the unequal distribution of income, goods, and services, and are aware of the existence and meaning of minority status. What is not as well understood is that it is not necessary for an individual to choose to operate consciously in a racist manner. The choice is already prestructured by the way the rules and procedures are set up. The individual only needs to conform and the institution will do the discriminating.[3]

We come up against inner resistance when we are forced to examine the ways in which the mental health field itself practices personal and institutional racism. We do not seem to appreciate the importance

29

and ramifications of the fact that social welfare practitioners define what are considered to be social problems and, in the process, these same institutions marshall the skills and resources of other professionals, paraprofessionals, and consumers in dealing with these problems.[4] Practitioners have, for example, discouraged the Latino population from utilizing services by not addressing such factors as geographical inaccessability, professional staff monolingualism, middle-class values entering both diagnosis and treatment, and lack of recognition of culture differences. Factors of social distance, prejudice, and dependence on a traditional system model of inquiry that pays no attention to potentially significant ethnographic data also enters into this underuse of service.[5] Service irrelevance and consequent underuse are common themes in the literature of all minority communities.[6]

In addition to assessing the reason for underuse of services, it is imperative that we also examine the organizational variables that are essential to quality service delivery. To ensure that this occurs as part of the process, it is essential that sensitization to racism, class, and cultural differences and values must be part of the ongoing training of all in the mental health field.[7]

Poverty and the Quality of Life

A model of service must deal with poverty as a concomitant of racism. That poverty affects all aspects of living—housing, food, clothing, medical care, recreation—has no need for elaboration, but it is also important to keep in perspective the psychological ramifications that often accompany poverty and serve as critical limitations in living. To be expected are feelings of powerlessness, deprivation, insecurity, and a relative simplication of the experience world. The individual under constant siege may well experience estrangement and become alienated. This alienation has the components of anomie, isolation, powerlessness, and meaninglessness.[8] Minority communities in this society often exist under deplorable conditions and are especially vulnerable to poverty and its psychological accompaniments. That there are differences between groups should, nevertheless, be noted as they have implications for our work with the various minority communities.

In 1977, the poverty rate for blacks was 31 percent, for whites, 9 percent, and for persons of Spanish origin, 22 percent.[9] These figures in relation to Spanish origin are deceptive in that persons of Spanish origin may be of any race or group.[10] It is important to recognize that there are great differences among the Spanish origin groups. The

1977 median income of the Puerto Rican was $8,000 compared with the Cuban's $14,200, and non-Spanish-origin income of $16,000.[11] It is unfortunate that the Bureau of the Census does not provide in its Consumer Income Report, issued in March 1979, comparable figures for the other ethnic minority populations. A government report states that for the Indian on the reservation the average family income is below the poverty level. The level of unemployment of the "more prosperous" reservations is about 20 percent to 60 to 70 percent in others.[12]

Sexism and Racist Practices

Sexism is another variable which, in combination with racism, has especially serious ramifications for minorities. In general, there is an increasing and significant concentration of the poor in families headed by women. As an illustration, in 1969 female-headed families accounted for 54 percent of poor black families, increasing to 71 percent of poor black families in 1977.[13] It is typical that the chances are greater for female-headed families to be below the poverty level when compared with other families of Spanish origin. In fact, about 50 percent of all female-headed families of Spanish heritage were below the poverty level.[14]

Intervening strategies must be focused on how racism and poverty combine in their specific consequences to victims and victimized group. As Lloyd Street points out, "Racism is not uniform. There is variation in racist practices and their impact on groups. The relative standings of groups change over time as a consequence of their location, power and so on."[15] The fact, for example, that the Hispanic community is growing in numbers and is expected to become the largest minority and, therefore, a greater voting force will by itself automatically afford the Hispanic community a different position in the power structure. Street recommends, for assessment of standing, a ranking system of the degree of structural similarity and departure on the traditional indicators of income, education, and occupation as compared with whites. Also, the evaluation should include an assessment of the group's level of cultural and political integrity. This refers to the extent to which the group has dominance over the social and cultural machinery that is necessary to its survival, and its ability to keep outsiders from "acting as agents of propriety for society."

Street goes on to state: "The utility of these data is that they provide a normative basis for intervention. It is generally accepted that some degree of parity should obtain and that intervention is 'fair' if it provides support for some 'parity'."[16] This assessment is essential for helping to make decisions about points of intervention and for setting

31

priorities for each specific group. Certainly, the struggle for "parity" with whites must be continued.

The Consequences of Racism and Poverty

Racism, poverty, and sexism are high-risk factors. There is considerable documentation linking mental illness with the devastating effects of racism and poverty.[17] The Joint Commission on Mental Health of Children has posited that poverty and racism are causes of major mental health problems.[18] A report on special populations—minorities, women, the physically handicapped—classifies minorities as having de facto second-class status in American society. Racism and sexism are acknowledged as factors known to compromise life's changes and to close off the opportunity to participate fully in society and to reach one's full potential. Minorities are consequently depicted as being overrepresented and inappropriately served in the mental health service system.[19] Mental illness is to be expected under present social conditions where there is a wide gap between the many tasks that need to be performed during the course of living and the complication and stress that results from not having necessary tools and services with which to work. This lack of resources promotes a vicious cycle in that it serves to diminish the individual's coping mechanisms, making it more difficult to work at securing the materials necessary to handle the stressful situation.

Credit must be given to those who have the strength to maintain an equilibrium under such odds. As an example of racism's toll, it has been reported that the Puerto Rican population in New York City, which has the largest concentration of mainland Puerto Ricans, has consistently had the highest rate of mental illness in comparison to other groups.[20] For blacks between 1950 and 1970, the rate of institutionalization increased in contrast to a decrease for whites. The data tend to show that blacks more readily than whites are committed, admitted, or sentenced for custodial care in mental institutions.[21] An examination of a number of research studies of Asian and Pacific Americans points to the underuse of services. Those who do receive services appear to have a higher severity of morbidity than other groups diagnosed.[22]

The elimination of both racism and poverty will serve as one of the most effective primary prevention measures. Racism itself should be perceived as a form of mental illness because pathological defensive mechanisms are employed and views and behavior reflect a distortion of reality.

32

The Impact of External Systems on Culture

The impact of external systems as related specifically to culture and lifestyle must also be dealt with in any service model. Although racism and poverty hurt ethnic minorities in many similar ways, there is a differential impact that relates to the value system of each group. It is insufficient, therefore, for practitioners to understand the mechanisms of racism and to find ways to deal effectively with the environment—this information must be used in combination with knowledge of the differences in value orientation between groups. The acknowledgment of differences must also be reflected in our work. For example, Derald Wing Sue and David Sue demonstrate the value of this approach through their examination and contrasting of the differences in value systems of several minority groups in terms of the cross-cultural barriers in the counseling situation.[23] This knowledge is essential in all other areas of work as well.

The differences of various groups from the white middle class create points of tension. Any plan of action, therefore, must address points of societal strain and assess their impact. For example, the Puerto Rican family has a traditional value system that stresses humanistic ideals and emphasizes extensive primary relationships. It also shows great respect for authority, difficult to maintain within the context of the wider American milieu. In contrast, the greater American society is materialistic and future oriented, and relationship patterns other than immediate familial ones are basically impersonal and business oriented. The Anglo family is a nuclear one, with an increasingly greater emphasis on "doing your own thing."

In fact, as the sociolegal structure of the wider society addresses itself basically to the nuclear family, a different family structure such as the extended one common to minority groups places ethnic groups and their individual members in jeopardy, as constraints are placed on their ability to assess members. Critical for survival to minority groups "will be the creative ways in which the kinship network is used by the poor to cope with the powerlessness created by racism and oppression."[24] The service delivery system must be continually aware of the impact of the sociolegal structure and work at being supportive of the kinship network, which is an essential coping mechanism for many minority group members in their efforts to maneuver the harsh environment in which they find themselves.

Because of these differences in value systems, present societal conditions, and societal constraints, we can well understand the high rate of mental illness for the Puerto Rican in New York City, referred to previously. A study by Judith Rabkin and Elmer L. Struening states

33

that "contributing to the individual's susceptibility to stress and illness are changes in lifestyles, the organization and role assignments of the family, social networks' memberships, and extent of the support of community."[25]

Value Conflicts

There are tension points for all groups that must be weighed. The black community is also under strain. Consider that African values stress affiliation, collectivity, respect for authority, and spirituality, with its accompanying belief in a higher power and a past-time orientation. These too are in contrast to such American values as differentiation, autonomy, independence, mastery, and a future-time orientation.[26] There are many who claim that value systems have their origins in economic factors and hence the similarities in cultural patterns of the oppressed. Whatever the origin of the value system of the minority group, the individual has to find ways of handling the conflicts caused by dealing with the different value systems and having to live in two worlds—the nutritive and the sustentative. The nutritive world is the world of community, family, and friends. The sustentative world is the world of status, education, and employment. There is the dilemma posed by the conflicting demands for survival in the broader society and maintaining one's psychological identity.[27]

The difficulties involved in this are underscored in a task panel report on the American Indian that addresses the issue of colonialization, where the white way is enforced as best. It discusses "the need to be colonialized to 'succeed' and the need to stay Indian to survive emotionally."[28] It reports on a study by Joseph Westermeyer that showed that Indians who had the best level of adjustment also had the highest level of cultural identification with their Indian heritage. The likelihood of social problems, imprisonment, or mental illness was highest for those with the lowest cultural identification.[29]

Biculturalism

Because each individual is different, knowledge of culture, lifestyles, stress points, and the impact of external systems on each particular minority group must not negate the need to understand the individual and his or her special situation. It is important that a practitioner having newly acquired knowledge regarding culture and lifestyles not make assumptions about an individual. A Chicano training center report discusses the importance of analyzing a person's biculturalism—the degree to which the person participates in both the ethnic and American cultures—because there is no way to avoid being part of both cultures. This discussion, although pointed to the

Chicano, is applicable to other groups and can be generalized to all minorities.

Biculturalism demands the bilateral bringing together of things, values, and behaviors. It is a lifestyle that integrates both ways of life. As this bilateral cultural fusion is tied into the individual's identity, each person has a unique configuration. Some people are able to move readily from one culture to another and be equally fluent and comfortable in either. In making the assessment of biculturalism, it is necessary to examine educational, economic, social, political, familial, and linguistic areas. Individuals may score differently in each of the spheres. The complexity is illustrated by a highly educated individual in American schools who retains his or her ethnic language as the primary language at home.[30] This examination will leave no doubt of the differences between individuals. The knowledge of the cultural values of each group should serve as a base line for the examination.

There will be those individuals who choose to assimilate. They deny their heritage and thereby negate their identity. The process of development of self not only has both conscious and unconscious psychological determinants, but also powerful ongoing societal determinants. People of color cannot become white, so that ethnic ties will need to be maintained if the individual is not to become a marginal person, belonging nowhere. As Pinderhughes states: "Since Afro-American identifying is not a matter of choice and Afro-Americans are never completely admitted to Americanization, any assumption of American identity means taking on an identity which is not validated by others who share it."[31] In the healthiest individual biculturalism is a matter of proud choice, but for all except those who pass for white it is a necessity and a reality.

Once having made this assessment or biculturalism, the fallacy of stereotyping becomes evident. Even family members may differ widely. As the external environment continues to have an impact on the individual and family, the configuration arrived at will be expected to alter. For planning and service delivery it is important to know the level of acculturation within the ethnic and American culture, the degree to which the individual is able to choose between two worlds, and the level of participation in each world that is desirable and obtainable by each client and client group. Freedom of choice must become the norm so that work must be done to open up societal options.

Minority Status and Ethnicity

The knowledge of the significance of minority status needs to be combined with information regarding its specific meaning and effect on each particular ethnic group. There are many factors to be considered and to which responses must be made; for example, whether the minority experience is a new or old role will have significance. The Puerto Rican who migrates to the mainland experiences shock at being in a minority role after having enjoyed a majority status in Puerto Rico. Additionally, it is of importance how the minority group perceives the issue of color. The Puerto Rican coming from a mixed heritage may well become traumatized by societal pressure to take on a definition of self as black or white, complicated further when other family members are of another coloring.

Of consideration too is immigration status—minority status can be expected to be somewhat different for those who have easy access between the United States and the country of their roots as opposed to those who are subject to immigration restrictions. This is bound to have some affect on the adjustment pattern. Columbians, who know that to leave may mean never being able to return to the United States and who wonder if and when there will be a reunion with relatives, will have a different mental set from Puerto Ricans, who may consider their stay transitory and know that they can easily see their families again. Whether the person is a legal resident or an illegal alien is also of significance; illegal aliens must put up with incredible abuses that they are in fear of reporting.

Being a political refugee and having a professional or upper-class status, as is true of many Cubans, has significance in the examination of minority status. The historical and governmental relationship will also have import in the understanding of the minority experience for a particular group. For blacks, the effects of a history of slavery and the struggle to maintain African cultural roots in a society where even the reality of its existence has been challenged gives a unique to the psychological reality of their minority experience. The colonial status of the American Indian—the knowledge that they are indigenous persons of the United States possessing dual citizenship—and members of sovereign nations again gives a different form to the minority experience. The amount of heterogeneity of any minority community will almost certainly affect their self-perception and affect their ability to acquire any degree of equity.

The Asian-Pacific community is extremely complex in terms of cultural, linguistic, and historical diversity and, as a result, they see themselves as largely having been overlooked by educational insti-

36

tutions, corporations, government agencies, and other societal sectors.[32] Ethnicity is a complex phenomenon and involves the individual's
identification with heritage and society, and governmental dealings
with community, group history, and present circumstances.

Ethnic Ties

In working with a particular minority community it is essential to
know the implications and ramifications of the ethnic ties as well as
to understand the multiple components of a particular group's minority status. Program planning and service delivery will have to
consider the degree to which there is a need for bicultural practitioners who can understand all the ramifications of this status and
with whom the community can feel trust. Important factors to be
assessed are the interracial climate and the critical nature of ethnic
identification.

Language

A model must take notice of the various functions of language. We
should be cognizant that language has played a significant social and
survival function and understand the ways it has served to foster
group solidarity.[33] Language helps to structure perception, organize
reality, and shape behavior. It is often comforting to speak one's own
language, particularly when under stress. The need for bilingual
workers is clear. Any model of service will need to examine the role
of the Anglo worker and that of interpreters. The use of interpreters
deprives the client of direct access to the helper.

Self-help

Any proposed service model must deal with the role of self-help and
tie itself into the natural helping networks.[34] It is evident that the
individual and community must have an active role in securing their
own destiny. This is a critical need and right and is of great therapeutic
value if we are not to destroy the sense of worth of a community and
foster a sense of powerlessness.

The tasks for any model of service within an Anglo setting are to
find appropriate ways to use ethnic workers, to create structures for
consumer input, and to develop partnerships with grass-roots organizations and indigenous helpers. As stated by Carel B. Germain,
"this matter of activity and personal decision making by the client
[and community] may be one of the most crucial issues in making our
services more responsive to human needs."[35] A guiding principle must

37

be for the minority community to input with power into the decision-making process.

Philosophical Underpinning

The philosophical underpinning that must be present in any model of service is that of the field working at the interface between man and environment. To achieve this end, an organization must accept as its responsibility working with outer systems that are either dysfunctional or are of insufficient help in maximizing human potential and creating innovative structures that foster growth. The ultimate goal for the practitioner is not only to alleviate this pain, but also to become a change agent. Case and cause must, therefore, be inextricably and circularly linked in any model of service delivery.

This philosophical underpinning, which has a long tradition in social work,[36] has to find expression through the organizational program components. At minimum, organizations must have advocacy, counseling, and family life education components. An agency will also, through a community assessment process, need to determine what other program components might be desirable.

Theoretical Base

The theoretical base should be grounded in systems and ecological concepts. These concepts help us to appreciate more fully how the outer environment impinges on people and how macro systems affect total populations. We become acutely aware that minority families and minority communities are social systems, "living systems [that] are acutely dependent upon their external environment,"[37] and that conditions for their existence are set by the broader society.[38] Pathology must, therefore, be defined in ecological terms, with behavior not being viewed as either sick or well. Instead, behavior must be defined in terms of transactional processes, an outcome of reciprocal interactions between specific social situations, and the individual and specific social situations and the community.[39]

The helping professions must concern themselves with helping people and environment achieve an adaptive fit and secure a mutuality and dynamic equilibrium. A life model for practice flows from a systems and ecological perspective. A life model would engage both the progressive and adaptive potentialities of people and activate and alter the environment to create a growth-producing milieu. Variations in lifestyles, the ways needs are perceived, and the importance of social networks must all be taken into account.[40] We must think less

38

in terms of psychic determinism, pathology, or disease. We need to concentrate more on how to foster human growth through the use of individual, family, and community strengths and the changing of environmental conditions that are presently playing havoc with minority families.

Implications

Implications stemming from this delineated framework lead to the recognition that any service delivery system developed to work with the minority communities must be one that deals both on the micro and macro levels and uses multifaceted strategies. It must deal both with the psychic pain experienced by people as well as the environmental situation impinging so destructively on the minority populations.

The interventions must be placed within an ethnic frame. Whatever strategies are implemented, whatever programs are developed, each community must have input into them, because the community has to define its own needs and the solutions cannot be superimposed. As Alfred Kahn points out, needs are, in effect, social definitions. The biological is very much supplemented by the cultural frame, to a point where the universal stable and biological core is but a small portion of the total. All in all, a value judgment enters into the process.[11] The minority communities, therefore, must have a role in the making of this value judgment and in determining the need task. It is essential that helping professionals work with minorities to help open up the opportunity structure.

Notes

1. The conceptual framework was originally developed by Emelicia Mizio, who believes that it can be applicable to other minorities, including poor whites. See Emelicia Mizio, ed., *Puerto Rican Task Force Report: Project on Ethnicity* (New York: Family Service Association of America, 1979).

2. Report of the Special Populations Subpanel on Mental Health of American Indians and Alaska Natives, *Task Panel Reports Submitted to the President's Commission on Mental Health* (Washington, D.C.: U.S. Government Printing Office, 1978), p. 956.

3. See Harold M. Baron, quoted in *Institutional Racism in America,* ed. Louis L. Knowles and Kenneth Prewitt. (Englewood Cliffs, N.J.: Prentice-Hall 1969), pp. 142-43.

4. See grant proposal for Golden Gate Chapter, National Association of Social Workers, "Proposal for a Program Development Grant on Institutional Racism," July 1971, p.2.

5. Amado M. Padilla and Rene A. Ruiz, *Latino Mental Health* (Rockville, Md.: National Institute of Mental Health, 1973), p.21.

6. See, for example, Anita Delaney, ed. *Black Task Force Report* (New York: Family Service Association of America, 1979); Kenji Murase, "Social Welfare Policy and Services: Asian Americans," in *The Dual Perspective*, ed. Dolores G. Norton (New York: Council on Social Work Education, 1978); Eligio R. Padilla and Amado M. Padilla, eds., *Transcultural Psychiatry: An Hispanic Perspective*, monograph no. 4 (Los Angeles: Spanish-Speaking Mental Health Research Centers, University of California, 1977); and Ronald G. Lewis and Man Keung Ho, "Social Work with Native Americans," *Social Work* 20, no. 5 (September 1975).

7. For materials useful in training, see Howard L. Fromkin and John J. Sherwood, eds., *Intergroup and Minority Relations: An Experiential Handbook* (La Jolla, Calif.: University Associates, 1976); Elaine B. Pinderhughes, "Teaching Empathy in Cross-Cultural Social Work," *Social Work* 24, no. 4 (July 1979); and G. Winifred Kagwa, "Utilization of Racial Content in Developing Self-Awareness," *Journal of Education for Social Work* 12, no. 2 (Spring 1976).

8. Lola M. Irelan, ed., *Low-Income Life Styles* (Washington, D.C.: U.S. Government Printing Office, 1968).

9. U.S. Bureau of the Census, Department of Commerce, "Characteristics of the Population Below the Poverty Level: 1977," *Current Population Reports*, Series P-60, no. 119 (Washington, D.C.: U.S. Government Printing Office, 1979), p. 1.

10. Ibid., p. 2.

11. U.S. Bureau of the Census, Department of Commerce, *Population Characteristics: Persons of Spanish Origin in the United States: 1978*, prepared by Edward Fernandez (Washington, D.C.: U.S. Government Printing Office, June 1979).

12. Report of Subpanel on American Indians and Alaska Natives, *Task Panel*, p. 962.

13. U.S. Bureau of the Census, Department of Commerce, *Consumer Income: Characteristics of the Populations Below the Poverty Level: 1977*, prepared by Carol Fendler (Washington, D.C.: U.S. Government Printing Office, March 1979), p. 3.

14. U.S. Bureau of the Census, Department of Commerce, "Persons of Spanish Origin in the United States: March 1978," *Current Population Reports*, Series P-20, no. 339 (Washington, D.C.: U.S. Government Printing Office, 1978), p. 13.

15. Lloyd Street, "Minorities," in *Encyclopedia of Social Work*, vol. 2, 17th ed. (Washington, D.C.: National Association of Social Workers, 1977), p. 940.

16. Ibid.

17. Morton Kramer, Beatrice M. Rosen, and Ernest M. Willis, "Definitions and Distributions of Mental Disorders in a Racist Society," in *Racism and Mental Health*, ed. Charles V. Willie et al. (Pittsburgh, Pa.: University of Pittsburgh Press, 1974), pp. 355-56.

18. Report of the Joint Commission on Mental Health of Children, *Crisis in Child Mental Health: Challenge for the 1970's* (New York: Harper and Row, 1970), p.44.

19. Report of the Special Populations Subpanel on Mental Health of Minorities, Women, Physically Handicapped, *Task Panel Reports Submitted to the President's Commission on Mental Health*, appendix (Washington, D.C.: U.S. Government Printing Office, 1978), p. 731.

20. Judith Rabkin and Elmer L. Struening, "Ethnicity, Social Class and Mental Illness,"

Working Paper Series, no. 17 (New York: Institute of Pluralism and Group Identity, 1976), p.11.

21. Report of the Special Populations Subpanel on Mental Health of Black Americans, *Task Panel Reports Submitted to the President's Commission on Mental Health* (Washington, D.C.: U.S. Government Printing Office, 1978) p. 831.

22. Report of the Special Populations Subpanel on Asian Pacific Americans, *Task Panel Reports Submitted to the President's Commission on Mental Health* (Washington, D.C.: U.S. Government Printing Office, 1978), p. 791.

23. Derald Wing Sue and David Sue, "Barriers to Effective Cross-Cultural Counseling," *Journal of Counseling Psychology* 24, no. 5 (1977).

24. Elaine B. Pinderhughes, "Afro-Americans and Economic Dependency: Implications for the Future," *The Urban and Social Change Review* 12, no. 2 (Summer 1979): 26.

25. Rabkin and Struening, "Ethnicity and Mental Illness," p. 31.

26. Pinderhughes, "Afro-Americans and Economic Dependency," p. 24.

27. Leon Chestang, "Environmental Influences on Social Functioning: The Black Experience," in *The Diverse Society, Implications for Social Policy*, ed. Pastora San Juan Cafferty and Leon Chestang (Washington, D.C.: National Association of Social Workers, 1976), p. 59.

28. Report of Subpanel on American Indians and Alaska Natives, *Task Panel*, p. 972.

29. Ibid., p. 968.

30. *Curriculum Schema*, vol. 3 (Houston, Texas: Chicano Training Center, 1977), pp 12-13.

31. Pinderhughes, "Afro-Americans and Economic Dependency," p. 26.

32. Report of Subpanel on Asian Pacific Americans, *Task Panel*, p. 785.

33. Marta Sotomayor, "Language, Culture, and Ethnicity in Developing Self-Concept, *Social Casework* 58, no. 4 (April 1977): 203.

34. U.S. Department of Health, Education, and Welfare, *Report on the Implementation of Task Panel Reports Submitted to the President's Commission on Mental Health, 1978*, No. ADM 79-848 (Washington, D.C.: U.S. Government Printing Office, 1979).

35. Carel B. Germain, "An Ecological Perspective in Casework Practice," *Social Casework* 54 (June 1973): 328.

36. See Katherine A. Kendall, "Signals from an Illustrious Past," *Social Casework* 58 (June 1977): 328:36.

37. Daniel Katz and Robert Kahn, *The Social Psychology of Organizations* (New York: John Wiley, 1966), p. 18.

38. William J. Goode, *The Family* (Englewood Cliffs, N.J.: Prentice-Hall, 1964), p.3.

39. James Kelly, "Ecological Constraints on Mental Health Service," in *Perspectives in Community Mental Health*, ed. Arthur J. Bindman and Allen D. Spiegel (Chicago: Aldine, 1969), p. 97.

40. See Germain, "Ecological Perspective," pp. 325-27.

41. Alfred J. Kahn, *Theory and Practice on Social Planning* (New York: Russell Sage Foundation, 1969).

The Theoretical Framework

Anita J. Delaney

In the field of human services, minority group social functioning has been a consistent topic of interest for researchers and planners seriously committed to the enhancement of human potential, and also for those whose primary aim has been to identify patterns of pathology and programs for remediation. Observations of functioning that seemed different from the norm of majority groups have often been interpreted as deficits, and services that flowed from such perspectives had limited compatibility with the psychosocial realities of the minority experience. The problem with such one-dimensional observations is that they derive from perspectives that do not give adequate recognition to the sociocultural context of the minority experience and the potential that exists in these communities to function in an adaptive way. With careful examination of the literature base, however, a number of concepts do emerge that promote greater understanding of larger systems' impact on minority social functioning and suggest the design of culturally sensitive strategies for growth, development, and change.

The purpose of this article is the development of a theoretical framework that has the breadth, sensitivity, and specificity to support models of mental health service delivery to the black and Puerto Rican communities.[1] To achieve such a goal requires knowledge of the commonalities as well as the differences of experience between the two cultures, a reduction of the highly specific functioning of individuals, groups, and institutions to manageable explanatory concepts, and the conceptualization of strategies to resolve the functioning problems of people and societal institutions.[2] In addition, it should be recognized that flexibility is required to accomodate the changing needs and resources of human and environmental systems.[3]

The Minority Experience

Puerto Ricans, black Americans, and other racial or linguistic minorities share commonalities of experience with external systems that clearly influence the development of similar structures and functioning patterns to cope with the hostile environments in which they exist.[4] The commonalities of minority status have been captured in Leon Chestang's conceptualization of the black experience: social injustice, societal inconsistency, and personal impotence.[5] Social injustice, or the denial of legal and human rights, is a well-documented legacy of the minority expereince on the American continent.

In today's era of enlightenment, there are laws that protect the civil rights of minorities, but the institutional policies and structures of the economic, political, and social systems continue to operate in a manner that denies equality of access and outcome for minorities.[6] The high unemployment rate, the high school graduation of functional illiterates in racially isolated communities, and the overrepresentation of minorities in our prison systems are indicative of the perpetuation of a pattern of social injustice.

Societal inconsistency refers to the individual and destructive forms of personal rejection experienced by minorities that attack self-esteem. Although social injustices can be dealt with legally or relieved through the group supports offered within the culture, the individual alone must assess the validity of direct assaults to his or her dignity and self-worth. A sense of impotence or powerlessness results when adequate supports are not available. Although majority group Americans have full access to the economic, political, and social systems that facilitate integration of the instrumental and expressive aspects of a culture, the experience of minority groups is one of depreciation, limited access to opportunity structures, and exclusion.

These threats to survival and self-esteem require adaptations from minorities that cause "a split in the acculturative process resulting in the development of a duality of culture."[7] For the minority consumer, the capacity to function effectively in *two* cultures is essential to survival. This primary coping mechanism serves to increase the opportunity for minority access to the goods and services vested in larger systems, while cultural relationships, behaviors, and institutions are strengthened and maintained to combat negative societal responses and promote the development of human potential.

43

System Concepts

The underlying philosophy of a mental health service delivery system to urban, low-income black and Puerto Rican communities recognizes that the interlocking processes of racism and poverty constrain the development of human potential. This model flows from an ecological systems perspective that widens the scope of assessment to include the transactions that occur between minorities and the systems within and outside their neighborhoods. Carel B. Germain supports the validity of this approach and states:

> Ecology is a science concerned with the adaptive fit of organisms and their environments and with the means by which they achieve a dynamic equilibrium and mutuality. It seems to furnish an appropriate metaphor for a helping profession concerned with the relationships between human beings and their interpersonal and organizational environments, with helping to modify or to enhance the quality of transactions between people and their environments, and with seeking to promote environments that support human well-being.[8]

The ecological systems approach draws on concepts from general systems theory, and its utility for human service systems has been described by William E. Gordon.[9] General systems concepts address our dual concern with minority families and the environmental systems containing the goods and services essential to survival, growth, and development. An ecological systems approach focuses attention on the quality of the transactions between individuals and external systems, highlights the life arenas where strengths are present and supports are needed, and promotes the design of helping strategies tailored to the identified needs of each situation.

Adaptation

The term "adaptation," when used in reference to minorities, has often carried the suggestion of passive submission to the values, lifestyles, and goals of the dominant society. It may further imply that if blacks and Puerto Ricans were to adopt a "melting pot" perspective and give up their cultural patterns, they could achieve greater success in their transactions with the larger environment. The historical and contemporary American experience indicates that the blending of racial minorities into the larger culture has been neither an achievable nor a desirable goal. A broader view of adaptation that recognizes the significance of cultural coping mechanisms and the need for external systems change seems more appropriate for a framework of service to minority communities.

Heinz Hartman's description of the ego's capacity for three types of adaptive maneuvers includes: the alloplastic changes individuals make in their environments to satisfy basic needs and to achieve the goals established for themselves, the autoplastic changes they make in themselves to meet the environmental requirements of desirable goals, and the search for new environments offering greater opportunities for the satisfaction of needs and goals.[10] These concepts relate to activity, collaboration, growth, and change, and give greater clarity to the minority development of cultural behaviors, family structures, institutions, and patterns of mobility to deal with the extrasystemic pressures experienced by racially and linguistically different populations. As planners and practitioners begin to integrate knowledge of the minority experience in America and the coping mechanisms essential to survival and self-esteem in such an environment, a perspective can develop that respects the consumer's capacity to participate actively in the assessment of need and the design of interventions to resolve problems in living.

Erik H. Erikson's concept of ego development through task resolution at identifiable stages in the life cycle stresses the importance of a supportive environment.[11] Individuals' genetic endowments, the knowledge they bring from the completion of successive developmental stages, and the opportunities or barriers they encounter in their environmental relationships are critical to the socialization process. These developmental concepts relate to the coping patterns of most people, but, for minority populations, the interlocking processes of racism and powerlessness bring additional elements to the assessment of social functioning and the identification of areas for intervention.[12] Human service givers should be attuned to the family socialization processes that serve to sensitize children to the realities of minority status and promote survival, self-esteem, and a sense of well-being.

Concepts from role theory support an understanding of the viable social and family networks in minority communities.[13] The family would be seen as an extended nurturing system, capable of changing its structure and functioning to meet the needs of its members. In addition to explaining the exchanges that take place within the cultural boundaries, role concepts clarify minority relationships with institutions and define a role for helping agents when the institutional response to minority status is destructive to the development of human potential.

If a service design is to address effectively one of the major causes of stress in minority communities—institutional barriers to the achievement of human potential—organizational theory provides

45

tools for utilization in the process of social change.[14] These concepts identify the functioning patterns of institutional structures and identity points of entry for change strategies. With information on the attitudes and power arrangements of specific organizations, change agents can model the role behaviors and strengthen the capacities of minority consumers to negotiate environmental resources with a sense of competence that will support the achievement of both current and future goals.

The minority experience in America requires that the adaptive mechanisms of blacks and Puerto Ricans, as well as other minorities, be well-tuned and in perpetual operation. Although these coping skills are essential to survival and must be durable under stress, in some instances, they may only serve to satisfy the demands of a destructive environmental situation while growth and development are inhibited. The dominant value orientations observed in black and Puerto Rican communities support inclusive family relationships, flexible family roles, and strong religious and work orientations.

To avoid depletion of these valued resources and to strengthen capacities to function successfully in two cultures, a developmental rather than a maintenance perspective holds greater relevance for minority communities. The objective of a developmental approach is to build upon the cultural strengths with a sensivitity that permits the minority development of alternative functioning patterns, as they seem indicated. This approach, however, does not lose sight of the noxious elements of environmental systems that must be eradicated if blacks and Puerto Ricans are to achieve their human potential.

Competence

An ecological systems perspective recognizes the destructive impact of racism and poverty on social functioning, and highlights the unique cultural supports adopted by blacks and Puerto Ricans for survival and achievement. The complexities of our contemporary American society require the development of bicultural competencies for sustaining life and developing a sense of well-being.

To some helping professionals, the concept of competence suggests a value judgment of individual or group deficit when it is used with reference to racial minorities. In our view, the term "competence" is broad enough to include an assessment of the functioning patterns of individuals, groups, and institutions within a cultural context that clarifies strengths as well as areas where support and change are needed. Cultural sensitivity does not mean that service givers assess all behaviors observed in black and Puerto Rican communities as

46

adaptive and useful. To overlook obvious deficiencies and pathologies would be a disservice to these communities, has racist overtones, and relieves the helping agent of any commitment to assist families experiencing internal stress, which may well have its base in the quality of their relationships with the environment. When human development has occurred in a noxious environment, it should come as no surprise to service providers that psychic as well as environmental problems will require their assistance.

Although it is essential for planners and practitioners to have a clear understanding of the sociopolitical ramifications of institutional racism and the internal dysfunctioning observed in minority communities, it is equally important to go beyond the labeling of these populations primarily as victims. The social forces that limit access to opportunities have been well documented in the literature,[15] but to dwell on minority victimization may obscure the potential for adaptation of self and the environment. A framework of service for minorities should address itself to a reduction in the sense of powerlessness through strategies that support the development and strengthening of individual and collective skills for survival and achievement.

Robert White defines competence as "the cumulative result of the history of interaction with the environment. Sense of competence is suggested as a suitable term . . . signifying one's consciously or unconsciously felt competence . . . in dealing with various aspects of the environment."[16] Ivy Bennet expands on this concept, stating that " . . . mastery is the result of experiences of competence and is a belief, based upon these feelings, that one can change one's environment by obtaining knowledge of how to change it."[17]

These concepts relate to man's innate push to have an affect on his environment and support our view of the potential for growth, achievement, change, and the enhancement of self-esteem in minority communities. The inclusion of social competence as a goal of mental health services to minorities does not, therefore, negate the strengths of cultural patterns, but instead promotes recognition of an existing base of competency that can be used to expand the range of coping skills available in these communities.[18] The selection of these health-focused concepts supports the view that consumer activity is vital to the resolution of tasks and the achievement of an adaptive fit which is good for the individual as well as the immediate and larger environments.

Service

The model of service that flows from an ecosystems perspective respects the capacity of the minority consumer to participate actively in the identification and change of the problems in living that interfere with growth, development, and achievement of human potential. Social work with minorities is often discussed informally among professionals as an overwhelming task that drains their strength and produces few outcomes that can be labeled successful. These assessments are often the result of adherence to a deficit view of minority functioning, and a view of the larger environment as a closed system that is highly resistant to change when the elements of racism and poverty are involved.

Planners and practitioners who succumb to this sense of powerlessness have minimal utility for effective service in black and Puerto Rican communities. What is needed is a cadre of helping agents who recognize that redistribution of the wealth and the eradication of racism are long-range goals. The intermediate accomplishments are vital components in developing and sustaining the strengths required in the struggle to achieve those goals.

Carol Meyer has described the complexities of contemporary urban living that affect all members of this society.[19] We live in a wage economy that is entirely reliant on money income; the institutional structures sustaining life make us interdependent rather than self-reliant; and the range of stresses occuring in areas of great population density produce needs for help and support in all families at one time or another. For low-income minority families who may be located in some of our most distressed urban areas, these problems in living are multiplied and the need for help is generally on multiple levels.

Human service givers can readily agree that the lack of money in minority communities to meet basic human needs has major consequences for the individual and the social systems within his or her sphere of interaction. Minority access to economic resources sufficient to provide a decent level of living is a right and a priority. This framework expands that view to include Alfred J. Kahn's concepts on social services as social utilities.[20] Kahn views the consumer of service as a citizen, rather than a client or a patient, who should have open access to an array of social services that will enhance his or her capacity to function effectively. The geographical locations, public relations efforts, and fee schedules of agencies should promote access to service for populations at risk, as well as the more affluent residents of a community.

The ecological systems approach requires that social work planners consult with communities to determine exactly what goes on between individuals and families, individuals and their neighbors, and individuals and the institutional structures that exist to meet the instrumental and expressive needs of our society. When we enter, for example, a low-income housing project to explore the need for help with problems in living, we note that some families are functioning more effectively than others. Although two single parents residing in the same building and sharing common racial and economic identities may appear to be in need of the same range of services, social planners and practitioners should be attuned to the individual dynamics of each situation. One parent may sit in her apartment all day with the shades down and a television set blaring, while a neighbor interacts effectively with a network of friends, relatives, and institutional resources in the community. The helping agent who has expanded his or her fundamental practice skills to permit a dual focus on the individual dynamics and the environmental reality is equipped to respond on multiple levels with strategies for mutual aid arrangements, therapeutic counseling, parent education, child care, and macrosystemic advocacy.

We have often assumed that common racial and socioeconomic conditions produce common problems in social functioning. Although sensitivity to culture and class is essential for work with minorities, it is equally important to retain the capacity to see individuals in their specific environments and to shape services to meet their identified needs. The individual biopsychosocial system causes variations in coping patterns, and behaviors that are adaptive in some instances and maladaptive in others. Helping professionals who are anxious to avoid the label of racism may be reluctant to diagnose pathology in minority clients and permit internal stress to proceed untreated until severe disturbance is manifested. The assessment of minority social functioning requires a delicate balance of skills to avoid stereotyping while maintaining an appreciation for cultural difference.

The competent helping agent must be equipped to respond to minority individuals, families, and communities with a knowledge and skills base seldom required when working with majority group clients, whose needs may relate to a more restricted sphere of functioning. Although a systems perspective is recommended for the assessment of all people in need of service, its use is essential for an accurate reading of the complex problems in living encountered by minority consumers.

A major objective of this framework is to develop greater sensitivity among human service givers to the progressive forces operative in minority communities. Comprehensive services designed to reinforce the strengths in minority families, to develop new modes of functioning, and to relieve stress-producing environmental situations should be accessible and accountable to the communities they hope to serve. An integrated program of culturally sensitive therapeutic counseling, advocacy, and preventive services supports a major thrust toward the eradication of some of the primary causes of social dysfunction in black and Puerto Rican communities.

Conclusion

Services to minorities often place the practitioner or social planner in the contradictory roles of consumer advocate versus social control agent. Gains for minorities may be seen by larger systems as losses for majority group members and controls are effectively employed to restore the equilibrium. Ecological systems concepts broaden the perspective to a humanistic level and suggest strategies with the potential for outcomes beneficial to both the consumer and the larger environment.

William Gordon sees theoretical systems as "open programs or proposals for inquiry rather than as closed channels."[21] This theoretical framework developed to support models of mental health service delivery to minority communities is not a closed system that speaks with definitive answers to minority problems in living. The populations discussed, blacks and Puerto Ricans, are living, human systems whose transactions with numerous environmental systems are frequently unjust and inconsistent. Because the institutional response to minority status shifts and changes with the social, political, or economic climate, it is expected that new cultural adaptations will develop for survival and achievement. A knowledge base that permits new definitions of need and new approaches to service is essential for the training of planners and practitioners committed to social justice and the enhancement of human potential.

Notes

1. See Anita J. Delaney, ed., *Black Task Force Report* (New York: Family Service Association of America, 1979); and Emelica Mizio, ed., *Puerto Rican Task Force Report* (New York: Family Service Association of America, 1979).

2. Carl M. Schafer, "Teaching Social Work Practice in an Integrated Course," in *The General Systems Approach: Contributions Toward an Holistic Conception of Social Work,*

ed. Gordon Hearn (New York: Council on Social Work Education, 1969), pp.26-36.

3. Dolores G. Norton, ed., *The Dual Perspective* (New York: Council on Social Work Education, 1978).

4. Emelicia Mizio, "Impact of External Systems on the Puerto Rican Family," *Social Casework* 55, no. 2 (February 1974): 76-83.

5. Leon Chestang, "Environmental Influences on Social Functioning: Experience," in *The Diverse Society: Implications for Social Policy*, ed. Pastora San Juan Cafferty and Leon Chestang (Washington, D.C.: National Association of Social Workers, 1976), p. 70.

6. For a perceptive study of this process, see Joel Dreyfuss and Charles Lawrence III, *The Bakke Case: The Politics of Inequality* (New York: Harcourt Brace Jovanovich, 1979).

7. Ibid., p. 70.

8. Carel B. Germain, "An Ecological Perspective in Casework Practice," *Social Casework* 54 (June 1973): 326.

9. William E. Gordon, "Basic Constructs for an Integrative and Generative Conception of Social Work," in *The General Systems Approach: Contributions Toward an Holistic Conception of Social Work*, ed. Gordon A. Hearn (New York: Council on Social Work Education, 1969), pp. 5-11.

10. Heinz Hartman, *Ego Psychology and the Problem of Adaptation* (New York: International Universities Press, 1958), pp. 19-20.

11. Erik H. Erikson, *Identity: Youth and Crisis* (New York: W.W. Norton, 1968); and Erik H. Erikson, *Childhood and Society* (New York: W. W. Norton, 1963).

12. For a description of these processes, see Barbara Bryant Solomon, *Black Empowerment: Social Work in Oppressed Communities* (New York: Columbia University Press, 1976).

13. Robert K. Merton, *Social Theory and Social Structure* (New York: Free Press, 1968); Elizabeth Bott, *Family and Social Network* (London: Tavistock Publications, 1957); and Bruce J. Biddle and Edwin J. Thomas, eds., *Role Theory: Concepts and Research* (New York: John Wiley, 1966).

14. Jack Rothman, *Planning and Organizing for Social Change* (New York: Columbia University Press, 1974).

15. See, for example, Delaney, *Black Task Force Report*; and Mizio, *Puerto Rican Task Force Report*

16. See Robert N. White, *Ego and Reality and Psychoanalytic Theory* (New York: International Universities Press, 1963); and Thomas Gladwin, "Social Competence and Clinical Practice," *Psychiatry* 30 (February 1967): 30-43.

17. Ivy B. Bennett, "Use of Ego Psychology Concepts in Family Service Intake," *Social Casework* 54 (May 1973): 291.

18. For expansion on this view, see Robert O. Washington, "Social Work and the Black Perspective," *The Journal of Applied Social Sciences* 3, no. 2 (Spring-Summer 1979): 149-67.

19. Carol H. Meyer, "The Impact of Urbanization on Child Welfare," *Child Welfare* 46, no. 8 (October 1967): 433-42.

20. Alfred J. Kahn, "Social Services in Relation to Income Security—Introductory Notes," *Social Service Review* 39 (December 1967): 381-89.

21. Gordon, "Basic Constructs for a Conception of Social Work," p. 6.

Reflections on the Dual Perspective

Samuel O. Miller

In 1903, W.E. DuBois, in his noted book *The Souls of Black Folks*, gave a poignant description of the socialization experiences of black (and, in reality, of all minority) individuals in the following words:

> One ever feels his twoness . . . two souls, two thoughts, two unreconciled strivings, two warring ideals in one dark body, whose dogged strength alone keeps it from being torn asunder. The history of the American Negro is the history of his strife. This longing to attain self-conscious manhood, to merge his double self into a better and truer self. In this merging he wishes neither of his older selves to be lost.[1]

No statement more cogently captures the thrust and significance of the dual perspective, to be defined and discussed in this article. In describing this theoretical construct, some of the knowledge contributing to its clarification will be identified, the rationale and necessity for its development will be addressed, and the implications of this concept for social work practice with minority clients and communities will be discussed.

Defining the Dual Perspective

For our purposes, the dual perspective is defined as the art, theory, and practice of consciously and systematically perceiving, understanding, and comparing, simultaneously, the values, attitudes, and behaviors of the minority client's immediate family, community, or cultural system with those of the larger social system.[2] It is the attempt to bring into conscious awareness what is believed and known about the similarities and differences between the client's immediate social situation and the larger system into which the former is embedded. Similarly, the social worker reaches for and attempts to grasp his or her attitudes and values in relationship to the client's cultural back-

53

ground and, in particular, how these mirror those generally held in society and their implications for the practice.

This concept of a dual perspective grows out of the confluence of several streams: role theory, systems and behavioral theories, and knowledge about minority people. For example, Robert Merton, whose reputation as a sociologist is impeccable, states that:

> A conception basic to sociology holds that individuals have multiple social roles and tend to organize their behavior in terms of the structurally defined expectations assigned to each role. Type cases are numerous and familiar: the Catholic communist subjected to conflicting pressures from party and church, the marginal man suffering the pulls of conflicting societies, the professional woman torn between demands of family and career. Every sociological textbook abounds with illustrations of incompatible demands made of the multiselved person.[3]

It is not difficult to draw parallel implications about the conflicts faced by minority individuals. They are inexorably associated with two worlds: the minority community out of which they emerge and the larger society in which they may be employed and to which they must turn for certain basic requirements in order to survive. Leon Chestang wrote of this duality and its implications. He called the larger and more dominant system of the individual experience the "sustaining system."[4] It houses the instrumental needs of man, the goods and services, the political power, and the economic resources, all of which confer status and power. Embedded in the larger system is the more immediate system, the physical and social environment of family and close community. A person's basic sense of identity grows out of this system, which Chestang refers to as the "nurturing environment." To consider a minority individual without reference to both of these systems is to hold a partial and rather limited view of him or her.

Systems Perspective

Another major source contributing to the development of the dual perspective is systems theory, the advent of which has opened a whole new set of vistas for the appreciation and understanding of individual and social functioning. It is difficult to select all the pertinent constructs from this theory-building tool, so a rather parsimonious mention of some selected notions will follow. Applied to an interest in understanding minority individuals and communities, this framework encourages a holistic view while simultaneously avoiding the risk of ignoring the reality or import of parts vital to the immediate situation.

54

This view highlights the interaction between minority individuals and their various environments, enhancing the selection of the most immediately impinging of these environments and simultaneously recognizing their unique qualities and their effect (or potential effect) on the environment.

The systems perspective also suggests that events of life are not random, but are shaped by the events of prior processes. Although not holding a predeterministic approach or suggesting that individuals are fixed by previous life events, systems thinking suggests that prior life processes shape the probable range of future patterns of interaction. To illustrate: the dual perspective assumes that one of its goals is to help workers recognize more clearly the institutional disadvantages directed toward individuals simply because they belong to a certain racial or ethnic group. Often, workers suggest that these barriers do not exist now as they did in the past or that they cannot be isolated. Professionals agree theoretically that social policies do not affect all groups equally in terms of degree of impact, but are sometimes unwilling to accept how certain patterns of deployment of resources as well as certain legislative and administrative decisions place heavier burdens on minorities than on the general population, simply because of the ethnic status and concomitant life experiences of minority individuals. Take, for example, the decision to tolerate a certain percentage of unemployment nationally, which means that young, urban minority youth frequently have an unemployment rate several-fold that of the nation at large. Further we can observe how human service delivery systems are imposed on clients and communities without knowledge or appreciation of the informal self-help resources already existing in the community, or the systematic refusal to uphold the tribal treaties enacted with the tribes of American Indians, or how Puerto Ricans who, although full-fledged American citizens, are viewed and treated as immigrants when they come to the mainland to seek a better life.

One last concept from the systems approach is worth mentioning here. This has to do with social-ecological attempts to appreciate how environments have an impact on individuals and communities. With the increasing elaboration of ecosystems, we have become keenly aware of how one dimension of the social environment depends very much on other aspects of that same environment. Similarly, we are aware that environments may limit or inhibit behavior or occurrences and that they may support or allow certain other behaviors to occur. Thus, a worker who seeks an accurate evaluation of why ethnic minority clients or communities appear unwilling to change their circumstances will need to consider how external forces in the environment

55

preclude or punish the efforts made previously. The worker may emphasize how the helping process can remove those obstacles and permit desired behaviors.

Research and Theory Building

Perhaps the single most important factor contributing to the development of the dual perspective is the ever-increasing knowledge regarding ethnic minority people, in particular the knowledge emerging from the research and theory building by minority scholars about their experiences, their people, and their coping and functioning mechanisms. Most social workers received their training through programs built on various models—psychoanalytic, medical, psychosocial, behavioral, and so on. The value and validity of this information have, however, been questioned, particularly the behavior and functioning of minority individuals and communities; it is clear that these models were developed with the dominant majority in mind. Consequently, hypotheses stemming from these models with reference to people culturally different from the dominant group are invariably interpreted as if all things are equal and based completely on the ethnocentrism of the theorist or observer.

Ethnocentrism

Ethnocentrism is the complete antithesis of the dual perspective, as it represents the tendency to evaluate people and experiences from the viewpoint of one's (the evaluator) individual group. This tendency unquestionably clouds one's objectivity and leads to a wide range of stereotypes about culturally different people, which gradually gain wide acceptance. For example, the following qualities are frequently associated with one or another ethnic minority groups:

1. *They* use force to settle arguments or to punish disobedient children.
2. *They* are generally antiintellectual and consequently fail to support their children's school activities or intellectual strivings.
3. *They* are unable to postpone gratification.
4. *They* are fatalistic in their view of the world and feel that they have little control over events, people, or institutions.
5. *They* do not make use of "talking therapies."

These qualities have been used in different places and at different times to characterize blacks, Puerto Ricans, Chicanos, and American Indians alike; they are generally extrapolated from research findings, or from theorizing about people living in poverty.[5] Although it is true that many ethnic minority individuals do live in poverty, those who

56

discuss this matter do not make the distinction between them and those minority individuals who are not poverty-stricken, nor do they acknowledge the obvious fact that it is the absence of money and the concomitant effects that lead to their observations, rather than the ethnic background of the group.

Edward Casavantes, writing about Mexican Americans, concludes that "the only true characteristics or attributes of most Mexican Americans are the following; they have come from Mexico, or perhaps from Spain via Mexico; they speak Spanish, many with an accent; they are Catholic and many have dark skin and hair. These are the things that a true Chicano, a real Mexican must possess."[6] After noting that the Chicano shares some of these qualities, especially Catholicism and dark skin and hair, with other groups, he says that the essence of being a Chicano emerges from the fact that his ancestors come, with their many customs and traditions, from Mexico and Spain and they speak Spanish.

The dual perspective seeks to help practitioners, researchers, theorists, and so on to burst out of their ethnocentric trappings; to abandon their stereotypes, and to look critically at the minority person or group with which they are concerned. They are then asked to identify the essential features of this individual or group, the essence of being a minority person. In doing so, practitioners or professionals seek to grasp the similarities and differences that the individual holds with others and to identify those most relevant to the current situation—a process that, when successful, leads to true individualization of the client.

Many observe that this is only good social work practice. Our response to this has been that when it comes to ethnic minority clients, good social work is not now and never has been good enough. It is true that the perspective is infused and informed by widely held social work values and principles. A quick perusal would help some to recognize such truisms as being able to start "where the client is," to view the client's situations nonjudgmentally, and to be critically appreciative of how individual self-awareness has an effect on efforts to help clients. When these principles are applied with the typical and somewhat natural ethnocentrism (as noted and defined above), they result in inadequate and often irrelevant social work services.

Reeducation for Practice

Building on and integrating such well-established social work principles as mentioned, the dual perspective demands greater professional responsibility and development in cognitive, attitudinal, and

57

behavioral spheres. It requires workers to identify consciously what they know or, most often and important, what they do *not* know about the cultural forms, interactional styles, and behavioral responses that are really characteristic of the group. Workers should be absolutely clear of how, when, and why clients are similar to and different from the dominant society, and what are the implications of the similarity and dissimilarity. When workers recognize the absence of knowledge, efforts should be made to fill in the gap through consultation with ethnic minority professionals, independent study, or engaging the client critically in ways that would add to knowledge. On the programatic plane, the dual perspective requires or pushes social work organizations to develop and create programs that are culturally responsive—employing ethnic minority professionals, providing opportunities for staff development of the nonminority staff members, encouraging citizen participation, and providing a climate that says loud and clear to ethnic minority clients, you are welcome here.

Attitudinally, the dual perspective requires professionals to examine their own and society's emotional responses to the client and his or her group, not solely to issues immediately relevant to the practice situation, but to issues about which workers and the profession as a whole may need to advocate on behalf of the client group. At the same time, workers need to inquire into the clients' attitudes regarding problem definition, practice objectives, process, and the climate in which services are provided. The major objective in this sphere is to establish the congruence (or to identify the lack of congruence) between clients' views and those of workers, the social work profession, and society in general.

The import of this process is reflected clearly in the general stereotypes regarding nonutilization of mental health services by minority clients. Interpretations of the data are frequently done with limited appreciation or recognition of the fact that ethnic minority individuals may have different attitudes regarding what social work or mental health services represent. The "blame the victim" attitude rigidly maintains service patterns that denigrate the potential receivers, their lifestyles, and their ambitions.

Culturally Relevant Service

In the last analysis, the value of the dual perspective will depend on whether and how it influences the behavior of professionals in their work with ethnic minority clients. Thus, workers who truly seek to use culturally relevant intervention methods will give serious consideration to the need for more actively supportive and highly personalized relationships, greater sharing and communication of values and expectations, and the provision of concrete services as needed to facilitate the helping process.

Practice with ethnic minority clients will be based on a clear differentiation between cultural paranoia and real pathology, between cultural resistance and depressive withdrawal, and traditional family needs and approaches and abnormal dependency needs. Workers engaged in such practices will not automatically seek to change survival mechanisms without full appreciation of how and why they developed. The worker's behavior will demonstrate actual respect for culturally relevant institutions (for example, families, including the important extended family members, churches, and self-help groups) and the role they play in a client's life situation, the need for space and time within one's own community during periods of stress and alienation or when one simply wants to desist from interacting with others who appear different, when and where one can see one's own kind, eat native food, hear one's language, and so on.

Ramiro Valdez, evaluating his academic experience at a noted Northeast university where he was extremely sucessful in achieving his educational objectives, says it most cogently:

> For a Chicano like myself it can be very hard. I have found that I am lonely for a people, a culture, a way of life—I have missed my people. Not just my family, but the Chicanos and the Chicano way of life. I miss speaking our language with a group of people. I miss our food and the many varieties of it, miss seeing others like me at restaurants and the movies, miss my people and culture. But aside from that, there is the matter of rethinking what I know and believe. Minority students who achieve high success in the educational system are often hurt most, because they have to exchange their way of life and their values so as to fit into the mold of that system. I have had to do that for a little while, but I have not given up my way of life and values. I have only placed them aside for a while. Once I return to San Antonio and the barrio, I will again be myself with one difference: I will know how to think like the people that are in control of things; and I will have credentials which they recognize. I will not think like them all the time; only when I want to communicate with them.[7]

The dual perspective can help workers make the critical choices necessary in their work with minority clients by forcing them to devote attention to the essential variables and by lessening the natural tendency simply and rigidly to follow one's favorite theoretical, personal, or social trend. The dual perpsective leads to a process of assessment that systematically includes examination of the dominant environment and institutional factors as well as those associated with client stress, assisting the worker to select whether the target of change should appropriately become the client, the larger system, or both, or whether to intervene at all.

At this point, the concept of the dual perspective is a system in process. There is a need for clearer definitions, specifications of how and when it is applied, and identification of the substantive knowledge that informs this construct. Despite its stage of development, the implications of adapting this perspective as a vital component of practice theory and skills are legion. Both the Puerto Rican and black task force reports respectively have described model programs, the structure and components of which constitute veritable embodiments of the dual perspective.[8] As one reads both models, one can visualize the flexibility, the relevance, and the use of multilevels and multifaceted strategies that would appeal to and positively affect a wide range of ethnic minority clients. The end result of such models will undoubtedly provide more efficient and useful services to ethnic minority clients and, in the process, affirm the essence of the minority person. And we come full circle to the DuBois statement. In whatever interaction they engage with the larger social system, minority persons wish not to have to relinquish their true selves, the self that evolves from ethnic identity.

Summary

Family service agencies, like most social welfare programs, are, in the main, white, in terms of service populations, staff, location, and funding sources. The question is, how can a basically white system be influenced to integrate within itself a potent minority perspective compatible with the total system? One obvious unequivocal answer is that the regular, incremental crisis-oriented approaches no longer represent truly adequate efforts. Rather, coping with the needs and expectations of minority people, including the need and demand for empowerment to deal with the issues that affect them, requires a radical, sustained, extraordinary, and vitally new response. The dual perspective offers some hope and gives impetus to developing such a response.

Notes

1. W.E. DuBois, *The Souls of Black Folk* (New York: Fawcett, 1903).

2. Dolores Norton, ed., *The Dual Perspective: Inclusion of Ethnic Minority Content in the Social Work Curriculum* (New York: Council on Social Work Education, 1978).

3. Robert Merton, *Social Theory and Social Structure* (New York: Free Press, 1957), p. 116.

4. Leon Chestang, "Environmental Influences on Social Functioning: The Black Experience," in *The Diverse Society: Implications for Social Policy*, ed. Pastora Cafferty and Leon Chestang (New York: Association Press, 1976).

5. Oscar Lewis, *The Children of Sanchez* (New York: Random House, 1961); *Five Families*, (New York Basic Books, 1959); and *La Vida* (New York: Random House, 1966).

6. Edward Casavantes, "Pride and Prejudice: A Mexican Dilemma," in *Chicanos: Social and Psychological Perspectives*, ed. C. Hernandez, Marsha J. Hang, and Nathaniel N. Wagner (St. Louis, Mo.: The C.V. Mosby Co., 1976).

7. Personal communication with Ramiro Valdez, 10 March 1977.

8. See Emelicia Mizio, ed., *Puerto Rican Task Force Report: Project on Ethnicity*, and Anita J. Delaney, ed., *Black Task Force Report: Project on Ethnicity* (New York: Family Service Association of America, 1979).

61

Racism and the Practitioner

Emelicia Mizio

To find strategies to eliminate racism and bring about necessary societal changes are herculean tasks. Racism permeates every person and every institution in this society; it is part of everyday life. The attempt to untangle this complex web of individual and institutional racism and free ourselves from it is not, I hope, to pursue an impossible dream.

To begin its elimination, it is first necessary to recognize the complexity of the problem. It is complicated not only because there are many powerful and vested interests who seek to maintain and benefit from the status quo, but also because self-interest is interwoven in the process. Many have reaped benefits that are, at minimum, material gains from a structure that keeps minority groups oppressed through racism in this country and other parts of the world. The exploitation of other countries has allowed the higher standard of living that this country has enjoyed and is now seeking to protect. This article will not, however, attempt an examination of our responses to global economics, nor will it focus on colonialization, although both are of great concern to the Puerto Rican and other communities.[1]

Racism serves not only economic purposes but psychic purposes as well. Minorities become societal scapegoats, an explanation for avoidance of dealing with the complexities of a faltering economy. It is easier for individuals to hold on to racist attitudes than come to terms with their own inadequacies, lack of self-esteem, or feelings of guilt or shame. Racism can be viewed as a form of mental illness, because racist attitudes are a distortion of reality. Counseling experience has shown that where a denial of racist practices exists, so also does a continuation of the discrepancy between thought and reality in other areas of life.[2] We should also be aware of the built-in discrepancy in American thought and behavior. We have all been taught of the democratic way of life, equality of opportunity, Horatio Alger, and the lack of ascribed class status. Yet, we find that minorities are basically placed in an underclass; opportunity structures are in great measure closed and, increasingly, we are moving back toward a stratified society. Civil rights gains are being eroded,[3] and all should be congizant of what Joel Dreyfuss terms a new racism. If "law and order" was the code of the 1960s, in the 1970s the code was "merit," and "Quotas versus qualification."[4]

We must be aware of the moral dilemma of those who seek to be fair and who stand for the American creed of insuring the equality of opportunity, but we must not forget that equality of opportunity, even when practiced, has not and will not insure equality of income. Instead, it serves to insure the status quo. Because of minority history in this country, there is a need for compensatory justice.[5]

Racism and Social Welfare

The field of social welfare is implicated in racist practices. Our services have reflected an anglo, middle-class ideology and have often been sparse and culturally irrelevant for ethnic minorities. It is necessary to assess the analysis that the "vast welfare bureaucracies and antipoverty programs are created to buy off and placate the rage of the black community. In the meantime, the white hegemony and wealth remain intact."[6] For example, an article in a community newspaper describes a social welfare organization as a "poverty kingdom."[7]

Social Workers as Change Agents

Social work does not have the resources to bring about the restructuring of society or the redistribution of wealth necessary to eliminate racism. Social work is not a powerful profession, but it does have more power than it has used up to this time because it has not been sufficiently organized to realize its potential. We have basically occupied a minority status in our many ancillary roles in host agencies. We have not been able to achieve recognition of our expertise, even in the general or personal social services where we are the primary profession.

We need to work toward a society that has social policies that reflect humanitarian values and minimize market values. We must work toward accepting and strengthening our roles as change agents in this society. To do so, however, we must first come to terms with ourselves in our roles as practitioners and with the functioning of the social welfare institution of which we are a part. Is it really in our own professional self-interest to work as agents of social change? Are we perhaps better off with social work as an instrument of social control, where we serve the purpose of helping to pacify the masses so as to prevent revolution or social upheaval and maintain our jobs?[8]

John B. McKinlay, in a discussion of the sociology of work, notes that there is no evidence to suggest that the professional in the human services is motivated differently or has different needs, stresses, and pressures from any other worker. His own studies suggest that in the present tight job market we all act to protect our own interests. This "is not necessarily a criticism of their altruism or ethicality but a recognition of the reality of life."[9] Thus, the attempt to maintain job security can inadvertently perpetuate racism.

The Linkage of Individual and Institutional Racism

There is no doubt that individual and institutional racism are interwoven and difficult to separate. Nevertheless, we must work to keep these distinct, especially as they pertain to our own functioning, if we are ever to come to terms with the eradication of racism and our complicity in the process, albeit unwilling. An often quoted definition of racism by Stokely Carmichael and Charles V. Hamilton avers that:

> Racism is both overt and covert. It takes two, closely related forms. Individual whites acting against individual blacks, and acts by the total white community against the total black community. We call these individual racism and institutional racism. The first consists of overt acts by individuals, which cause death, injury or the violent destruction of property. This type can be reached by television cameras; it can frequently be observed in the process of commission. The second type is less overt, far more subtle, less identifiable in terms of specific individuals committing the acts. But it is no less destructive of human life. The second type originates in the operation of established and respected forces in the society, and thus receives far less public condemnation than the first type.[10]

Institutional racism refers to what Walter Stafford and Joyce Ladner have spoken of as: "The operating policies, properties, and functions of an ongoing system of normative patterns which serve to subjugate, oppress, and force dependence of individuals or groups by (1) establishing and sanctioning unequal goals, objectives, and priorities for blacks and whites, and (2) sanctioning inequality in status as well as in access to goods and services."[11]

It is essential to recognize the interrelationship and manner in which institutional and individual racism sustain and reinforce each other. "In a reciprocating fashion, racist attitudes helped to establish racist social attitudes."[12] It is critical to recognize that, even without

64

racist attitudes, we will have difficulties in operating in a nonracist manner. As Harold M. Baron points out:

> Maintenance of the basic racial controls is now less dependent upon specific discriminatory decisions. Such behavior has become so well institutionalized that the individual generally does not have to exercise a choice to operate in a racist manner. The rules and procedures of the large organizations have already prestructured the choice. The individual only has to conform to the operating norms of the organization and the institution will do the discriminating for him."[13]

The idea that the institutions for which we work and in which we function and live are the discriminators and we are innocent is a cop-out. We are all in complicity. Becoming aware of how we are really part of these ongoing mechanisms is a difficult task and calls for agonizing and painful examination. Unwittingly, we fall into racist postures, and minority communities fall into their assigned roles. John Longres points out that "both sides assume and accept the existing authority structure and act accordingly. Usually this is the case, because socialization patterns have led to the internalization of the authority pattern such that it becomes the normal state of affairs."[14]

Empowering the Client

Imagine the conflicts for those of us who have been assigned both roles—oppressor and oppressed. For we too, having been socialized by a white society, are racist. We must now look at the importance of gaining power, a critical factor in reducing racism. Although ultimate power resides with those who control production in this country and in the world and, thus the wealth, power certainly exists in various forms wherever there is a superior-to-subordinate relationship and rules and value systems that maintain such roles. Power components are present in the relationship of the therapist with a client, the welfare worker with a recipient, the administrator with a worker, and the professor with a student. We all exert power in some way, and its misuse is common. If we do not find ways of rectifying present inequities by transferring power, we too are perpetuating racism. We must ask ourselves: How hard have I been fighting for community input and using consumer feedback in my work? How much by way of decision-making power am I willing to share with the people who use or need services?

It is not sufficient to talk about redistribution of the income of others or restructuring society without consideration of how this will or does affect us. We must bring our theories down to a very personal assessment at all levels. Will we all be willing to accept less and pay more taxes, as higher taxes for the rich alone will not bring sufficient equity? Do we get caught up in accepting unemployment to fight inflation? Would we be willing to vote, if need be, for the elimination of the program employing us if the money were to be used instead for guaranteed income or guaranteed jobs for our clients?

Making the Personal Assessment

To deliver racist-free services, each and every practitioner must be able to make an honest self-appraisal. Each must acknowledge his or her own racist hang-ups and question where and how these are being reflected. Barbara E. Shannon speaks, for example, of the "alien-anxiety self-interest theory as a cause of white racism. Differences from ourselves are used as rationalizations to exploit others and, thereby, serve our self-interests."[15] This concept is of interest in that it provides a framework for making a self-evaluation. It is important to ask how similar to and how different from clients we see ourselves in general. How much social distance are we maintaining in such areas as relationships, housing, work, and recreation? How would a true upward change in the status of minorities affect my career, my benefits, my life? Am I willing to risk my property values going down? How much am I willing to listen to that community board? What will I allow paraprofessionals to do? We need to face that none of us likes our position threatened. Thus, how much are we willing to give? How much are we willing to risk? If you are willing to risk little, you should know it and find ways of working around it.

As a minority worker, and, accordingly, implicated in racism, I have also experienced oppression from colleagues. Thus, I would ask colleagues to consider the following: If ideas like having a Puerto Rican colleague or marrying a Puerto Rican or even having a "spic" live near you are distressing, you should recognize your prejudice. This acknowledgment will probably conflict with an ego ideal of yourself as the humanitarian social worker. If you are unaware of your own prejudices, you will act in contradictory ways, experience guilt and anger, and tend toward rationalization. Minorities don't need workers to love them, but to work with them.

Ethical Behavior

As already pointed out, it is unrealistic to think that most people will go against what they consider self-interest. Nevertheless, the profession counts on your use of professional self to find ways that will threaten you as little as possible and not make you feel that your survival is jeopardized. At the same time, your professional self also depends on your ability to find ways to act in an ethical fashion, to be of help to the minority community, to be true to your humanitarian ideals. For example, if you don't want Puerto Ricans in your community, help them live more comfortably in their own. If you are disturbed about the number of Puerto Ricans coming to the United States, recognize that many Puerto Ricans would prefer not to be here. A good part of migration is related to economic factors, so perhaps you could work toward programs that would enable people to remain in their homeland.

There are many Puerto Ricans who are in America to stay, so why not work toward programs that will improve their lives? Many minority people prefer to live in their own communities, and all they want to have is a better quality of life there. So work toward improvement of housing, education, police protection, sanitation conditions, and so on, in areas where minorities do live.

It is imperative to recognize the parts of us that are racist and see how these may be balanced with social work ethics. The practitioner who has made the commitment to self-appraisial needs to proceed as well to the assessment of the organization by which he or she is employed. In making this assessment, an important beginning question is: What group is the population at risk in your agency's service area? If this group is not being served, or if there is service underuse, you need to explore why? Find out if this group is represented at all the various agency levels, such as board, administration, and staff. The practitioner could work toward helping the agency have a bicultural presence.

Equality between Worker and Clients

It is insufficient to view a minority person only from the perspective of helper or client. There must be a view of the minority person as an equal. If a minority client group has never been dealt with as an equal in a relationship between peers or as a superior as in a relationship with an administrator, it cannot be really experienced as having any true worth or potentiality. It is only through experiential processes and differing power relationships from those which society has accustomed us that we can be expected to work through the racist attitudes prevalent in all of us. These novel role relationships would help to assure agency relevance, as it would be difficult under such conditions to superimpose alien value systems on minority clients. In this manner, agency personnel would have to come to terms with a group's rights and abilities to define its needs and solutions. We cannot afford as a philosophical underpinning the concept of doing *for* rather than doing *with*.

67

There are also questions to be tackled in regard to society and the whole social welfare system. This examination must encompass areas as knowledge base, value system, policies, programs, service delivery (including methodology), resource allocation, and staffing patterns. There are multiple areas of concern and an infinite number of issues to be raised. A small sampling of what needs to be scrutinized is: How valid is the theoretical model based on psychoanalytic concepts when a person is dealing with harsh environmental realities? How valid is a model that focuses on self-actualization when the person is is struggling with issues of self-determination? What happens to the oedipal complex in an extended family system where there may be a multiplicity of caring figures? How do day-care regulations affect those who prefer leaving a child with a trusted individual instead of a center? How do public policies using the definition of family in nuclear terms affect extended family systems? Should we be teaching casework or should we be teaching community organization? Is there a need for workers skilled in integrated methods, and what kind of service programs should we be designing and implementing that would be culturally sensitive and deal with the person in his or her situation?

Conclusion

There is much that the honest practitioner can find that needs to be changed. Becoming a change agent requires first and foremost self-change: coming to terms with one's own racism. We will constantly have to ask and answer: How ethical can we be? How much organizational wrath as a practitioner are we willing and able to endure to fight racist practices? How much can an organization itself afford to take on the white power structure? How much martyrdom can and should we display? Finally, how do we balance our commitment to cause with our protection of self-interest?

Notes

1. See Manuel Maldonado-Denis, *Puerto Rico: A Socio-Historic Interpretation* (New York: Random House, 1972).

2. Judy H. Katz and Allen Ivey, "White Awareness: The Frontier of Racism Awareness Training," *Personnel and Guidance Journal* 55 (April 1977): 486.

3. Robert Reinhold, "Study Traces Progress of Blacks Since 1790," *The New York Times*, June 19 1979, p. 18.

4. Joel Dreyfuss, "The New Racism," *Black Enterprise* 8 (January 1978): 41-54

5. Ruth C. Macklin, "The Moral Dilemma of Racism," *The Journal of Applied Social Sciences* 55, no. 8 (April 1977): 1-16.

6. Louis L. Knowles and Kenneth Prewitt, eds., *Institutional Racism in America* (Englewood Cliffs, N.J.: Prentice-Hall, 1969).

7. *Our Town*, New York, 17-23 June 1979, p. 2.

8. Frances F. Piven and Richard A. Cloward, *Regulating the Poor: The Functions of Public Relief* (New York: Random House, 1972).

9. John B. McKinlay, "The Limits of Human Services," *Social Policy* 8 (January-February 1978).

10. Stokely Carmichael and Charles V. Hamilton, *Black Power* (New York: Vintage Books, 1967), p. 4.

11. Walter Stafford and Joyce Ladner, "Comprehensive Planning and Racism," *Journal of the American Institute of Planners* 35 (March 1969): 70.

12. James P. Comer, "White Racism: its Root, Form and Function," in *Boys No More: A Black Psychologist's View of Community*, ed., Charles Thomas (Beverly Hills, Calif.: Glenroe Press, 1971).

13. See Harold M. Baron in *Institutional Racism in America*, ed. Knowles and Prewitt.

14. John Longres, "Impact of Racism on Social Work Education," *Journal of Education for Social Work* 8, no. 1 (Winter 1972): 33.

15. Barbara E. Shannon, "Implications of White Racism for Social Work Practice," *Social Casework* 51, no. 5 (May 1970): 270-76.

Family Social Policy and Cultural Pluralism

Emelicia Mizio

The imperative need to develop a coherent family social policy is recognized by many, even if debated by those who fear government interference in family life. It has been pointed out, however, that "analysis to date suggests . . . family policy does exist and consequences for the family are inevitable concomitants of policies at every level of government."[1] As government policies do affect family life, explication can only serve to clarify what is already in existence. If we are to improve the quality of life in this country, we must face that families are important to individual well-being, thus, we cannot afford a social policy that focuses on the individual alone. By social policy, I am referring to the "principles and procedures guiding any measure or course with regard to social phenomena that govern social relationships and the distribution of resources within society."[2]

The purpose of family social policy should be to establish a framework for the provision of support to the family in its tasks of socialization, acculturation, and physical and emotional sustenance for its members. If family policy is to be relevant, consideration must be given to the fact that the family structures differ. Thus, the family must be defined in other than nuclear family terms if it is to conform to reality and the requirements of today's society. Family is, perhaps, best defined in functional terms:

> A familial constellation is a person-to-person mutual aid system which intends to provide on a sustained basis for a variety of necessary functions: the provision of emotional support to all its members and the assurance of economical and physical survival of the total constellation. Functional familial behavior is characterized by intimacy, commitment to the constellation, and continuity and intensity of the relationship over time.[3]

All people have similar life tasks and common human needs, but there are differences in how people express these needs and seek

70

their fulfillment. Needs are expressed through cultural filters and value systems come into play. Reflections of value systems in governmental policies may, however, differ from the value systems of various groups. This makes it essential that values be made explicit rather than implicit, so that they can be supported, challenged, or modified. This would also provide a framework in which the impact of policy on families could be more easily studied and outcomes assessed.

Cultural Pluralism

That this same family policy must then be cast into the context of a pluralist society, allowing options for many diverse ethnic groups, is not readily acknowledged, even by those who support the need for a formalization of family policy. The fact that the White House Conference on Families took so long to come to into being speaks to society's difficulty in accepting differences relating to other than white middle-class America.

It is imperative that policymakers truly understand and show acceptance of the belief that individuals are sustained by their families and the groups to which they belong. The myth of the melting pot has resulted in the underestimation of the importance of ethnicity and group membership. Joseph Giordano rightly asserts that:

> Ethnicity . . . is more than the distinctiveness of race, religion, national origin or geography. It involves conscious and unconscious processes that fulfill a deep psychological need for security, identity and a sense of historical continuity. It is transmitted in an emotional language within the family and is reinforced by similar units in the community. There is a significant interrelationship between ethnicity, family and neighborhood.[1]

As such, ethnicity encompasses and affects the sense of self, the relationship to all others, including family, group, and society, and incorporates societal view of self, kin, and group. We are also aware of how the personality core is formed in the early years; consequently, even if an individual denies his or her heritage, this ethnic identification remains a part of the inner being. No matter what the degree of assimilation, the ethnic cannot fully succeed in obliterating his or her cultural background.

Policymakers must help preserve ethnic ties or, at least, not destroy through public policy the fabric of these groups. Minorities of color, especially in this society, have a difficult enough time with survival and gaining of the acceptance and support of the wider society, so that it is critical that the support they receive from their own group be enhanced and not diminished. Housing policies that allow only

71

nuclear family members to dwell together, income tax provisions regulations that do not allow kin deductions broadly defined, health insurance limited to traditional family definitions—all serve to render people impotent in their attempts to help each other and insure survival of self, family, and group. The extended family, which is so important to minorities of color and to white ethnics, must be protected.

Diversity in Lifestyle

As noted earlier, we are a pluralistic society. Diversity is enriching, and lifestyle differences allow a broader scope and range of choices. We are provided with alternatives for attitudes and behavior and need not be boxed into set patterns. We can learn from each other and are, thus, enabled to expand our own coping repertoire. We have the opportunity to learn new skills through differing role models. An important goal of public policy should be "maximizing freedom of choice as a prerequisite for increasing the capacity of people to be responsible for their own lives and for insuring the continuation of a pluralistic society."[5]

Not only government, but, for too long, the field of social welfare has also acted as if there were an idealized prototype of an American family with which it worked and for whom it had to advocate, we have paid lip service to the notion of cultural differences. Although some of us might have taken a course or two in the area of cultural issues, in actual practice we promptly dismissed all learning in this area. Despite protestations to the contrary, we too have subscribed to the notion of the melting pot. In our attempt to help people find a more satisfactory level of adjustment, we have often challenged their lifestyles if they did not reflect an Anglo middle-class ideology—our hope has been to Americanize all.

Institutional Racism

Robert W. Habenstein and Charles H. Mindel present a historical perspective on ethnicity: The term "melting pot" was first developed by Isreal Zangwill in a 1906 play of the same name. The melting-pot ideology expresses the belief that somehow all the best of the cultural contributions of each immigrant group would come together in a superior amalgam. In contrast, the concept of cultural pluralism was explicated by Horace Kallen in 1915: An individual becomes American but is able at the same time to retain his or her heritage.[6]

The degree to which either ideology has, in fact, been in operation is questionable. There are many of us who agree with the view that

72

Mindel and Habenstein describe as the feeling that "what we have here in America is a highly ethnocentric coercion toward 'Anglo conformity,' implying the downgrading and elimination of ethnic and incorporation of the dominant anglo culture."[7] Mindel and Habenstein further point out what an ethnic minority person knows only too well—that historically the concept of assimilation has indeed reflected ethnocentricism and has carried a value-laden assumption. The assumption has been that of the superiority of the host American culture and the inferiority of all those who are different.[8] We should note that assimilationist theory in effect "denies or obscures the minority group's preference for its own culture and community."[9] In reality, there has never been any way for people of color to melt and metamorphose as white. No matter if the person succeeds in becoming part of the quota of those permitted to enter the upper classes through admission to such fields as medicine, law, dentistry, and so on, he or she will get a lower score based on color.

Institutional Racism in America traces the notion of white supremacy as far back as the first English immigrants who came seeking religious freedom in this country. The colonists at first tried unsuccessfully to "civilize" and make Christian the Indians, which led to their near-extermination and oppression. The same kind of thinking led to the American enslavement of blacks, who were seen as "savages." Social Darwinism has permeated American thinking, along with the notions of manifest destiny and the white man's burden.[10] Attitudes toward Puerto Rico have reflected the same type of thinking.[11] Today, most proponents of white supremacy are much more subtle in their approach. Institutional racism is just as insidious and has served to maintain white supremacy.

Institutional racism is defined by Walter Stafford and Joyce Ladner as "the operating policies, properties, and functions of an on-going system of normative patterns which serve to subjugate oppress, and force dependence of individuals or groups by (1) establishing and sanctioning unequal goals, objectives and priorities for blacks and whites, and (2) sanctioning inequality in status as well as in access to goods and services."[12] Through this process, minorities of colors have remained fixed in poverty and, in good measure, have been relegated to a position of an underclass. In many ways, we must view this society as a stratified one for minorities of color. Despite the gains made by civil rights activists, even in the black community, which is thought of as having made the greatest gains of the minority communities, we note that:

The economic gains of many middle and upper income black families

73

have eroded in recent years. The numbers of unemployed and poor persons in the black community are at their highest level. And the economic cleavage between black and white families is widening and not narrowing. In fact, the gaps between the jobless rates and family income of Blacks and Whites are the widest they have been in this decade. Meaningful job opportunities continue to be denied disproportionately to black women and family heads and to black youth.[13]

Even if we did succeed in assuring equality of opportunity, public policy must demand ongoing and structured compensatory mechanisms to insure equality of outcome. An ongoing assessment of the impact of public policies must be made.

White Ethnics: Common Cause with Minorities

We should be clear that when we speak of the need for social policy to reflect cultural pluralism, we are not only relating to the concern for the quality of life of minorities of color. Social policy has the potential to serve either as a constructive or destructive force in the lives of all people. Policies will shape programs that affect all aspects of individual, family, and community living. Programs "are indicators and assumed policies, and also, indicators of how stated policies are working."[14]

Donald Fandetti, in a discussion of the European white ethnic, talks about the increasing concern that too much standardization and uniformity in service delivery will serve to prevent the use of public services by the various ethnic communities. There cannot be any question that there are differences between groups. "Even to the most casual observer, a stroll through 'Little Italy' should reveal social patterns and local arrangements in the central city and suburbia."[15]

It is essential that these differences between groups be addressed in service delivery. Policies must allow for service individualization, services tailored to the social ambiance of the community. Social ambiance refers to the lifestyles of the ethnic group, its family structure, the social communication system, and the community's perception of itself.[16] For service relevance, policies shaping programs must not run counter to the institutional fabric of the neighborhood or its existing social networks. A simple but meaningful example of a violation of institutional fabric is in the tearing down of housing with front stoops, which had served as meeting points for the neighbors to rest and chat, and the setting up housing units where no one is allowed "to loiter" in front of the building. An example of faulty relating to the institutional fabric is the offering of counseling services

74

for white ethnics in nonsystemized settings—they would best be in the form of social utilities through schools, labor unions, or churches.[17]

The 1960's concept of maximum feasible participation in policy-making, program design, and implementation and delivery is worthwhile: community involvement is a must. Policymaking should not be the sole province of experts. People whose lives are affected need to have a meaningful role in shaping their own destinies. Ideally, self-help groups should be funded by the government. Consumer enpowerment needs to be incorporated into the organizational behavior of all sectors. This would help to minimize service alienation and consumer helplessness and to insure appropriate service—underuse of services in minority communities and white ethnic communities is common.

The Dual Perspective

Along with working toward increasing consumer input, experts must develop cultural sensitivity and attempt to work toward achievement of what is termed the "dual perspective":

> The dual perspective is the conscious and systematic process of perceiving, understanding, and comparing simultaneously the values, attitudes, and behavior of the larger societal system with those of the clients' immediate family and community system. It is the conscious awareness on the cognitive and attitudinal levels of the similarities and differences in the two systems. It requires substantive knowledge and empathic appreciation of both the majority societal system and the minority client system, as well as a conscious awareness of the social worker's own attitudes and values. Thus, the dual perspective allows one to experience from the point of view of the other . . . The intent is to broaden the social worker's understanding and sensitivity to the totality of the life situation of the client group and to build services on the needs of that particular situation.[18]

It should be understood that not all members of a particular ethnic group will perceive their needs and solutions in a similar way. We cannot be too careful about avoiding stereotyping. Care must also be taken not to limit ethnics to choices made by the majority of their community. For example, although family members in Puerto Rican culture are expected to help each other with child-care responsibilities, a social agency should not demand this of an aunt who refuses to help look after her sister's child.

Policymakers should not use culture as an excuse for not providing funds for program development, particularly in areas of common human needs and readily available information on these needs. It is well known, for example, that, "largely as a result of ageism older persons constitute the largest deprived group in America. They are deprived in terms of income, health care, nutrition, transportation, acceptance, dignity, and even spiritual well-being."[19] Further, it should not be assumed, for example, that because blacks have strong kinship ties and desire in good measure to keep problems within the family, that they will take "care of their own."[20] Some individuals or families may not wish to do so or may not be in a position to do so.

The needs of the black and other ethnic minority aged must be recognized, not obscured, by cultural considerations. Policymakers need to pay attention as well to statistical data regarding income, housing, health, and so on, which show quite clearly that the ethnic minority aged suffer from multiple jeopardy as a result of minority status compounded by the usual problems of the aged in our society.[21] The knowledge of a cultural group will enable policymakers and service providers to make their own educated predictions about consumer needs and possible service use patterns.

Framework for Consideration of Cultural Pluralism

In order to achieve an explication of a coherent family social policy that gives the necessary recognition to cultural pluralism and to the present social and economic plight of minorities and other populations at risk, the following questions should be addressed by policymakers:

1. How do policies potentially affect the many family forms, with special reference to the nuclear family, extended family, single-parent family, or family as defined by minorities of color and white ethnic groups: *Value*: People are entitled to select the family form in which they wish to live.

2. How do these policies affect populations at greatest risk in terms of whether they serve to minimize or maximize the service and income gaps between the rich and poor, lessen or increase nonrisk category? *Value*: Priority must be given to the needs of populations at risk.

3. Do these policies serve to restore or substitute family function? *Value*: For individual survival and family well-being in this depersonalized society, restitution of family functions rather than institutional substitution must become the theme of this decade.

4. What research evidence is there to support the effectiveness of the policy decision? *Value*: Research is necessary to avoid continued dependence on untested assumptions.

5. How much input is there from the groups to be affected by the decision? *Value*: People have a right to be instrumental in shaping their own destinies.

6. Was there an attempt made to maximize the options available to the consumer? *Value*: It is important to maximize options.

8. What provisions are being made for ongoing assessments of impact and use of this information for policy reformulation? *Value*: Ongoing consumer and professional feedback is essential to viable policy formulation.

7. What provisions are made to educate the consumer with reference to the options available? *Value*: People are entitled to know their rights and to be as informed as possible in order to make educated decisions.

Conclusion

It is quite a challenge. It will not be an easy task to create a unified body of family policy that clearly expresses the value system which serves as its underpinning. There is no need to fear that this will foster totalitarianism if we are committed to cultural pluralism, providing options, allowing freedom of choice, and "unjamming" the opportunity structure. We must see as our framework working toward family health and individual well-being, while curbing disorganization, and enhancing family life.

Notes

1. Sheila B. Kamerman and Alfred J. Kahn, "Explorations in Family Policy," *Social Work* 21, no. 3, (May 1976): 183.

2. Shirley Zimmerman, "The Family and its Relevance for Social Policy," *Social Casework* 57 (November 1976): 54.

3. Definition approved by the Board of Directors of the Family Service Service Association of America, June 15 1977.

4. Joseph Giordano, *Ethnicity and Mental Health* (New York: Institute on Pluralism and Group Identity, 1973), p. 4.

5. Advisory Committee on Child Development of the National Research Council, *Towards a National Policy for Children and* Families (Washington, D.C.: National Academy of Sciences, 1976), p. 11.

6. Charles H. Mindel, and Robert W. Habenstein, eds., *Ethnic Families in America: Patterns and Variations* (New York: Elsevier North-Holland, 1976), pp. 1-11.

7. Ibid., p. 2.

8. Ibid.

9. Lloyd Street, "Minorities," in *Encyclopedia of Social Work* (New York: National Association of Social Workers, 1977), p. 934.

10. Louis L. Knowles and Kenneth Prewitt, eds., *Institutional Racism in America* (Englewood Cliffs, N.J.: Prentice-Hall, 1979).

11. Manuel Maldonado-Denis, *Puerto Rico: A Socio-Historic Interpretation* (New York: Random House, 1972).

12. Walter Stafford and Joyce Ladner, "Comprehensive Planning and Racism," *Journal of American Institute of Planners* 35 (March 1969): 70-71.

13. Robert B. Hill, "The Economic Status of Black Families," in *The State of Black America, 1979* (New York: National Urban League, 1979), pp. 38-39.

14. Leo F. Hawkins, "The Impact of Policy Decisions on Families," *The Family Coordinator* 28 (April, 1979): 265.

15. Daniel V. Fandetti, "Ethnicity and Neighborhood Services," in *Reaching People: The Structure of Neighborhood Services*, ed. Daniel Thursz and Joseph L. Vigilante (Beverly Hills, Calif.: Sage Publications, 1978), p. 113.

16. Thursz and Vigilante, "Neighborhoods: A Worldwide Phenomenon," in *Reaching People*, p. 17.

17. William McCready, "Social Utilities in a Pluralistic Society," in *The Diverse Society: Implications for Social Policy*, ed. Pastora San Juan Cafferty and Leon Chestang (New York: National Association of Social Workers, 1976), p. 20.

18. Dolores G. Norton, *The Dual Perspective* (New York: Council on Social Work Education, 1978), p. 3.

19. Harriet Pipes McAdoo, "Black Kinship," *Psychology Today*, May 1979, p. 110.

20. M. Alan Sheppard, "A Federal Perspective on the Black Aged: From Concern to Action," *Aging* (September-October 1978): 29.

21. Ibid., p. 13.

A Black Historical Perspective

Howard J. Stanback

Most traditional approaches to studying the history of black people in America have followed either an assimilationist or a white prejudice perspective. The assimilationist perspective suggests that the position of black people in America has essentially followed the lines of other immigrant populations. According to this school of thought, black people's past and future will be seen to reflect the experience of other immigrant groups, even though there has been some uniqueness in the history of blacks compared with that of European immigrants.[1] The white prejudice perspective suggests that antiblack prejudice predates salvery and has been an integral part of European culture since it came into contact with black and other nonwhite people. This perspective further contends that slavery was a natural extension of such prejudices.[2]

This article roots the development of racism as an organized system of racial oppression (as opposed to ineffectual and random prejudice) in capitalism. The development of capitalism was highly dependent on the slave trade and slave production. Organized oppression of Africans by Europeans represented the ideological, and, thus, the cultural, justification for the slave system. Racism serves capitalism by allocating disproportionate unemployment burdens to black people, by isolating them, and by leaving them to do the dirty work of society. In turn, racism leads to political impotence, which makes the availability of this type of labor more likely.

Racism, although rooted in capitalism, reaches much farther than the economic character of the nation. In order to maintain black labor in a state of subservience, whether in slavery or not, racism has to affect all aspects of black and white life. It is essential that culture, family, education, and all other aspects of life be ingrained with racist theory. However, appropriate political and theoretical connections are seldom made between the economic base and the role of black labor in capitalism. Yet, the conditions and experiences of black people cannot be understood without these connections.

The shaping of the current social condition of black people is both the product of an oppressive political and economic system and of the struggle of blacks to overcome it. This dialectical relationship forces the system to oppress as well as to relax or alter the forms of oppression.

Historical Patterns of Racism

Evidence of the historical pattern of racism gives credence to the strength of black resistance as a shaping element of both black life and major changes in social policy. Within the capital-labor relationship system, black people have overwhelmingly been assigned to the position of labor. The shape of the economic organization and production process of a particular period have provided the material rationale for the particular use to which black labor would be put. In turn, the sociocultural rationale for such use develops and becomes the prevalent racial ideology of that particular period. Over the years, the interaction between the ideology and the material rationale generates an ever-changing character in both the material base and in the structure and ideology within the political and social arenas.[3]

The economic organization of the late fifteenth century in Western Europe was characterized by a declining feudalist mode of production and a slowly emerging capitalist mode of production. In the late sixteenth and early seventeenth centuries, the growing role of merchants and their increasing use of Africans as slaves coincided with the growing demand for labor in the colonies of European nations. Although there were many battles fought between these nations over control of the slave trade, the British use of slaves facilitated the development of colonial production of tobacco and, later, of cotton.

The Slave Trade

The introduction of the slave trade by the Portuguese in 1452 did not go unchallenged by either the source of slaves or by elements of the political-social structure of European society. The tribes from which slaves were captured put forth tremendous amounts of violent resistance and, eventually, forced the traders to develop more sophisticated methods for obtaining their commodity.

The Church condemned the slave trade, and, in 1402, the Pope threatened the excommunication of those engaging in such trade. However, by the time the British dominated the trade, church resistance had buckled to the point of blessing the slave ships that sailed from British ports. Church policy was critical in providing the moral justification of an already economically justified institution. Because the enslavement of human beings was contrary to church doctrine, it was necessary to develop some rationale that categorized slaves as "heathen" in order to justify slavery. It was this concept of blacks that dominated up until and throughout the eighteenth century; the "mission" of slavery was to save the heathen blacks from their own self-destruction.

The development of this ideology was important because all societies require some ideological justification for economic practices. In European societies it was not too difficult, given ethnocentrism and preexisting prejudice related to color, but it had to be shaped and organized into a full-blown system of values, belief, and laws that controlled the lives of a racial category of people. This system developed with the institution of slavery.

The slave system in the Western hemisphere varied from North America to the West Indies to South America because the southern colonies of North America were settler-colonies, while most of the British, French, and Spanish colonies in the West Indies and South America were not. The British who settled in the southern colonies of North America came primarily to settle the land, not to engage in slavery. Subsequently, however, slavery become a way in which the wealthy were able to organize production. Thus, although black slaves were the majority population of most West Indian and South American slave colonies, only one-fourth of the whites in the southern part of North America owned slaves.[4]

By 1860, the true planter aristocracy was made up of only 10,000 families who each owned fifty or more slaves.[5] Their control over the political economy of the South was predicated on their ability to dominate all aspects of southern life, including the lives of white non-slaveholders.

Racism as Unification

Control of slaves was legal in the form of property relations; control over other whites was not so structurally simple. The planter class faced the following contradiction: on the one hand, if they allowed the advancements of technology and urbanization to penetrate the South on a large scale, their control system of slaves and slave production would be damaged by the nature of a wage labor system; on the other, the material conditions of nonslaveholding whites varied from a little better to worse than the conditions of black slaves.[6] The method that planters used to maintain the allegiance of poor whites

81

was racism. Although material status did not necessarily come from being white, social status certainly did. The poorest white farmer saw himself as better off than the black; because he was white, he was not only free from bondage, but he was also free from the various stereotypes associated with blackness. Racism worked to unify the whites across class lines, in spite of their own inherent conflicts.

By the nineteenth century, with the ending of the slave trade, slavery was coming under strong attack from various fronts. Much of this attack was associated with the principles on which the American Revolution was fought. Much of it was also, however, associated with the economic and political motivations of northern merchants and emerging industrialists to strip southern planters of their national political power and expand the wage labor system. In the face of such attacks, and with the growing economic rationale for slavery resulting from the invention of the cotton gin in 1793, southern planters bulwarked their position by placing more and more emphasis on a so-called biological inferiority of blacks in an effort to solidify the unity of the white South.

Such unity was necessary not only for defense from the outside, but also from potential rebellions from slaves. There have been hundreds of slave revolts historically documented that contradict the docile image often projected for slaves. Some of the most dramatic slave and antislavery revolts occurred during the nineteenth century, including those led by Gabriel Prosser, Denmark Vesey, John Brown, and Nat Turner.[7]

Black Labor

During the nineteenth century, and before the ending of slavery, black slaves and free blacks in both the North and South had assumed many skilled labor roles, in direct conflict with white workers. However, white workers in the North and Midwest were better able to challenge these roles. Immigrant laborers from Ireland were able legally and physically to drive black workers from the docks of Boston and New York; white workers in the South were not able to prevent blacks from working because they were hired out cheaply as slaves. Once slavery and Reconstruction were over, black workers were successfully prohibited from most skilled labor occupations in the North and South through various versions of Jim Crow laws. Such laws were predicated on the notion of biological inferiority. Nonetheless, black workers were assuming roles that dispelled the myth of biological inferiority.

By the twentieth century, changes in the economic organization of production began to change the role that black labor played. Three critical changes in the economic character of society prescribed the new role of black labor that persists to the present day:

1. Growing mechanization of southern agriculture made much black labor superfluous and led to northern migration.

2. Industrialization of the North required more and more cheap labor, especially with the strictures against immigration during World War II, and led to the further pull of black labor from the South into the Industrial North.

3. United States capital began to be poured into nonwhite countries around the world in a search for both resource and product markets.

The first two changes led to black workers being disproportionately represented among the unemployed. This meant that black workers could be called during periods of expansion and laid off during cutbacks.

Capitalism and Racism

Capitalism requires a population that can absorb the bulk of the shocks of the instability of the system. If the burden of such instability were to be spread among all workers it would foster political instability. Racism becomes, therefore, a mechanism for allocating unemployment. Capitalism also requires politically impotent groups to take on the lowest paying, least desirable work in the economy. Racism is one way of establishing political impotence and designating such roles. More politically potent groups can and do refuse such jobs. The industrializing North in the early twentieth century established such lines of impotence on the basis of race and ethnicity.

The third factor listed above had a direct role in the changing ideology of racism. An early justification for the economic and military occupation of nonwhite lands was the philosophy of the "white man's burden." The presence of the United States in such places was rationalized as representing cultural and economic uplift; that without this intervention, the populace was doomed to permanent backwardness. The emerging racial ideology was that of the culturally disadvantaged. This began to replace biological versions of racism and became dominant in the 1960s. It asserted that nonwhite people are of an inferior culture and, thus, must be "saved" from that state of inferiority. Integration into or equality within American society would come with the adoption of the Euro-American standards of behavior and values.

83

The Fight for Civil Rights

Throughout the twentieth century, black people have resisted oppression. The forms of resistance have ranged from the semi-separationist line of Booker T. Washington to the more nationalist line of Marcus Garvey to the civil rights line of W. E. B. DuBois. The form and degree of success that such struggles had were in part dependent on the political atmosphere and economic conditions of a particular period and the objective and subjective conditions of the black masses. The turn of the century was a particularly brutal period for blacks in terms of Jim Crow violence in the South and black-white labor conflicts in the North. A Washingtonian program would clearly have more success during such a period, while a more activist civil rights program as advocated by DuBois and by organizations such as the N.A.A.C.P., could only achieve significant success when issues related to black-white labor competition had been fundamentally resolved. Jim Crow laws were created primarily out of the efforts of white workers to control the movement of black workers and their access to certain jobs.

By the mid-twentieth century, inferior education, discrimination by employers, and migration to the North had structured the black working class in such a way as to pose no serious threat to white workers in the South, particularly during periods of economic growth. World War II, the Korean War, and the Vietnam War spurred periods of growth that reduced competition between black and white workers. And, even though there was massive resistance by the white working class to civil rights laws, especially in the South, the civil rights movement achieved some success.

Affirmative Action

The economic growth of the 1960s appeared to resolve many issues related to racial discrimination. The establishment of affirmative action programs, civil rights and voting rights laws, and massively funded social welfare and urban development programs signaled to many that significant progress had and would continue to be made. The sometimes life and death struggle of black people to win these laws and programs made it clear that dramatic, positive changes in racial stratification were on the way. The media, supported by scholarly interpretations of census reports, has made a concerted effort to note the progress of black people as indicated in the growth of a black middle class.[8] Such contentions directly or indirectly give an image that racism is not as forceful or prevalent as it was ten or twenty years ago, and that black society is becoming a social mirror of white society, especially in terms of class. The limits of this article do not allow a thorough analysis of these contemporary assertions of the declining role of race and changing racial structure. However, a few comments are required that set a framework for an alternative view—one that dispels most and confirms some of these assertions.

Racial and Capitalist Dynamics

One of the major premises of this article is that racial dynamics are linked with capitalist dynamics. When there is a decline in the material forces that make racism so functional to capitalism, it is likely that, given intense struggle, the legal and political forces of racism will also decline, or at least retreat. When job competition is least intense, racial antagonisms, especially in legal forms, are more readily disposed of as happened in the 1960s and 1970s. The Vietnam War, together with federal social expenditures, reduced such competition and liberalism prevailed.

However, when the forces of growth are no longer at work, a different set of powers emerge. The protests of the 1960s helped to bring on large-scale federal spending which, in turn, exacerbated the deeply rooted capitalist contradictions of inflation and unemployment. When the federal government could no longer support expansion, the props were pulled and a recession began, the deepest since the 1930s. The liberal cure for the political crisis was the catalyst for an economic crisis. Such crises are normal capitalist phenomena, but this one was unique in that it emerged after a period of significant alteration in the laws governing racial discrimination. By 1974, affirmative action programs had been introduced in most major economic and educational institutions in the country. Additionally, most state governments had expanded the human services share of their budgets. The recession of 1974-75 established the basis for an attack on both of these and other products of the 1960s.

The 1974-75 recession brought on material forces that brought racism to the fore again as a critical variable in society. Increased job competition brought charges by white workers of reverse discrimination. The United States Supreme Court case of *Bakke versus University of California-Davis* was decided in favor of Bakke, endorsing a charge of reverse discrimination, although the Court ruled in favor of affirmative action in the case of *Weber versus Kaiser Aluminum*. The Court's lack of consistency, however, and the general open season challenge on affirmative action leave many unanswered questions. Affirmative action program administrators are freed to proceed cautiously.[9]

85

Affirmative action alone does not represent a solution to racism. It does, however, make it possible to redistribute the burden of unemployment. In other words, if there is to be unemployment then it must be shared equally. Therefore, attacks on affirmative action programs represent a new racism in that they attempt to force black workers to remain in disproportionate numbers among the unemployed.

The economic crisis of 1974 also brought attacks on public human service expenditures and high taxes. To pay for human services governments have recessively taxed middle- and low-income citizens. The tax revolt and the "Proposition 13" spirit, however, has not redistributed the burden of taxation, but instead has jeopardized those heavily dependent on human services. Cutbacks on such services amount to attacks on the jobs and incomes of a large portion of the black community.[10] These programs, like affirmative action, do not solve the problem, but they do represent major avenues of employment or income alternatives for black people at this time.

Current Political Climate

The combination of these attacks, plus attacks on minority leadership, growing discriminatory practices in suburban housing programs, and so on, indicate growing, not declining, racism. It is true that there are more black people in positions that separate them from the masses of black people in terms of income, education, and occupation, although not as drastically as suggested by William Wilson.[11] Their ability to remain in such positions, however, is dependent on the very programs now under attack: affirmative action and human services spending. Additionally, the movement of blacks into these positions seems to represent as much a political concession to blacks as a result of the 1960s, as an economic achievement. If this is so, then such concession, like all political concession, is likely to be removed when the climate is appropriate.

The political climate in the United States today is decidedly to the right. The crisis of 1974-75 represents the basis of that rightward move. At that point in time, a move began to give various concessions to white America as a result of Vietnam, Watergate, and the economic crisis. Such concessions are eventually aimed at a consolidation in the political strength of the government. They involve the retreat on issues related to black people and other oppressed racial minorities, as well as the growing strength of racism.

Implications for Service Delivery

For those agencies, institutions, and individuals recognizing the social, economic, and political shifts occurring in this society and committing themselves to the fight against the growth of a climate destructive to the well-being of blacks and other minorities, there are specific implications with regard to the field of mental health service delivery. These implications emerge at three levels: client services, agency personnel practices, and political action.

Client service providers must be cognizant of the nature and effort of the racist, political, economic, and cultural forces that impinge on the lives of black clients. Such knowledge must be actively sought through a variety of educational methods, such as local universities or regular and frequent in-service training.

Any treatment service must integrate the knowledge both to help build coping abilities and to move people to change these forces. It is simply not enough to get people to live comfortably with a persistent problem. The root of the problem—racism—must eventually be destroyed; otherwise, the mental health symptoms will persist.

Agency personnel practices must include an aggressive affirmative action program. A successful program will not only help black employment, but will provide expertise for working with black clients. The black worker can be an invaluable resource for expanding consciousness as well as for providing services.

Human service agencies have long had the luxury of remaining fairly parochial in the political struggles in which they have chosen to engage. A strong stand against racism, however, requires agency presence in multiple arenas. This would obviously include active political advocacy of the rights of black people within the agency's own particular service field. It would also require active political or affirmative action directed toward federal and state policies and programs on employment; minimum wage and public assistance benefits, and other policy issues that affect clients.

An agency must seriously examine its efforts at all of these levels—client services, personnel policies, and political action. In other words, it must actively involve itself in the struggle to eliminate racism, utilizing its capacity to link individual victims and the resources for employment and political action. Until this is done, an agency cannot claim full commitment to the rights of victims of racism.

Notes

1. Nathan Glazer and Daniel Moynihan, *Beyond the Melting Pot: The Negroes, Puerto Ricans, Jews, Italians, and Irish of New York City,* 1st and 2d eds. (Cambridge, Mass.: M.I.T. Press, 1963 and 1970); Oscar Handlin, *The Newcomers: Negroes and Puerto Ricans in A Changing Metropolis* (Cambridge, Mass.: Harvard University Press, 1959); and Irving Kristol, "The Negro Today is Like the Immigrant of Yesterday," in *Nation of Nations: The Ethnic Experience and the Racial Crisis,* ed. Peter I. Rose (New York: Random House 1966), pp. 197, 210.

2. Winthrop D. Jordon, *White Over Black: American Attitudes Toward the Negro 1550-1812* (Baltimore, Md.: Penguin Books, 1968). For a summary of the white prejudice and assimilationist schools, see James A. Geschwender, *Class, Race and Worker Insurgency: The League of Revolutionary Black Workers* (Cambridge, Mass.: Cambridge University Press, 1977).

3. Paul Baran and Eric Habsbaum, "The Method of Historical Materialism," and Karl Marx, "The Materialist Conception of History," in *The Capitalist System: A Radical Critique of American Society,* 1st ed., ed. Rich Edwards, Michael Reich, and Thomas Weiskopk (Englewood Cliffs, N.J.: Prentice-Hall, 1971); and "Fundamentals of Historical Materialism," in *Dynamics of Social Change: A Reader in Marxist Social Science,* ed. Howard Selsam, David Goldway, and Harry Martel (New York: International Publishing, 1970).

4. See Harold Baron, *The Demand for Black Labor* (Cambridge, Mass.: New England Free Press, 1971); and Robert Allen, *Black Awakening in Capitalist America* (Garden City, N.Y.: Doubleday, 1969).

5. William J. Wilson, *The Declining Significance of Race: Blacks and Changing American Institutions* (Chicago: University of Chicago Press, 1978).

6. See Robert Fogel and Stanley Engerman, *Time on the Cross: The Economics of American Negro Slavery* (Boston: Little Brown, 1974); and Eugene Genovese, *The Political Economy of Slavery: Studies in the Economy and Society of the Slave South* (New York: Pantheon, 1965).

7. Herbert Aptheker, *American Negro Slave Revolts* (New York: International Publishing, 1943).

8. See, for example, Wilson, *Declining Significance of Race*; Ben J. Wattenberg and Richard M. Scamman, "Black Progress and Liberal Rhetoric," *Commentary* 3 (April 1973): 35-44; James P. Smith and Finish R. Welch, *Race Difference in Earnings: A Survey, New Evidence, and The Convergence to Racial Equality in Women's Wages* (Santa Monica, Calif.: The Rand Corporation, 1978); and *The New York Times,* "Two Societies: America Since the Kerner Report," series, published in March 1978.

9. The Affirmative Action Coordinating Center in New York City has documented over 200 court cases in which affirmative action programs have been challenged.

10. Howard J. Stanback, "The Move to the Right: Implications for Ethnic Minorities." Paper presented at the Annual Program Meeting, Council on Social Work Education, Boston, Massschusets, 4-7 March 1977.

11. An excellent statistical rebuttal to William Wilson is presented by Robert B. Hill in *The Illusion of Black Progress* (Washington: National Urban League, 1978).

The Black Cultural Process

Anita J. Delaney

The purpose of this article is to establish a framework for under-standing the cultural psychosocial process that shapes the develop-ment and functioning of black Americans in a hostile environment. A focus on "cultural process" rather than "cultural traits" enhances the capacity to assess more accurately the variety of behaviors, atti-tudes, and beliefs observed in the black community and avoids the trap of stereotyping, which so often occurs when a list of traits is the foundation of one's knowledge about blacks.

Prior to the 1970s, there were few schools of social work willing to acknowledge the existence of distinct black cultural patterns and minimal attention was given to the development of a cadre of prac-titioners who could approach black communities with the cultural sensitivity, knowledge, and skills needed for maximum effectiveness in the delivery of service. Although there were two graduate schools of social work with core curricula reflecting a service commitment to the black community—Atlanta, University, Atlanta, Georgia and Howard University, Washington, D.C.—most schools responded with elective courses in "Black Studies," leaving it to the students to decide whether they could afford to sacrifice the inclusion of a "high-value" clinical course on their schedules. These courses were selected pri-marily by black students, and the few white students who were neither threatened by the content nor by their minority status in the class-room. It was generally left to the students to integrate the black cultural material with the psychodynamic theory and treatment mo-dalities being taught. The attitudinal stance of educators made clear to the students that ethnicity was of secondary importance in the assessment of consumer needs and the design of helping strategies.

The historical experience of blacks in America has been well doc-umented in the literature with the collection and interpretation of statistical data to describe the nonstatic social and economic conditions of black American life.[1] It is not within the purview of this article to restate data that are adequately detailed and readily available for an ongoing assessment of social conditions in the black community.[2] Robert Staples has observed that:

> The problems black people face are essentially the same as for the past century. Those problems are not related to family stability but to the socioeconomic conditions that tear families asunder. In general, the problems are poverty and racism . . . . Blacks are still singled out for discriminatory treatment in every sphere of American life. Moreover, while whites are in agreement about the racial discrimination blacks are subjected to, any national effort to further remedy these racist practices has a low priority among white Americans.[3]

As institutional patterns of racism change, black people adapt, using a variety of highly specific coping behaviors. A conceptual framework that demonstrates how black cultural patterns function within a shifting social context has greater utility in the design of strategies to address the human service needs of the black community.

Ideological Perspective

It should be safe to assume that most social workers who are practicing in the United States today have some knowledge of the black experience, either through articles that appear in the professional literature from time to time, the occasional workshop that focuses on service to minorities or the poor, or direct service delivery to black individuals, families, and communities. Many, however, are only peripherally aware that knowledge gained has been screened through the ideological perspective of the researcher, the lecturer, or the service giver, whose value orientations strongly influence the perception of black family life. Because value-free findings are impossible to achieve, it is important to develop an awareness of the major perspectives that have influenced the study of black people and to understand that which has guided the development of material for this article.

From a review of the literature, Walter R. Allen has identified three distinct ideological perspectives that appear to characterize black family research: the cultural equivalent perspective, the cultural deviant perspective, and the cultural variant perspective.[4] Those researchers who tend to deemphasize the distinctive qualities of black families and look instead for commonalities with white families are using the cultural equivalent perspective.[5] This view recognizes black family structures and functioning as valid cultural patterns *only* as they parallel the white middle-class norm. The cultural deviant perspective gives recognition to the distinctive patterns of black family life but, using the white middle-class family as the cultural ideal, black families who deviate or function differently are labled pathological or dysfunctional.[6] The present framework rejects these two perspectives as they ignore the social context of the black experience and " . . . the role of ethnicity in shaping behavior and defining social competence."[7]

The Cultural Variant Perspective

The cultural variant perspective recognizes the different experience of blacks and whites with external systems that demand a unique set of responses for blacks. This view permits one to see black cultural patterns as adaptations within a specific social context and does not presuppose pathology; this model does not subscribe to the deficit view of black family life. The perspective holds that the experience of blacks, being unlike that of any other group in America, has required creative psychosocial responses for survival, for protection of self-esteem, and for enhancement of potential for growth and achievement in this society.

The concept of culture is generally regarded as the specific adaptive patterns developed by human beings to cope with or master their environments. The terms "coping" and "adaptation" are sufficiently general to go beyond the autoplastic changes that black people make internally to satisfy the requirements of a harsh and unyielding environment. These concepts are broad enough to incorporate the black potential for dynamic change of those external elements that interfere with social functioning, as well as the development of value orientations and styles of living to combat the inconsistent and unjust institutional responses to minority status. Leon Chestang has discussed two aspects of culture, indicating that:

> The sustentative aspects of culture [food, shelter, and jobs] are objective cultural expressions, but offering livelihood, physical comfort and safety. In essence, the sustentative aspects of culture are those that respond to man's basic instincts, survival. The nutritive aspects [values, social organization, institutions] are the expressive features of culture embodying and influencing thinking, feeling, and behavior—in other words, the social character of a people. It is through these facets of culture that the individual experiences psychological, and social gratification, derives an identity, feels intimacy and finds a haven from the assaults of the larger society.[8]

The family unit, a social system, assumes the overall responsibility for providing the needs of its members. Many of these family functions are shared with larger social organizations, and the family's capacity to interact effectively with these systems determines the quality of life experienced. For majority group Americans who have open access to the economic, social, and political systems, the integration of the instrumental and expressive aspects of culture is more readily achieved. The experience of many black Americans who seek transaction with these systems is, however, one of depreciation and exclusion, which threatens survival and the maintenance of self-esteem. These threats require black adaptations that split the acculturative process and result in the development of a duality of culture, or bicultural patterns.[9] The larger environment potentially holds the means of satisfying basic survival needs if acceptable behaviors and skills are offered, but nutrients for self-esteem are limited for people of color, who are considered outsiders. Blacks recognize, therefore, the value of maintaining relationships within their familial and community networks that support positive identity, afford protection from the assaults of a hostile environment, and enhance the capacity to negotiate both internal and external systems for survival, growth, and achievement.

Afro-American Value Orientations

For black Americans, the difficult task of survival with a measure of self-esteem is accomplished with a unique set of responses derived from an African value system combined with adaptations deemed essential to existence in the larger Anglo-American society. The African value orientations brought to this country emphasized "affiliation, collectivity, obedience to authority, belief in spirituality and acceptance of fate and past time . . . ."[10] African communities, guided by principles that supported "the survival of the tribe," reflected a high regard for interpersonal connectedness, cooperation, and collective responsibility. A respect for the wisdom of ancestors and the elderly and a strong belief in religion and magic were major themes of the cultural base. Those behaviors, attitudes, and beliefs that encouraged order and productivity for the powerful planter aristocracy were tolerated or reinforced, while those that threatened the successful operations of the slave system were targets for destruction through physical and psychological brutalities.

Whether contemporary black family systems display residuals of African value orientations is a matter of continuing debate among traditionalist and revisionist scholars. In a recent empirical study, Wade Nobles compared the African principles of human connectedness and interdependence with the thoughts and behaviors ex-

92

pressed by the black American families he had studied and found such organizational elements as the kinship network, role flexibility, and the socialization of children toward humanistic values to support his conclusion that the African cultural base continues to be operative.[11] The documentation of African cultural connectedness has been a positive force in the development of black self-identity. However, the social conditions experienced by blacks on the American continent have strongly influenced the development of a socialization process that represents an African peoples' effort to survive, maintain a sense of integrity, and achieve their human potential.

The dominant value orientations within contemporary black American family systems permit an openness to the inclusion of significant others, related or nonrelated, and a sharing of economic and psychological resources. These humanistic, inclusive, and cooperative orientations transcend the biological definition of family and offer comfort, understanding, and protection in situations that threaten the physical or psychological well-being of the kin network. The sense of "we-ness" that has grown out of the shared experiences that accrue to black status in this society has also shaped the development of family structures, roles, relationships, and institutions that support survival and the achievement of human aspirations and goals.

Strengths of Black Culture

Robert B. Hill has identified the strengths of black culture— strong kinship bonds, flexible family roles, strong religious orientations, and strong work and achievement orientations.[12] Black kinship networks are vital supports for the sharing of households, food, money, and child-care services. The nontraditional family structures observed in the black community offer a helping network that goes beyond the satisfaction of instrumental needs.[13] HarriettePipes McAdoo's study of black middle-class families revealed that family and community supports continued to be valued after achieving financial security because of racism in larger society institutions.[14] Geographic mobility and urbanization may decrease the level of direct support once offered by the kin-help system, but, with adaptive creativity, that former sense of security may be reestablished in other settings.

> The family network concept expands in the Black community to include others who are not related by blood or marriage. "Play sister," "cousin," or "home boy" describe relationships with origins in a former neighborhood or a common birthplace in the South that gives a sense of closeness. In several northern urban centers, social clubs have been organized to reproduce the sense of community and to reduce the feeling of isolation.[15]

93

The commonalities of experience in growing up black in America have produced a socialization process that internalizes a world view that supports the development of positive identity and affords opportunities for life satisfaction in an environment that may seem grossly inadequate to outsiders. The struggle to secure basic needs from wider society institutions has promoted egalitarian roles and relationships within the black family.

Although some students of the black family continue to interpret the black woman's strength in dealing with social realities as dominance, most scholars now label such findings as myth.[16] When the earnings of both male and female are required to survive in a system of limited opportunities, the commonsense approach of most black families suggests a functional adaptation of roles to meet the needs of its members. Children reared in such families observe a sharing of responsibility and decisions in the model of two employed parents. The strong work orientation promotes aspiration toward achievement goals and education is seen as essential to the attainment of jobs that bring dignity and respect in the community.

Group Identity

The socialization of black children for adequate functioning in two cultures is a family task shared with the black community and the institutions of the larger society. Institutional racism brings an additional component to the developmental process with which black parents must deal to prepare children for survival with a positive sense of self in a hostile environment. Although overt acts of racism have diminished to some degree, institutional barriers to achievement imply that blacks do not function as well as other groups.

The implication of basic inferiority would do serious damage to self-esteem were it not for the opportunities provided within the black community to express the talents and competence of its members. The sense of "we-ness" among black people finds expression in the development and staying power of such institutions as the black Church and fraternal organizations. It is also a major element in such observable phenomena as the "black table" in cafeterias of predominantly white universities and the unqualified expressions of pride when a black person is the winner in black/white competition. When individual accomplishments in academia, business, entertainment, or athletics are applauded, the esteem is shared throughout the group and others are motivated to develop their potential for achievement.

94

Bicultural Adaptation

It is clear that the dominant Afro-American value orientations are in conflict with the Anglo-American emphasis on individualism, differentiation, independence, mastery, and concern with the future as desirable assets for achieving the American dream.[17] Although acculturation has been a comparatively simple processcfor other immigrant groups, the complexities of racism require that blacks maintain the delicate balance of living in two cultures for survival with a sense of self esteem. For black Americans, acculturation, or the internalization of mainstream behaviors, attitudes, and values promotes a loss in the humanistic and cooperative themes so vital to survival, security and self-esteem. Jessie Bernard has described the "externally adapted" black family that adopts superficially those white middle-class behaviors and attitudes needed for access to mainstream opportunities.[18]

Although such behaviors do not resolve the value conflict and may result in strain, dealing with stress is not an unknown quantity to black people who learn to cope within the natural helping systems. Bicultural adaptation or "two ways of coping with the socialization tasks, expectations and behaviors"[19] is the most viable solution for adequate functioning in the black community.

Blacks in America have obtained physical survival needs using strategies that served to protect their humanity and self-esteem. Limited access to employment commensurate with skills and potential promoted instrumental adaptations to jobs for the economic benefits provided, but a cultural wariness and limited emotional investment was required to function effectively in a society that sanctioned unequal status for blacks. The civil rights actions of the 1960s and recent affirmative action commitments have permitted a few blacks to move into the economic mainstream and have increased the hopes and aspirations of untold others that their individual achievements would reduce the need for the cultural psychosocial patterns that supported them in the past.

An increasing number of young black people in recent years have been trained for access to positions in organizations previously closed to minorities. When overt responses from coworkers and superiors imply an acceptance and respect for one's competence, a value orientation toward individualism tends to develop. The recipient of such accolades may begin to feel secure enough in his or her job and organizational relationships to invest emotionally in the dominant culture and to reduce ties to family networks and the black com-

95

munity. When issues of racism are confronted, however, such an individual is left unprotected and may no longer have the cultural behaviors and relationships that serve as a haven from such assaults to the integrity, promote the renewal of strength, and also serve as a base for the development of power to address the destructive impact of external systems.

Maintaining Bicultural Functioning

The documentation of rising black suicide rates has given cause for speculation that the loss of these cultural supports may in some instances mean the loss of life.[20] Although suicide is only one of a range of possible behaviors, it is useful in illustrating the survival function of the cultural process. Most blacks are aware of the tenuousness of their relations with external systems and approach them pragmatically with few illusions about the social reality in which they live. Education, jobs, and housing are pursued in the larger environment for the economic and physical security they potentially offer, but the family and the black community continue to be major psychological support systems.

The eradication of racism, poverty, and inequality continue to be worthwile long-range goals, but blacks increasingly develop high blood pressure and experience depression and other response patterns that could result in death. Black cultural patterns support life and have demonstrated an enduring capacity to integrate sustenance and nurturance needs. As long as the forces of racism continue to be operative (events of the 1970s revealed a change in form but not in substance), all blacks must develop, strengthen, and maintain their skills for bicultural functioning.[21]

Conclusion

The time has passed for continuing the debate among human service professionals on the relevance of black cultural patterns to survival and achievement in an urban, technological society. Although it is recognized that there has been a decline in the official constraints on black participation in mainstream systems, the shifting barriers of institutional racism continue to control the opportunities for life satisfaction in the black community.

The creative adaptations observed in the black community are vital elements of a durable support system that enhances the capacity to function within the larger social context, where the response to racial difference is frequently unjust and inconsistent. Advocacy to eliminate the forces of racism and poverty must continue, but human

96

service givers would be well advised to recognize the potential that exists within the natural support systems of the black community to reduce the sense of powerlessness, to enhance the sense of competence, and to resolve their own problems in living.

Notes

1. See, for example, Herbert Gutman, *The Black Family in Slavery and Freedom: 1750-1925* (New York: Pantheon Books, 1976); and U.S. Bureau of the Census, Department of Commerce, *The Social and Economic Status of the Black Population in the United States: An Historical View, 1790-1978* (Washington, D.C.: U.S. Government Printing Office, 1979).

2. An excellent source of current information on the socioeconomic, educational, and political status of blacks is the National Urban League's annual publication, *The State of Black America*.

3. Robert Staples, "The Black American Family," and Howard J. Stanback, "A Framework for Understanding Black History in the United States," in *Ethnic Families in America*, ed. Charles H. Mindel and Robert Habenstein (New York: Elsevier North-Holland, 1976), p. 241; and Robert B. Hill, "The Illusion of Black Progress," *Social Policy* 9, no. 3 (November-December 1978); 14-25.

4. Walter R. Allen, "The Search for Applicable Theories of Black Family Life," *Journal of Marriage and the Family* 40 (February 1978): 117-29.

5. See Jessie Bernard, *Marriage and Family Among Negroes* (Englewood Cliffs, N.J.: Prentice-Hall, 1966), and John Scanzoni, *The Black Family in Modern Society* (Boston: Allyn and Bacon, 1971).

6. See Daniel P. Moynihan, *The Negro Family: The Case for National Action* (Washington, D.C.: U.S. Department of Labor, Office of Planning and Research, 1965); and Lee Rainwater, "Crucible of Identity: The Negro Lower Class Family" in *The Negro America*," ed. Talcott Parsons and Kenneth B. Clark (Boston: Beacon Press, 1966).

7. Robert O. Washington, "Social Work and the Black Perspective," *The Journal of Applied Social Services* 3 (Spring-Summer 1979): 152.

8. Leon Chestang, "Environmental Influences on Social Functioning: The Black Experience," in *The Diverse Society: Implications for Social Policy*, ed. Pastora San Juan Cafferty and Leon Chestang (Washington, D.C.: National Association of Social Workers, 1976), p. 69.

9. Ibid., pp. 65-67.

10. Elaine B. Pinderhughes, "Afro-American and Economic Dependency: Implications for the Future," *The Urban and Social Change Review* 12, no. 2 (Summer 1979): 26.

11. Wade W. Nobles, *A Formulative and Empirical Study of Black Families*, Grant no. 90-C-255 (Washington, D.C.: U.S. Government Printing Office, 1976).

12. Robert B. Hill, *The Strengths of Black Families* (New York: Emerson Hill 1971).

13. Andrew Billingsley, *Black Families in White America* (Englewood Cliffs, N.J.: Prentice-Hall, 1968).

14. Harriette Pipes McAdoo, "The Impact of Upward Mobility on the Reciprocal

Obligations of Kin-Help Patterns in Black Families." Paper presented at the National Urban League Conference on Black Families, Chicago, Illinois, 4 November 1977.

15. Anita J. Delaney, ed., *Black Task Force Report* (New York: Family Service Association of America, 1979), p. 9.

16. Joyce Ladner, *Tomorrow's Tomorrow: The Black Woman* (Garden City, N.Y.: Doubleday, 1971); Hill, *Strengths of Black Families*; and Elizabeth Herzog and Hyland Lewis, "Children in Poor Families: Myths and Realities," *American Journal of Orthopsychiatry* 40 (April 1970): 375-87.

17. John Papajohn and John Spiegel, *Transactions in Families* (San Francisco: Jossey-Bass, 1975).

18. Bernard, *Marriage and Family Among Negroes.*

19. Leon W. Chestang, *Character Development in a Hostile Environment*, Occasional Paper, no. 3 (Chicago: University of Chicago, School of Social Service Administration, 1972).

20. Alvin F. Poussaint, "Rising Suicide Rates Among Blacks," *Urban League Review* 3, no. 1 (Winter 1977): 22-30.

21. For a useful discussion on contemporary forms of racism, see Joel Dreyfuss, "The New Racism," *Black Enterprise* 8, no. 6 (January 1978): 41-54.

A Puerto Rican Historical Perspective

Melvin Delgado

It is essential to view the presence of Puerto Ricans in the United States within a historical context that takes into account social, economic, and political factors. Failure to understand the impact these factors have had on Puerto Rican migration to the United States seriously undermines any effort at analyzing the ramifications of migration on Puerto Rican mental health.

For the purpose of analysis, this article will focus specifically on the post-1898 period of Puerto Rican history. In addition, a brief overview of pre-1898 United States will be presented to set the context in which to examine the factors leading to the colonization of Puerto Rico.

The limitations inherent in briefly summarizing eighty years of history are prodigious and must be taken into account in reading this article. The author, admittedly taking a "left of center" approach, will provide a foundation from which to examine the social and economic status of Puerto Ricans residing in the United States.

The U. S. at the Time of Spanish-American War

The war in the Caribbean between the United States and Spain was the culmination of various factors that had shaped American attitudes toward Spain and her colonies. These factors represented a wide range of interests, which ranged from humanitarian concerns over Spanish acts of atrocities in Cuba to purely imperialistic intents.

There were six major factors influential in precipitating the Spanish-American War of 1898: (1) social Darwinism as a prevailing North American philosophy, (2) the need for the United States to recover from the effects of a devastating depression, (3) rapid industrialization, (4) military interests in the Atlantic and Pacific, (5) the need for reunifying the nation over a common cause, and (6) pressure from liberal elements to intervene in Cuba to protect lives.

The years 1890-1898 were a crucial period in American history, a period that saw the maturing and operationalization of social Darwinism in American thought.[1] This philosophical position represented the unification of imperialistic and racist concepts. In essence, it held that the United States had survived and prospered because of a natural selection process. Consequently, it was morally correct to absorb weaker nations under the guise of benevolence.[2] This righteous sentiment, in combination with capitalistic concerns, provided the moral foundation for United States expansion overseas.

Economic Developments

This period also witnessed two important economic developments, which, in combination with social Darwinism, necessitated expansion of American industry. First, the United States was in the midst of a great depression such as had never been experienced in its brief history.[3] Second, rapid developments in industry facilitated industrialization to proceed at an unprecedented pace. This, in turn, required a plentiful supply of raw materials and cheap labor. In addition, a market for manufactured goods was essential. The following two statements, the first by Foraker and the second by Beveridge, two powerful senators of the times, surmise the predicament of American industry during this period:

> We have reached the point in the development of our resources and the multiplication of our industries where we are not only supplying our home demands, but are producing a large surplus, constantly growing larger. Our greatest present and prospective commercial need is for markets abroad. We cannot find them in the countries of Europe. Their demand upon us is limited. They strive to supply themselves and to compete with us in the markets of the world.[1]

> Today we are raising more than we can consume. Today we are making more than we can use. Today our society is congested; there are more workers than there is work; there is more capital than there is investments. We do not need money—we need more circulation, more employment. Therefore, we must find new markets for our products, new occupation for our capital, new work for our labor.[5]

These two quotes capture the essence of America's industrial dilemma—the need for expansion through implementation of a new "manifest destiny."

The expansion of United States interests overseas required the development and expansion of military outposts to protect United States interests. Puerto Rico, as with other Spanish territories, played a pivotal role in these plans. Its strategic position in the Caribbean had traditionally made Puerto Rico a key military island for both Spain and the United States. Relatively recent historical developments, particularly Cuba's socialistic orientation, have reinforced Puerto Rico's military attractiveness.

There was an additional factor that made a war with Spain an attractive proposition at the time. Namely, a short and popular war that would end in a clear victory for the United States would serve a valuable psychological function for the nation. There are those who contend that the Vietnam War became unpopular with Americans because of its length and its increasingly hugh expenditures of funds and human resources. Its length and its requirements increased the possibility of dissention. In contrast, the Spanish-American War served a unifying function at a time in American history when "poor" economic conditions threatened the nation. The Spanish-American War lasted only several months and culminated with a clear victory for the United States. In fact, several prominent American figures firmly established their imprint on American history as the result of this war. The most notable was Theodore Roosevelt, who not only served two terms as president, but also influenced who his successor would be and, in 1912, was nearly elected for an unprecedented third term.

In conclusion, it would not be wholly fair to give the impression that the Spanish-American War of 1898 was fought purely on imperialistic grounds. The repressive nature of Spanish rule in Cuba had resulted in thousands of deaths. News of these Spanish atrocities eventually found their way into the American press, resulting in indignation on the part of many Americans. Consequently, there were many Americans who favored war with Spain for purely humanitarian reasons.

Spanish-American War of 1898

The Spanish-American War of 1898 was prompted by the blowing up of the United States battleship *Maine*, which was anchored outside Havana. There have been numerous accusations over the past eighty years concerning who blew up the ship: Spain said it was the Cubans; the Cubans contended it was Spain; others said it was the United States. Nevertheless, "Remember the *Maine*" served as a rallying cry for military intervention.

The Treaty of Paris, recognizing the United States victory, was signed on December 1, 1898. Spain agreed to sign over possession of the Philippines, Guam, Cuba, and Puerto Rico. Several Cuban and Puerto Rican historians contend that these islands were for all intents and purposes politically autonomous at that point in history, and Spain and the United States had no right to use these islands as barter.[6] As for Puerto Rico, it took approximately fifty years before Puerto Ricans could exercise any influential degree of control over its internal issues.

United States Presence in Puerto Rico

The introduction and impact of American capital on Puerto Rico can best be illustrated through the analysis of sugar production. The most rapid growth of the sugar industry occurred during the early decades of the twentieth century.[7] This was the result of exceedingly high world demand for sugar. Growth was spurred as a result of Puerto Rican sugar being regarded as a high-profit crop and preferred risk because Puerto Rican products could enter the United States without payment of duties.

It must be noted that prior to 1898, Puerto Rico was reliant on three major crops—sugar, tobacco, and coffee. However, since 1900, sugar production held a privileged position among the industries of Puerto Rico. Puerto Rico's inclusion within the American tariff system had pronounced impact on the profitability of its major crops. Cane and tobacco prospered, while coffee, a low profit crop during the period, floundered as a result of no tariff protection and higher production costs.

Economic Shifts

By 1930, Puerto Rico became a typical sugar island. By that year, close to $120 million in American capital had been invested in the island. Sugar, in turn, was responsible for approximately 78 percent of all capital invested in manufacturing (five times the amount invested in coffee and tobacco combined). In addition, sugar constituted 65 percent of all products exported to the United States.[8]

The economic shift to a primarily one-crop economy had, and continues to have, prodigious impact on the Puerto Rican economy. A shift in land utilization to a one-crop dependence results in the alienation of resources normally allocated for subsistence food growth, and the importation of food. Consequently, the cost of food is multiplied; in Puerto Rico it is higher than in the United States.[9] In addition to the added cost of food, the increased reliance on "absentee ownership" of land by United States corporations affected the society as a whole. As will be noted below in the section on industrialization, the concept of absentee ownership is still prevalent, although a different product is involved.

102

United States Citizenship

Puerto Ricans have been United States citizens since 1917 as a result of the Jones Act, which granted citizenship to all Puerto Ricans who desired it.[10] However, the expedience of this Act has been seriously debated in some circles because shortly afterwards Puerto Ricans were required to perform military duties (World War I).

United States citizenship for Puerto Ricans has carried some rights and privileges, but not others. For example, Puerto Ricans can enter the United States without passports or visas, just like any other United States citizen. However, in the area of elections, there are major differences between residing in the United States and in Puerto Rico. Puerto Ricans do not have any representation in the Congress, with the exception of a resident commissioner who has a voice but no vote. In addition, Puerto Ricans can vote in primaries, but cannot vote in United States general elections. Consequently, they have no say over presidential preferences. It must be noted that Puerto Ricans do not pay any federal taxes; thus, no representation without taxation.

The fact that Puerto Ricans cannot assist in determining who occupies the presidency has far-reaching implications. First, Puerto Ricans, as noted, can be drafted into the United States military and be required to fight for the United States; however, Puerto Ricans do not have a choice over who is their commander-in-chief.

Puerto Ricans are eligible to receive health and education benefits, but only some welfare benefits. For example, food stamps are made available, but public assistance is not. The judicial system is closely tied to that of the United States, and legal appeals must follow procedures similar to those in the United States, with the Supreme Court having the final decision on all such matters. In essence, citizenship for Puerto Ricans can best be classified as being 'quasi', with limited rights and privileges.

Development of Tourism

Up until the early 1940s, all major administrative positions in Puerto Rico were held by Americans appointed by the political leadership of the United States. An appointment in Puerto Rico was often regarded as a political plum. The administrative costs of maintaining a government in Puerto Rico were paid for by the Puerto Rican people. Needless to say, the use of political appointees without regard to qualifications does not insure effective administration.

It was not until several political uprisings and a visit by President Roosevelt had taken place that Puerto Rico was assigned an administrator with the necessary qualifications to administer. It was during this period that Rexford Tugwell was assigned to Puerto Rico.[11] Under his governership, tourism as an economic venture was developed in Puerto Rico. Through the investment of American capital into the service industry, Puerto Rico became a major tourism center for North Americans.

In similar fashion to the sugar industry, however, Puerto Rico once again had to rely on outside funding, had limited control over funds, and was very dependent on the economic swings of the United States. In essence, a focus on tourism served an immediate need, but it also had long-term consequences.

Industrialization

Puerto Rico has industrialized at such a rapid pace over the past thirty years that it is considered one of the twenty most industrialized areas in the world.[12] United States industry was attracted to Puerto Rico through tax exemptions, cheap labor, and assurances of political stability.[13] Industrial development, in turn, resulted in increased employment for Puerto Ricans and a corresponding increase in income per capita; Puerto Rico has the highest per capita in Latin America.

However, progress has not been made without social consequences for Puerto Rico. These social costs can be categorized into three major areas: (1) failure to develop indigenous industries sufficiently, (2) an increased reliance on the United States that has perpetuated absentee ownership, and (3) rising expectations that have further accentuated a dependency on United States manufactured goods.

Puerto Rican industry has, as a result of no tax exemptions, been forced to compete with United States companies, which has made the development of indigenous industry very difficult to accomplish. An increased reliance on the United States has fostered the perpetuation of absentee ownership of resources. As noted by Gordon Lewis, absentee ownership of Puerto Rican resources has not changed dramatically over the past few decades:

> In 1948 some 78 percent of local capital investment activities were in Puerto Rican hands; in 1966 some 77 percent of these activities, including manufacturing, were in the hands of nonresidential North American entities, while by 1970 some 65 percent of housing construction, some 60 percent of banking activities, some 90 percent of insurance activities, and almost all internal traffic operations and external passenger and goods operations were concentrated in the same nonresidential entities.[14]

Thus, absentee ownership of Puerto Rican industrial resources will play an influential role in Puerto Rico's future. Failure to address successfully this reliance on the United States will seriously restrict development of indigenous industry.

Urbanization

Rapid industrialization and urbanization have also resulted in both a dramatic increase in the standard of living and an uprooting and disruption of family stability. Minimum wages have increased steadily over the years and are currently $2.30 an hour. Along with this increase, there has been an increase in consumption of manufactured products—cars, appliances, and so on—in fact, Puerto Rico is the fifth largest consumer of American goods in the world.[15] However, as a result of an increase in minimum wage and the expiration of tax exemptions, American industry is slowly leaving the island for other parts of the world where minimum wages are still relatively low and tax exemptions are readily available. Consequently, Puerto Ricans must contend with high expectations of and poor prospects for a "better life."

Uprooting families from rural sections of Puerto Rico to urban areas has affected family stability. The depersonalization process often associated with major urban areas has been prevalent in the Puerto Rican experience. Lack of adequate employment, housing, and other basic human resources has not facilitated the transition process successfully. Crime, drug addiction, poverty, and school drop out rates have increased dramatically during the period of industrialization.

Political Status of Puerto Rico

The political status of Puerto Rico is of concern to every Puerto Rican, regardless of socioeconomic stratum. The choices for Puerto Rico are relatively simple: (1) continue its status quo existence as a commonwealth, (2) elect statehood, or (3) elect independence. Since 1952, Puerto Ricans have been able to cast a vote concerning the political status of the island. Its commonwealth status can best be classified as a quasi-colonial existence. However, over the past few decades, with two exceptions (statehood party candidates were elected governors), Puerto Ricans have preferred this type of political affiliation.

Commonwealth status allows Puerto Rico to receive federal funds for various social-health programs, a continuance of citizenship, and representation in the Congress; Puerto Ricans, in turn, are not required to pay federal taxes. There are many Puerto Ricans who feel

105

that commonwealth status is a second-class status, and that a choice of statehood or independence is necessary for the country to survive in future years. Those who argue for statehood feel that Puerto Rico has for all intents and purposes been a part of the United States for over eighty years; those who argue for independence feel that Puerto Rico will lose economically and culturally by becoming a state. Clearly, any of the choices will result in controversy within Puerto Rico and the United States.

Interpretation of Historical Events

This article has focused thus far on presentation of facts. It is essential to interpret this information in light of implications for mental health. Clearly, the fact that Puerto Rico has not enjoyed "freedom" from foreign powers in over 450 years has prodigious implications for self-image and sense of control over one's destiny.

The effect of United States control over the island's economic, social, and political systems cannot be underestimated. Mass migration to the United States has resulted from this control; the same can be said for the conditions that have awaited Puerto Ricans in this country. Puerto Ricans in the United States must contend with social welfare institutions that are at best unresponsive to their needs.

In examining the benefits bestowed by the United States on Puerto Rico, inherent contradictions seriously limit the advantages Puerto Rico has as a result of her association with the United States. Citizenship, as pointed out, is not full-fledged. It remains to be seen whether, if Puerto Rico decides to become a state, the United States Congress would allow it to enter the union. An increase in the standard of living has been accomplished, but there are many Puerto Ricans who believe that the price has been too high and Puerto Rico is now feeling the consequences.

It is imperative, therefore, for human service providers to have an understanding of the social, economic, and political factors that have made Puerto Rico dependent on the United States for food, manufactured goods, employment, and social welfare programs. Failure to appreciate the interface of these factors with Puerto Rican migration to the United States will increase the likelihood of developing stereotypes that denigrate an entire ethnic group.

Summary

In summary, the social, economic, and political conditions in Puerto Rico have necessitated mass migration to the United States. Recent

106

studies indicate that some return migration to Puerto Rico is occurring. However, dispersal within the United States is also prevalent, and this has an impact on human service programs throughout the country.[16]

Puerto Rico currently finds itself in the midst of an economic depression that will require major restructuring of social, economic, and political institutions in order to achieve a lasting recovery. The cost of food, as noted, is higher than in the United States, requiring a high dependence on United States food stamps for subsistence. Unemployment is conservatively estimated at 18 percent.[17] Fortunately, the island is experiencing a boom in tourism, keeping unemployment rates from rising further.

As a result of industrialization, major population shifts have occurred from rural to urban areas. In turn, urbanization has resulted. However, so have the social ills normally associated with urban living: crime, substandard housing, transportation limitations, and so on. Finally, expectations for a better life have increased prodigiously over the past three decades. However, just as in the United States, prospects for an increased standard of living are becoming more dim.

It is essential for human service workers to have an appreciation of the factors influencing Puerto Rican migration to and within the United States. The process has had deleterious impact on those who have chosen to leave Puerto Rico, as well as on those who were forced to stay behind. This uprooting influences all members of the family.

Notes

1. Richard Hofstader, *Social Darwinism in American Thought* (Boston: Beacon Press, 1944).

2. See Manuel Maldonado-Denis, *Puerto Rico: A Socio-Historic Interpretation* (New York: Random House, 1972), pp. 55-62; and Gordon K. Lewis, *Puerto Rico: Freedom and Power in the Caribbean* (New York: Monthly Review Press, 1964), pp. 85-122.

3. Richard Hofstader, *The Age of Reform: From Bryan to F.D.R.* (New York: Alfred A. Knopf, 1955).

4. Maldonado-Denis, *Puerto Rico*, pp. 89-90.

5. Lincoln Bergman et al., *Puerto Rico: The Flame of Resistance* (New York: People's Press, 1977) pp. 28-29.

6. See Juan Angel Silen, *We, The Puerto Rican People: A Story of Oppression and Resistance* (New York: Monthly Review Press, 1971), pp. 27-36; Maldonado-Denis, *Puerto Rico*, pp. 47-51; and Gordon K. Lewis, *Notes on the Puerto Rican Revolution* (New York: Monthly Review Press, 1971).

7. Bailey Diffie and Justine Diffie, *Puerto Rico: A Broken Pledge* (New York: The Vanguard Press, 1931).

8. See Lewis, *Power in the Caribbean*, pp. 88-90; Thomas C. Cochran, *The Puerto Rican Businessman: A Study in Cultural Change* (Philadelphia: University of Pennsylvania Press, 1958); Silen, *Puerto Rican People*, pp. 53-54; and Maldonado-Denis, *Puerto Rico,* pp. 72-76.

9. Lori Larkin and Eric Langdon, *Puerto Rican Independence* (New York: International Socialist Press, 1972), p. 24.

10. U.S. Commission on Civil Rights, *Puerto Ricans in the United States: An Uncertain Future* (Washington, D.C.: U.S. Government Printing Office, 1976), p. 13.

11. Rexford Tugwell, *The Stricken Land: The Story of Puerto Rico* (Princeton, N.J.: Princeton University Press, 1961).

12. Bergman et al., *Flame of Resistance*, pp. 66-68.

13. Lewis, *Power in the Caribbean*, p. 51.

14. Ibid.

15. Larkin and Langdon, *Independence*, p. 24.

16. See Guy Gugliotta, "The End of the West Side Story," *Worcester Sunday Telegram*, 9 December 1976, p. 11; Jon Nordheimer, "Puerto Ricans Return to Crowded Homeland Accelerating," *The New York Times*, 10 May 1978, p. 1; and A.J. Jaffe and A. Carreras-Carleton, *Some Demographic and Economic Characteristics of the Puerto Rican Population Living on the Mainland, U.S.A.* (New York: Columbia University Applied Research Center, 1974), pp. 9-49.

17. Jon Nordheimer, "Food Stamps Buoy Economy in Puerto Rico," *The New York Times,* 12 May 1979, pp. 1, 9.

Puerto Rican Culture

Emelicia Mizio

Healthy families are the sine qua non of a healthy society. They are critical to the preservation of our societal structure and its effective functioning. Families cannot exist in isolation and maintain their health without societal supports. There is a reciprocity between society and its members that must be recognized.[1]

To understand a family and its operations one must study it in transaction with its environment. The Puerto Rican family must, therefore, be examined from this perspective. The family is an extremely vulnerable institution affected by and responsive to societal conditions. The family must be provided with the resources to manage its changing tasks in a society which seems ever in flux.

The degree of a family's vulnerability relates closely to its socioeconomic status. The effects of poverty in terms of physical and mental malaise and feelings of helplessness, hopelessness, and alienation have been well documented. We know that the Puerto Rican family is in jeopardy. The Puerto Rican family is, for the most part, in jeopardy because of poverty and because the structural difference of its extended family system and value differences place it in conflict with the sociolegal system of this country, which addresses itself basically to the nuclear family. Society, in turn, jeopardizes itself when it does not meet the needs of its citizenry and provide the necessary supports—hence, for example, the problems of the inner cities. Major cities such as New York, Chicago, Philadelphia, Cleveland, Newark, and Boston have large Puerto Rican populations (as well as other minorities). The quality of life of the Puerto Rican (and other minorities) and key urban centers must be viewed as inextricably linked.[2]

A coherent and just national family social policy must evolve to address ethnic differences and rectify societal inequities that have given minority status its meaning. Social policy deals with the principles and regulations that govern any measure or activity, with reference to social relationships and the distribution of resources in our society. Social policy deals with the kinds of benefits that are to be

109

distributed, with the people to whom they are to be distributed, with the amounts to be distributed, with the ways in which benefits are to be financed, and with the cost for providing a specific benefit.[3] Social policies that only relate to the Anglo Saxon, nuclear family and make no provisions for compensatory justice will continue to perpetuate racism. It is important, therefore, that the helping professional appreciate the significance of ethnicity.

Ethnicity fulfills deeply embedded psychological needs for security, identity, and a sense of historical continuity. Within the family it is transmitted in an emotional language and is reinforced by similar units in the community.[4] Ethnicity carries with it a sense of peoplehood and community. It is critical in the development of self-esteem, self-image, and the sense of belonging. Ethnicity refers to a common culture. It forms the basic values, norms, attitudes, and lifestyles of the group's members, despite its modification by such factors as class, race, religion, sex, region, and generation.[5]

Ethnicity serves an inherently supportive function. Society can, however, enhance this support. The identification with one's group also tends to encompass, in part, the societal perception of one's community. Under present conditions this view contributes to negative self-esteem in the minority community. This societal perception and its individual and communal consequences is one for which policy experts will have to make provision in planning if the status quo of inequality is to be eroded.

The Puerto Rican Family

The Puerto Rican family is a patriarchal one in which roles are clearly defined and carefully monitored. There are important reciprocal obligations and strict enforcement of controls. Each individual's worth is guaranteed by the fulfillment of his or her role responsibilities.[6] The Puerto Rican family espouses extended family patterns; its elderly are respected and its children are deeply loved. They are never held accountable for their parent's "sins."

In Puerto Rican culture, the male is seen as innately superior to the female, who is overprotected, has limited freedom, and, even today, is encumbered by the traditional virginity and machismo cults. Parents view their children as completely dependent, and dependency is generally encouraged throughout age groups. Parents demand obedience and respect from their children. Achievement is less important than conformity—this is especially true for the female. In the middle and upper classes there is less emphasis on subordination patterns, but they are still interwoven into the fabric of all Puerto

110

Rican society. To understand something of the Puerto Rican family it is important to understand the interrelated Puerto Rican cultural values of *dignidad, respeto,* and *personalismo.*[7] A person has *dignidad* (dignity) in a broad sense. They have an innate worth and inner importance. The spirit and the soul are more important than the body. The focus is on the inner qualities of uniqueness and goodness.

Because people are born into their socioeconomic role, they are not held accountable for their status. There is often a *fatalismo* (fatalism) about one's position in life.[8] What a person has or their station in life is, therefore, not crucial—he or she has an innate status just by being. Future rewards will come in heaven.

People must, however, be treated in this life with *respeto* (respect), which is the esteemed acknowledgment of an individual's personal attributes, uninfluenced by wealth or social position.[9] *Respeto* also connotes hierarchal relationships. Elders and superiors are to be accorded respect and, in turn, they must always be cordial. Puerto Ricans are very sensitive to violations of their dignity. A person affronted must always handle him or herself in an honest, dignified, and upright manner. The attempt is to settle the situation *a la buena* (in a nice way). There is generally an attempt to avoid direct confrontation and *palea monga* (passive resistance) is often employed. Aggression is permitted only when a man's honor is challenged. In family situations the hope is always that love will elicit the desired behavior.

Tied in with dignity and respect is the concept of *personalismo* (a strong preference for face-to-face contact and primary relationships).[10] It is not the organization that one counts on or trusts, but the individual. The concept of a collective welfare generally has little meaning. One thinks instead in terms of the effects on Pablo, Jose, and Juan. Even in terms of ties to the church, Puerto Ricans have a very individualistic relationship with the saints. Involvement in group activity usually depends on strong ties to individual group members rather than ties to a cause per se.[11] Puerto Ricans seem to look to charismatic leadership and show a high rate of participation in elections, but there is a tendency to idolize their leaders and leave too much policymaking to those they have elected. This relates as well to other leaders such as in labor and religious bodies[12] All in all, it is a requirement of *personalismo* that all social, economic, political, and religious relationships proceed on a basis of face-to-face contact.[13]

Wider Relationships

Because Puerto Ricans feel most comfortable with family-type relationships, it is not surprising that the Puerto Rican extended family

111

encompasses more than those related by blood and marriage and includes those tied to it by custom in reciprocal bonds of obligation and feeling. *Compradazgo* is the institution of *compadres* (companion parents), a network of ritual kinship whose members have a deep sense of obligation to each other. These responsibilities are taken quite seriously and include economic assistance, encouragement, support, and even personal correction. Sponsors of a child at baptism and confirmation take on the role of *padrino* (godparents) to the child and *compadres* to the parents. Also assuming this role are witnesses at a marriage and close friends. The relationship is deemed to have a religious and even mystical quality.

Hijos de crianza (children of the upbringing) is the cultural practice of accepting responsibility for another's child without the necessity of blood or even friendship ties. This child is raised as if it were one's own. Neither the parent nor the child is stigmatized for the surrender of this child. It is important to take note that there is no stigma either on an illegitimate child. Following the Roman law tradition there is no concept of illegitimacy; rather, the child is viewed as a natural child.[14] This institutional practice serves as an economic and emotional safety device for the family and makes it often possible for the child to have a better life. In such situations, the family will probably be without any legal documents pertaining to the child. The helping person must often be prepared, if need be, to handle the legal complications in work that includes these children.

Societal Strains on the Puerto Rican Family

The points of tension on the Puerto Rican family have been classified as follows:

1. A traditional system of relationships based on social class and family background for social status, versus an industrial system based on personal competition, initiative, and conspicuous consumption as a basis for status.
2. High aspirations and low achievement.
3. The value of dignity, pride, and honor contrasted with the increasing emphasis on material wealth and consumption.
4. A value system that reveres the *jibaro* (an idealized folk hero) as opposed to one that reveres the successful entrepreneur.[15]
5. The present commitment to democracy compared with the traditional methods of power that prevailed in the colonial system.[16]

Other important societal tension points present in Puerto Rico that have ramifications for Puerto Ricans on both the island the mainland include the great population explosion, unequal distribution of wealth, cultural fusion and its accompanying conflicts, federal relations with the United States, and the ongoing issue of Puerto Rico's political status.[17]

There is no universal model that applies to the Puerto Rican family living in the United States or even in Puerto Rico. Families are affected by and deal with potential strains in different ways. The Puerto Rican family system must be viewed as being a continuum that at one end is an extended family system with traditional Puerto Rican values and at the other end is the nuclear family system with an American value system. Perhaps helpful in understanding differences in family structure and values is seeing industrialization and the penetration of the Anglo culture as different streams of influence.[18] Strains may be caused by either stream. The interconnections of both streams cannot be denied. One therefore finds in Puerto Ricans a middle-class suburban nuclear family that may have an open-door policy to friends and relatives from other areas. Also, the traditional patterns are often augmented by other friendships such as those formed at work.[19] Business firms may be quite paternalistic and highly centralized in authority, following a preindustrial form.[20]

A study of dealing with acculturation among Puerto Rican women on the mainland showed that even among those who scored high on acculturation there was evidence of respect for and adherence to traditional family-related values.[21] The nuclear family pattern in both structure and functioning is on the increase in Puerto Rico. It has been observed, however, that despite this trend the traditional ties to parents and grandparents remain. The pattern described as being resistant to change is the one of child-parent obligation.[22]

Urbanization

Under the impact of American colonialization, the family in Puerto Rico has often undergone considerable cultural shock. Even before emigrating, the poor family in moving from a rural community to an urban area may have already encountered Americanization and suffered the effects of a clash of value. The required lifestyle in an urban area in Puerto Rico and the lifestyle of those who are prospering around them is different from anything experienced in a rural past. Puerto Rican families, who may often find themselves living in urban shanties, at times within the shadow of sleek new office buildings, have to exist on odd jobs and meager welfare payments.[23] Problems in the United States become considerably more complex than in urban Puerto Rico. A lack of proficiency in English, limited education and

113

occupational skills, and exposure to prejudice are added to existing strains.

The traditional family structure and value system comes into immediate conflict with the demands of the mainland environment. Women must act independently, work in Anglo settings, and carry the same types of burdens as men. They must deal with external systems such as the school, police, hospitals, and so on—men cannot shield them from external sources. Children must also become assertive to survive and begin this pattern with parents, thus challenging parental views. These exchanges and others need not be critical, but may become so when compounded by a society denying access to the resources necessary to newly defined roles.

Certainly, these strains result in a critical situation for the Puerto Rican. Judith Rabkin and Elmer Struening, in revewing the research on mental health among New York City residents, reported that epidemiological studies consistently show higher rates of mental illness for Puerto Ricans than for other ethnic groups or for the total population.[24] In addition, their findings may not reflect the degree of the problem, because Puerto Ricans have great tolerance for the "peculiarities" of others and will lend support to keeping the person at home and in the community.

Also, for many Puerto Ricans spiritualism[25] is practiced hand-in-hand with Catholicism, the predominant religion. Thus, spirits are believed to be the cause of mental illnesses and seances are attended. Puerto Ricans may find community support in dealing with psychic problems, which, in their perception, is externalized into a spiritual cause. However it may well be that not seeking psychiatric help quickly may allow for the further breakdown of individuals.

The Puerto Rican as a Minority Member

The Puerto Rican family often finds itself in a hostile environment that makes life a struggle for existence at every turn. Racist practices, along with the highly technological, stratified, closed society, delays the upward mobility of the Puerto Rican family. It is defined as a minority group, whereas in Puerto Rico it was part of a majority. The label of minority is synonymous with a deprecated and stereotyped lifestyle. Minority indicates blocked access to the fraternity of the "in-group" and the full benefits of the American way of life. The Puerto Rican family's chances for success in America seem related to its ability to obscure all differences from the majority group. Puerto Ricans will even attempt to be defined as white or black, the standardized categories for color in the United States, because no allowance is made for the Puerto Rican's Indian, Spanish, and African heritage. The Puerto Rican who, by placing himself into the proverbial melting pot, is able to metamorphose as "white," with an Anglicized name and lifestyle, makes it finally possible to provide for his family an American standard of living. The price he must pay is denial of self and heritage and a sacrifice of personal integrity.

The racial experience on the continent goes beyond the individual and the family, however, and must be viewed as a collective one. The color question persists as a psychological dilemma, even among the seemingly assimilated.[26] For those who pass as Anglo, there is, for example, a need to decide whether to confront or let pass a remark about Puerto Ricans, and always at issue is can one accept racism in one's friends. Such Puerto Ricans need to constantly reassess the Puerto Rican stereotype to try and place themsevles and others in perspective. Puerto Ricans with a negative internalization of self as Puerto Ricans may also work against the interests of their own in their attempt to deny their own heritage and the attempt to secure their new "chosen" identity.

The problems created in the individual and in the family by society's measurements of worth by color is vividly portrayed in *Down These Mean Streets*. Piri Thomas's autobiography describes how his painful identity problem and destructive relationships with his siblings and his father were related to the differences in color between him and his siblings and feelings about self and others tied to these color differences. In his words, a Puerto Rican who was dark like his father and different from the rest of his family speaks:

> It wasn't right to be ashamed of what one was. It was like hating Momma for the color she was and Poppa for the color he wasn't. . . . Man do you know what it is to sit across a dinner table looking at your brothers that look exactly like paddy people? True, I ain't never been down South, but the same crap's happening here. So they don't hang you by your neck. But they slip an invisible rope around your balls and hang you with nice smiles, and 'If we need you we'll call you' I wanna feel like a 'Mr.' part time . . . You and James [his brothers] are like houses painted white outside and blacker'n mother inside. And I'm close to being like Poppa—trying to be white on both sides.[27]

Search for the Pot of Gold

Because Puerto Ricans are United States citizens there is little preparation involved if they wish to come to the mainland. As a result, there is an airborne migration and a back-and-forth flow that has significance because the feeling of the need to adjust to the mainland environment is less than if travel were restricted. In fact, it is difficult to find a Puerto Rican adult who has not spent some time in the United States.[28] There are many reasons why Puerto Ricans come to the States, but most of all economics serves as the primary motivation for migration. However, the Puerto Rican is by no means doing well on the mainland. In 1976, the U.S. Commission on Civil Rights reported that Puerto Ricans are poorer, have less education, and are more dependent on welfare than the national average.[29]

In 1977, the median income of non-Spanish men was $10,300 and non-Spanish women $4,000 as compared to the $8,100 median income for Puerto Rican men and $4,200 for Puerto Rican women. In 1977, 9 percent of families of non-Spanish origin had incomes of below $5,000 in comparison to 16 percent of Spanish-origin families. About 50 percent of all Spanish-origin families with a woman as a head of household were below the poverty level.[30] In March 1978, the unemployment rate for the Spanish-origin labor force was 10 percent in comparison to the general United States rate of 7 percent. The male unemployment rate was 9 percent in contrast to 6 percent and the female rate was 10 percent unemployment in comparison to 7 percent.[31]

Education

In educational attainment, March 1978 figures show that 3 percent of non-Spanish persons twenty-five years and over had completed less than five years of schooling. Sixty-seven percent of the non-Spanish population twenty-five years old and older had completed four years of high school. This contrasts with 15 percent of Puerto Rican origin persons who completed less than five years of schooling and 36 percent who were high school graduates.[32] For Puerto Rican youth there is a severe drop-out problem. A Puerto Rican is only 50 percent as likely to be attending school as his or her young adult peers. Studies in both Chicago and New York City schools showed that schools with heavy Puerto Rican enrollments had students' reading averages lower than predominantly black or Anglo schools. Lags increased with each succeeding grade. Birthplace, language, and drop-out rate were interwoven. Young Puerto Ricans born on the island are more likely to be doomed to a life of poverty.[33]

Bilingual programs and bicultural representation are inadequate, and, consequently, there are insufficient role models and communication links to students and staff. Teachers often expect too little of minority students and this becomes a self-fulfilling prophesy. Students needing special education programs are undercounted and, thus, underserved. There is also a lack of commitment by adminis-

116

tration to bilingual programs, and an inbalance of experienced teachers to inexperienced teachers, with majority communities claiming the experienced teachers. The odds are usually stacked against the student remaining in school.

Despite these burdens, however, the majority of Puerto Rican families have been able to adjust somewhat to their new environment, recreate some of their cultural ambiance (for example, food, religion, and recreation), and create communal institutions and organizations that contribute to the community's well-being and progress. In addition, a baseline of 1.2 million people, the United States 1978 Census figures show 369,280 people completed high school, 36,928 completed college and 84,242 had one to three years of college,[34] and 11,540 people earned $25,000 or more, with 174,165 people in white-collar occupations.[35] In 1975, technical, professional, or managerial jobs were held by more than 42,000 people.[36] Another very important fact to remember is that, despite the high numbers on welfare, 75 percent of all mainland Puerto Ricans do not receive any governmental aid and are wholly self-sufficient.[37]

Conclusion

To understand the Puerto Rican family it is important to know its cultural heritage and the degree of each individual's family's identification with the Puerto Rican and Anglo culture. There is a unique blending found in each individual and family that is affected by class factors. The term *ethclass* has been formulated by Milton M. Gordon to describe the subsociety created by the intersection of social class and ethnicity. He speaks of two types of identification: the historical, that has its focus on the ethnic group, and the participational, the *ethclass*. He points out that members of similar ethnic groups but different social classes share peoplehood (historical identification), but do not necessarily have similar behavioral styles (participational identification).[38]

All classes in Puerto Rican society seem to maintain to some degree both the historical and participational identification. On the mainland it is difficult to identify the numbers of those who have completely assimilated to an Anglo lifestyle. No culture will remain static, especially if it is to remain viable, and all cultures have functional and dysfunctional aspects. The subordination patterns in male-female roles must continue to undergo changes as in all societies, but without females developing into superwomen. Extended families remain critical to individual members in an alienated world, but should not negate a person's individuality. The humanitarian value system of

117

the Puerto Rican needs to be adopted by the Anglo culture. The Puerto Rican should not, however, accept the concept of material goods only in heaven. A humane standard of living must be available to all.

Caution must be taken not to stereotype any individual, class, or group. To affirm Cafferty and Chestang's view, just as it is dangerous to ignore an individual's ethnic identity, it is equally dangerous to assume certain behavioral characteristics based on that identity.[39] Therefore, the characteristics of the Puerto Rican culture that have been discussed should be used as a base for comparisons and treated with a respect for the differences and similarities between the Puerto Rican group itself and the Anglo group.

The helping professions cannot by themselves restructure society and achieve a more equitable distribution of opportunities and rewards. They can, however, help the Puerto Rican family to deal with suffocating external systems, and through joint advocacy efforts work toward systems change. The helping professional and professions must examine with honesty their own delivery system to the Puerto Rican consumer. They must examine the ways in which their services are both functional, dysfunctional, or are nonexistent. Services must be culturally syntonic and not geared to an Anglo value system.

The Puerto Rican family must be allowed and helped to use its own strengths, draw on its humanitarian values, and support its kin and the Puerto Rican community. The helping professions must work as change agents if they are to be instrumental in the Puerto Rican's family efforts to manage tasks effectively, in harmony with its values and lifestyles.

Notes

1. Shirley Zimmerman, "The Family and its Relevance for Social Policy," *Social Case-work* 57, no. 9 (November 1976): 548.

2. U.S. Commission on Civil Rights, *Puerto Ricans in the United States: An Uncertain Future* (Washington, D.C.: U.S. Government Printing Office, 1976), p. 5.

3. Zimmerman, "The Family and Social Policy," p. 547.

4. Joseph Giordano, "Ethnics and Minorities: A Review of the Literature," *Clinical Social Work Journal* 2, no. 3 (Fall 1974): 209.

5. Joseph Giordano, "Introduction," *International Journal of Mental Health* 5, no. 2 (Summer 1976): 3.

6. Raymond Scheele states that in Puerto Rico, a person, be he a bootblack or a bank president, by successfully fulfilling the expectancies of his various statuses, maintains *dignidad*. See Raymond Scheele, "The Prominent Families of Puerto Rico,"

in *People of Puerto Rico*, ed. Julian Steward (Urbana, Ill.: University of Illinois Press, 1969), p. 431.

7. Sidney W. Mintz, "Puerto Rico: An Essay in the Definition of National Culture," in *The Puerto Rican Experience: A Sociological Sourcebook*, ed. Francesco Cordasco and Eugene Buccioni (Totowa, N.J.: Littlefield, Adams, 1973), pp. 26-90.

8. Fatalism and Puerto Rican values should be examined in the context of Catholicism and colonialism. The notion of a "colonialized personality" is found throughout the literature. It would be essential for an understanding of the Puerto Rican situation to become acquainted with the history. See, for example, Karl Wagheim, *Puerto Rico: A Profile* (New York: Praeger, 1970). For an interpretation from the view of an independent, see Manuel Maldonado-Denis, *Puerto Rico: A Socio-Historic Interpretation* (New York: Random House, 1972). For an understanding of how fatalism comes into play in the helper relationship, see Ligia Vasquez de Rodriguez, "Social Work Practice in Puerto Rico," *Social Work* 18, no. 2 (1973): 32-40.

9. Vincent Abad, Juan Ramos, and Elizabeth Boyce, "A Model for Delivery of Mental Health Services to Spanish-Speaking Minorities," *American Journal of Orthopsychiatry* 44, no. 4 (July 1974): 584-95.

10. As an illustration of the importance and extent of this preference, the supermarket may be much cheaper but the *bodega* (neighborhood grocery store) in many communities takes on the characteristics of a social institution. See J.D. Vasquez, "La Bodega—A Social Institution," in *Puerto Rican Curriculum Workshop: A Report*, ed. Angel P. Campos (New York: Council on Social Work Education, 1974), pp. 31-36.

11. For a look at the difficulties in community organization efforts statewide and how this relates to cultural patterns, see Lloyd L. Roger, *Migrant in the City: The Life of a Puerto Rican Action Group* (New York: Basic Books, 1972).

12. Theodore Brameld, "Explicit and Implicit Culture in Puerto Rico: A Case Study in Educational Anthropology," in *Sociology in the Cultural Context*, ed. Joan I. Roberts and Sherrie K. Akinsanya (New York: David McKay, 1976), pp. 44-57.

13. Mintz, "Puerto Rico: Definition of National Culture," p. 68.

14. Joseph P. Fitzpatrick, *Puerto Rican Americans* (Englewood Cliffs, N.J.: Prentice-Hall, 1971).

15. Wagheim, *Puerto Rico*, pp. 217-19.

16. These points of tension have been quoted in a number of publications by various authors for several years. They still continue to be perceived as strains affecting the Puerto Rican on the Island or Mainland. See Carmen Lydia Norciga de Santa, "The Family As a Social Welfare Institution in Puerto Rico," in *The Social Welfare System in Puerto Rico: Institutions and Problems* (Rio Piedras Campus: University of Puerto Rico, Beatriz Lassalle School of Social Work, 1976), pp. 8-9.

17. Ibid., p. 9.

18. This distinction is drawn by Maldonado-Denis in *Puerto Rico*, p. 85.

19. Wagheim, *Puerto Rico*, p. 191.

20. Scheele, "Prominent Families," p. 420.

21. Torres Matrullo, "Acculturation and Psychotherapy Among Puerto Rican Women

119

in Mainland United States," *American Journal of Orthopsychiatry* 46, no. 4 (October 1976): 710-19.

22. Carmen F. Quinones Rodriguez, "The Family As a Social Welfare Institution in a Changing Society: Its Sharing Functions with the Government," in *The Social Welfare System in Puerto Rico: Institutions and Problems* (Rio Piedras Campus: University of Puerto Rico, Beatriz Lassalle School of Social Work, 1976), p. 99.

23. Wagheim, *Puerto Rico*, p. 8.

24. Judith G. Rabkin and Elmer L. Struening, "Ethnicity, Social Class and Mental Illness," Working Paper Series No. 17. (New York: Institute of Pluralism and Group Identity, 1976), pp. 10-14.

25. For mental health practitioners working with the Puerto Rican population it is critical to have an understanding of this belief system and the way in which the profession can cooperate with the spiritualism. See Pedro Ruiz, and John Langrod, "The Role of Folk Healers in Community Health Services," *Community Mental Health Journal* 12, no. 4 (Winter 1976): 392-98; and Melvin Delgado, "Puerto Rican Spiritualism and the Social Work Profession," *Social Casework* 58, no. 8 (October 1977): 452-58.

26. John F. Longres, "Racism and its Effects on Puerto Rican Continentals," *Social Casework* 55, no. 2 (February 1974): 67.

27. Piri Thomas, *Down These Mean Streets*, (New York: New American Library, 1967), pp. 97, 125-126, 131.

28. U.S. Commission on Civil Rights, *Puerto Ricans in the United States*, p. 28.

29. Ibid.

30. U.S. Bureau of the Census, Department of Commerce, "Persons of Spanish Origin in the United States: March, 1978," *Current Population Reports*, Series P- 20, no. 339 (Washington, D.C.: U.S. Government Printing Office, 1979), pp. 8-13.

31. Ibid., p. 6.

32. U.S. Bureau of the Census, "Persons of Spanish Origin," p. 6.

33. U.S. Commission on Civil Rights, *Puerto Ricans in the United States*, pp. 92-99.

34. U.S. Bureau of the Census, "Persons of Spanish Origin," p. 23.

35. Ibid., p. 10.

36. U.S. Commission on Civil Rights, *Puerto Ricans in the United States*.

37. Ibid.

38. Milton M. Gordon, as discussed by Pastora San Juan Cafferty and Leon Chestang, "Introduction" in *The Diverse Society: Implications for Social Policy*, ed. Pastora San Juan Cafferty and Leon Chestang (Washington, D.C.: National Association of Social Workers, 1976), p. xi.

39. Ibid., p. xiii.

Culturally Specific Mental Health Programs

Melvin Delgado

The development of mental health programs for racially and linguistically distinct groups in the United States must be based on concepts that take into account the specific needs and value orientations of the community. Failure to be sensitized to the unique sociocultural attributes of these distinct groups will result in the minimal use of the services offered.

The material and experiences delineated in this article focus specifically on Puerto Ricans and other Hispanic groups. However, the issues and concepts raised are also applicable to other racial and linguistic communities. Culturally specific mental health programming is based on the premise that the services offered must reflect the needs and values of the target population.

This article will present an overview of Hispanic and other racial groups' sociodemographic statistics, describe a culturally specific program, and examine the planning principles on which the program is based. In addition, an attempt will be made to address the common planning pitfalls encountered by organizations wanting to deliver mental health services to culturally distinct communities.

Demographic Characteristics

Blacks and Hispanics, the two largest racially and linguistically distinct groups in the United States, number approximately 30 million.[1] In focusing on Hispanics, several salient characteristics of this population indicate that they are a rapidly expanding group. Hispanics constitute approximately 5.6 percent of the total population in the United States.[2] It is expected that Hispanics will reach numerical parity with blacks sometime between 1980 and 1990.[3]

Hispanic populations are concentrated in four states (California, Texas, New York, and Florida), with several other states having sizeable concentrations. Approximately 85 percent of all Hispanic families live in metropolitan areas, compared with 65 percent of families nationwide.[4] In comparing the age of the average Hispanic with the national average, it becomes apparent that Hispanics are very young: their median age is twenty-two, as compared to thirty for the population as a whole.[5] In comparing Mexicans and Puerto Ricans, the two largest Hispanic groups in the United States, to the rest of the population, it was found that children under the age of nine represent 26 percent of the Mexican population and 25 percent of the Puerto Rican population. Nationwide, only 15 percent of the population is under nine years of age.[6]

In examining income statistics, the average black or Hispanic family lives in poverty. Approximately 28 percent of the black families in America live below poverty level;[7] 21 percent of Hispanic families do[8]. However, the prevalence of poverty is not uniform throughout all Hispanic groups: 39 percent of the Puerto Rican, 19 percent of the Mexican, and 15 percent of the Cuban families live below the poverty level.[9]

The data presented are meant to convey the need for administrators and planners to be aware of demographic factors in developing mental health programs. The groups addressed in this section will not disappear in the United States; statistics on age characteristics alone indicate a rapidly growing population.

Hispanic Program of a Youth Guidance Center

The Hispanic Program of the Worcester Youth Guidance Center was developed during the fall of 1974 to address the needs of the rapidly growing Puerto Rican population in Worcester, Massachusetts. During the five-year period from 1970 to 1975, the Puerto Rican population increased from under 2,000 to over 8,000.[10] It will number over 12,000 by 1982, representing close to 6 percent of the city's total population. This compares with a black population of 3 percent.

In the five years since it began, the Hispanic Program has expanded from a paraprofessional staff of three to a staff of ten, of which seven are professionally trained. The Hispanic Program is multidisciplinary and multifaceted and provides a wide range of primary and secondary intervention programs. The program offers basic services that have a direct and indirect impact on the Hispanic community of Worcester: community education and training, clinical consultation, program consultation, research, and clinical case management and clinical intervention.

The Hispanic Program places heavy emphasis on consultation and

122

education activities as a means of reaching a large sector of the human service field. Approximately one-half of its resources are targeted at consultation and education and the other half allocated for direct client services.

Planning Principles

For the purposes of analysis, factors pertaining to program development will be addressed in the section related to community-specific variables (external). Internal factors, in turn, reflect agency-related variables that either facilitate or hinder day-to-day operation of a program.

External

In reviewing the literature on Hispanic mental health services, several significant approaches to program planning were noted. Following a review of the various models that have been developed to increase Hispanic utilization of services, Amado Padilla, Rene Ruiz, and Alvarado Alvarez noted three basic models: progressional adaptation, family adaptation, and the "barrio" service center model.[11] These models are also applicable to blacks and other racially and linguistically distinct groups.

The professional model concentrates on assisting staff to adapt themselves to the population they are serving by using sociocultural concepts relevant to their clients. The family adaptation model provides relevant services through effective use of family and other primary social relationships in devising treatment plans. The barrio service model focuses on providing important social broker services with complementary counseling.[12]

Although each of these models emphasizes a slightly different orientation, several factors are common to all. Culturally specific mental health programming must take into account several variables regardless of its target population: (1) awareness of the role of environmental factors on mental health, (2) appreciation and sensitivity regarding cultural values, (3) recognition of the impact of racism on the daily lives of service consumers, (4) provision of services by individuals familiar with the language of the clients, (5) neighborhood-based services with community input into program planning, (6) an appreciation of the valuable role of folk therapists and religion within a culture, (7) flexibility in program design for provision of a wide range of services.

The Hispanic program developed at the Youth Center incorporated these factors into its service delivery pattern. In addition, it

123

developed six principles, which have guided its expansion over the past five years: (1) interagency collaboration in program development, (2) flexibility in program design to accommodate changing mental health needs, (3) multifaceted programming stressing micro- and macro-approaches, (4) primary prevention as an integral part of service delivery, (5) community-based services accessible to all geographical areas and segments of the population, and (6) counseling in generic settings whenever possible to eschew the stigma associated with mental health services.

Interagency collaboration in program development offers great potential for underserved populations. The concept of interagency planning lends itself to better coordination of existing resources, narrowing of service gaps, and maximizing resource utilization. Combining the resources of two or more agencies facilitates the development of a wider political base for securing funds. In addition, it allows for the undertaking of more ambitious projects.

Flexibility in program design to accommodate changing mental health needs is an essential element in any mental health program. Program flexibility, however, takes on added significance in racially and linguistically distinct communities. Changing community characteristics necessitate the development of a community "barometer" that is attuned to needs and sociodemographic variables.[13] The failure of planners and administrators to respond to these changes results in limited utilization of services. As a result, mental health programs must be viewed as dynamic.

Mental health programs must not restrict services to psychotherapy. Instead, they must maintain a balance between micro- and macro-oriented intervention. It is essential to provide micro-oriented services such as therapy; however, a macro-oriented approach takes into account the person within his or her environment.[14] Efforts must be made to restructure a client's environment through effective intervention in the major systems impacting on their lives.

Mental health programs for culturally specific groups must do more than treat symptoms; instead, efforts must be directed toward preventing problems from emerging. This requires a prevention orientation whenever possible. Prevention-oriented programming must stress development of self-help skills,[15] systems change, development of healthy role models, and programming to reach high-risk groups.

It is essential that services be community-based and within easy access to all geographical areas and segments of the population. Accessibility of service plays a prodigious influence on utilization. If a program is based in the community, it increases the probability of service utilization and conveys a sense of input and control over the services to the community. If clients must rely on public transportation to reach the setting, the cost and time expended in getting there may outweigh its potential usefulness. Consequently, accessibility takes on real meaning in planning service provision.

Counseling should take place in community-based settings that are not traditionally associated with "mental illness."[16] The failure of program planners to recognize the potential impact of stigma on the recipient of mental health counseling can seriously undermine a program. Therefore, it is imperative to develop counseling programs within settings that have both a "positive" image within the community and a mandate to provide a variety of services, for example, health, social service, recreation, education, and so on. Thus, an individual seeking counseling may enter the setting for a variety of reasons other than "mental illness."

Internal

The efficient day-to-day operation of a program is contingent on many factors. Three key factors are: (1) the recruitment of staff, (2) the source of funding, and (3) administrative support. Each of these factors influence program operation. Improper staffing, short-term funding, or a lack of administrative support will undermine a program's ability to serve its target population.

Culturally specific mental health programs must actively seek to recruit staff that reflect the target population's racial and linguistic background.[17] Individuals from different racial and cultural backgrounds can be hired; however, they must have a sound base from which to function; that is, an understanding of culture, language, and so on.[18] Using multiracial and ethnic teams can be a valuable asset to the agency and community.

Agencies must be careful not to overburden staff treating special communities. Based on the experiences of the Hispanic Program, agencies have a propensity to hire just one member of a racial or linguistically distinct group. In the sites served by the Hispanic Program, eleven out of the fifteen sites hired only one Hispanic. Hiring only one minority is often insufficient to insure the provision of quality services and may result in low staff morale and a high turnover rate. Being the "only one" places a staff member in a highly pressured and vulnerable position. Agencies must work to insure that minority staff are given every opportunity to succeed in their position.

The issue of funding is central to any programming. The funding source not only expresses the goals of the program but also the agency's commitment to service. Total reliance on what is referred to as "soft funding" for racial and linguistically distinct programs

125

raises questions about the agency's goals for the program. Does the agency have only a short-term commitment while funding for the program lasts or a long-term commitment to continue once initial funding terminates?

Relying on soft funding for program and staffing purposes places programs in a precarious position of year-to-year existence. In essence, initial work (recruitment, planning, implementation, and so on) often requires a long period of time before a program becomes operational. Consequently, if funding is contingent on annual renewal, it is not uncommon to see low staff morale, high turnover rates, and minimal impact on the community.

It is essential that the agency planning these programs develop contingency plans to insure that the program is continued beyond the initial contract period. The transfer of staff from "soft" to "hard" funds conveys a sense of commitment toward the community. Thus, staff can be assured of continued enployment through the grant period. In addition, the agency must not rely on staff members to locate and obtain new funding sources if they wish to remain with the agency. Thus, an agency administrator and board must actively seek alternatives rather than rely exclusively on staff to engender funding.

Host agencies must provide necessary administrative support to special programs. It must be kept in mind that special programs may present needs and goals that are not usually encountered in a traditional service setting. The uniqueness of these programs demands sensitive and cooperative administrative structures. Lack of administrative support may be manifested in various ways: lack of culturally sensitive clerical and receptionist staff, uninviting waiting rooms, inflexibility for staff in making home visits, and so on. Staff who do not enjoy proper administrative support experience additional position-related frustrations not experienced by colleagues dealing with "traditional" clients.

The Hispanic Program's Developmental History

The Worcester Youth Guidance Center's Hispanic Program has been in existence for over five years. Its developmental history illustrates many of the external and internal factors described in this article.[19] As noted earlier, the program was initially staffed by three paraprofessionals; currently, the program consists of ten staff members who are bilingual/bicultural, and seven of these are professionals. The expansion of staff has resulted in the expansion from a primarily outreach program to a program providing a wide range of primary and secondary intervention services.

The program's expansion can be examined in stages during which major administrative and planning decisions were made that have ultimately had impact on staffing and service delivery patterns. The program has experienced three major phases: (1) inception, (2) transitional, and (3) multifaceted and multidisciplinary.

The inception phase can best be described as a rudimentary attempt at service delivery. It focused exclusively on outreach with no attempt at culturally specific programming once the Hispanic client was contacted. This phase met with minimal success both in service delivery and retainment of Hispanic staff. The transition phase followed and represented a shift from an emphasis on outreach to planning. During this period, the Hispanic outreach staff left the program and an Hispanic mental health planner was hired. Planning, in turn, focused on needs assessment, relationship building between the youth guidance center and the Hispanic community, minimal service delivery (consultation and crisis intervention), and the development of culturally specific program plans for service delivery. This phase lasted approximately one year. The multifaceted and multidisciplinary phase was based on the plans developed during the transition phase and represented the operationalization of a culturally specific mental health model that took into consideration community needs and specific cultural variables.

Each of the phases served as a valuable learning experience. However, this process was far from smooth with consistent progress; issues external and internal to the program both facilitated and hindered its development.

The internal factors experienced by the program correspond to those raised earlier: recruitment of staff, source of funding, and administrative support. Each of these factors represent crucial points in the development of any mental health program, regardless of the target population. However, these factors take on prominence in culturally specific programs.

Staff recruitment efforts were both time-consuming and laborious. The paucity of Hispanic mental health professionals in the area required a redifinition of what constitutes a "mental health professional" and the use of unusual methods of recruitment. The program planners were willing to expand the definition of mental health professional to include professionals in other disciplines. In addition to psychologists and social workers, the program hired Hispanics with school counseling and early childhood training backgrounds, with the intention of undertaking extensive inservice training to upgrade and develop consultation techniques. Recruitment methods varied widely and ranged from newspaper advertisements to contacting Hispanic organizations throughout the state and region, as well as personal contacts with Hispanic professionals. Personal contacts proved to be the most successful; however, they also proved to be the most time-consuming.

The administrative support received for the program proved to be invaluable, particularly during the transition phase. The support of the center's director facilitated both board and staff acceptance of the program. The director provided various ways of communicating the plans and progress of the program to staff in all sectors of the center. The board, in turn, was kept informed through periodic presentations at board meetings.

The external factors that played influential roles in the program's success are the six program principles outlined earlier. These principles can be summed up as community acceptance and services. Community acceptance or rejection determines the ultimate success or failure of any program.

Communities, regardless of cultural or linguistic differences, are composed of various subgroups. Each of these subgroups will vie for services, often in competition with others. Consequently, it is imperative not to align a program with any particular faction for fear of jeopardizing a program's attempt to reach the wider community.

The nature and geographical location of services must also be considered. The Hispanic Program did not have the luxury of providing only one type of service. In addition, the projected increase in population further required the development of innovative and relevant services. The program therefore attempted to reach the Hispanic community through programs which stressed direct and indirect contact. Consultation and education services served to upgrade the skills of other agency staff to better serve the community. Direct intervention, in turn, not only focused on therapeutic intervention in various modalities, but also on advocacy.

In providing services, an attempt was made to locate these services in areas that did not require clients to rely on public transportation. In addition, program staff were assigned to several "host" agencies to provide culturally specific services. These host agencies provided generic services, that is, education, day care, health, social services, and so on, and did not have the "stigma" of mental illness.

Conclusion

As evidenced by the Hispanic Program's experience, culturally specific programs bring with them inherent satisfactions and frustrations. The development of culturally specific programs presents agencies with new challenges and experiences. The failure to identify and address the specific issues involved will result in unsuccessful mental health programming for culturally and linguistically distinct populations.

Racially and linguistically distinct groups are often unable to use services that were planned for very different groups, for example, middle-class, English-dominant, and so on. Instead of focusing on how to make blacks and Hispanics "fit" into these programs, effort must be made to develop programs that take into account particularistic factors. Agency administrators must be prepared to make serious commitments to culturally specific programs through allocation of time, funds, and support. A failure to make this commitment will result in programs of at best secondary importance and minimal impact on the community they seek to reach.

Notes

1. Neal R. Pierce, "The Hispanic Community—A Growing Force to be Reckoned With," *National Journal* 11 (April 1979): 549.

2. Ibid.

3. Ibid., p. 548.

4. Ibid., p. 549.

5. "Hispanics: Fastest Growing Minority in the U.S.," *The New York Times*, 18 February 1979, pp. 1, 16.

6. Ibid., p. 16.

7. U.S. Department of Housing and Urban Development, *How Well are we Housed? Blacks* (Washington, D.C.: U.S. Government Printing Office, 1979), p. 3.

8. "Hispanics," *New York Times*, p. 16.

9. Ibid., p. 16.

10. Melvin Delgado, "Puerto Rican Dispersal within the United States: A Study of Worcester, Massachusetts," unpublished paper, 1978.

11. Amado Padilla, Rene Ruiz, and Alvarado Alvarez, "Community Mental Health Services for Spanish-Speaking Surnamed Population," *American Psychologist* 30 (September 1975): 892-905.

12. Ibid.

13. Melvin Delgado, "A Grass-Roots Model for Needs Assessment in Hispanic Communities," *Child Welfare* 58 (November 1979): 571-76.

14. See, for example, James P. Comer, *Beyond Black and White* (New York: Quadrangle, 1971); Anita J. Delaney, ed., *Black Task Force Report*, pp. 25-28, and Emelicia Mizio, ed., *Puerto Rican Task Force Report* (New York: Family Service Association of America, 1979), pp. 12-13; Melvin Delgado and John F. Scott, "Strategic Intervention: A Mental Health Program for the Hispanic Community," *Journal of Community Psychology* 7 (July 1979): 187-97; Carel B. Germain, "An Ecological

Perspective in Casework Practice," *Social Casework* 54 (June 1973): 323-30; and Carel B. Germain, "An Ecological Perspective on Social Work Practice Health Care," *Social Work in Health Care* 3 (Fall 1977): 67-76.

15. William McCready, "Social Utilities in a Pluralistic Society," in *The Diverse Society: Implications for Social Policy,* ed. Pastora San Juan Cafferty and Leon W. Chestang (Washington, D.C.: National Association of Social Workers, 1976), p. 17; and Mizio, *Puerto Rican Task Force Report,* p. 11.

16. Delaney, *Black Task Force Report,* p. 18; John F. Scott and Melvin Delgado, "Planning Mental Health Programs for Hispanic Communities," *Social Casework: The Journal of Contemporary Social Work* 60 (October 1979): 451-47; and Mizio, *Puerto Rican Task Force Report,* pp. 18-19.

17. Delaney, *Black Task Force Report,* pp. 19-21; Scott and Delgado, "Planning Mental Health Programs"; and Mizio, *Puerto Rican Task Force Report,* pp. 19-22.

18. Delaney, *Black Task Force Report,* p. 21; Melvin Delgado, "Hispanic Staff in Non-Hispanic Settings: Issues and Recommendations," *Administration in Social Work* 3 (Winter 1979): 465-75; Emelicia Mizio, "White Worker—Minority Client," *Social Work* 17 (May 1972): 86,; and Mizio, *Puerto Rican Task Force Report,* pp. 20-21.

19. The following material on the Hispanic Program is based on an article by John F. Scott and Melvin Delgado. See "Planning Mental Health Programs for Hispanic Communities," *Social Casework: The Journal of Contemporary Social Work* 60 (October 1979): 451-56.

Integration of Methods

Salvatore Ambrosino

In the provision of social services, there are an almost endless variety of program designs. The position presented here is that counseling, family life education, and family advocacy are a logical and powerful combination of services that create a synergistic impact.

The development of a program is the result of many factors. There is the mission and philosophy of the agency, how it perceives the scope of its activities, the extent of existing community resources, and funding possibilities and staff capability, to mention a few.[1]

The long-range planning structure of an agency must weigh the question of the proper service mix. It must also incorporate changing conditions into its deliberations and be prepared to reshape programs. Although this analysis should be systematic and include a review of pertinent criteria and information, the decision about the best collection of services for an agency to offer is ultimately a value judgment.[2]

Counseling, family life education, and family advocacy are fundamentally related and are relevant to many kinds of service organizations, especially to the family service agency, which helps individuals and families to cope with different kinds of emotional and social problems. It is difficult to categorize family problems as essentially emotional, which requires counseling, or as a lack of understanding of human relations, which requires a program of family life education, or as a critical social problem, which requires advocacy intervention. Most often, the problems presented to a family service agency are a complex blend of emotional and social problems, which require involving the family in more than one service.

This article is based on an article by Salvatore Ambrosino, "Integrating Counseling, Family Life Education, and Family Advocacy," which appeared in Social Casework: The Journal of Contemporary Social Work, *60 (December 1979): 579-85.*

Three Service Components

Before discussing their integration, it is helpful to examine more closely the three service components. Counseling in family service agencies usually focuses on relationships that cause distress; on reality problems, such as the need for housing, employment, health care, which often necessitate referral to another resource; or a conflict with another agency, which may involve an unjust policy or a serious deficiency in services. The distinction between a family service agency and other counseling programs, such as mental health clinics, varies from one community to the next. For the most part, family service agencies assist families struggling with problems about marriage, parent-child conflicts, and the aged, with the focus primarily on interpersonal relationships.

Distinctions between Counseling and Family Life Education

It is important to clarify the difference between counseling and family life education. Counseling is directed primarily to conflicts that bind and misguide energies. The client is helped to become aware of feelings and of the conditioning of past relationships or expectations that create stress, with the objective of freeing energy for more rational and appropriate behavior. "Education is aimed at those faculties of the ego which are undisturbed by conflict. It is oriented to healthy factors of the personality, and appeals to the ability to judge, to learn by experience, to gain understanding, to plan, to make choices, to adapt to changing circumstances."[3]

Although their basic goals are different, there is some overlap between counseling and family life education. The counseling process in its various forms of one-to-one, conjoint, group, or family also appeals to the conscious ego strengths of clients by providing information about personality development and interpersonal relations. In turn, it is possible in family life education programs for members to acquire greater understanding of their behavior or the dynamics of stressful relationships, both of which open avenues for improved functioning. The therapeutic effect of a family life education program may be similar to positive life experiences, such as exchanges in close relationships or the impact of literature, theater, or other arts.

The Process of Family Life Education

Although the gains from a successful counseling or family life education experience may appear similar, it is critically important to understand the differences in process and to safeguard these in offering the respective services. It is necessary to establish a clear idea of what

132

the agency is offering and what the client can expect. For example, the leader of a family life education group might explain the sessions as an opportunity to talk about the areas of most common and urgent interest and an exchange of ideas, feelings, and experiences. The leader should emphasize that the group cannot solve individual problems but will focus instead on increasing participants' understanding of selected problem areas. If, despite this explanation, members at times ask the group to solve individual problems, the leader is obliged to remind the group of its purpose.

Assume, for example, that a group of parents of preschool children focus on the subject of toilet training, which is a common concern for all parents. As the discussion unfolds, one of the parents expresses tremendous anger at the inability of her three-year old to become toilet trained. She requests the group to help her understand why she is so upset. After reminding the member that this is not an appropriate focus for the group, the leader guides the group to explore the many aspects of the subject: what toilet training means to children, how the various parents react to the adjustment, the range of parent approaches (both helpful and not helpful), when sphincter control is developed in children, and so on. The leader poses questions, solicits responses to contributions, and furnishes information to balance the content so that important dimensions are included. This overall review enlarges the members' understanding of this particular developmental period so that all are in a better position to understand and deal with their individual family situations. Each contribution is helpful to this effort; the parents who are successful and those who are struggling both help to develop a full perspective of the subject area.[4]

Family life education programs may employ reading materials, films, skits, or plays and take the form of a single meeting, a series of meetings with different topics, or an ongoing discussion group (usually eight to fifteen members) that establishes its own agenda and meets regularly, usually on a weekly basis, for anywhere from six to ten weeks.

There are a variety of home-based programs as well that teach parents how to improve the cognitive and social development of their preschool children. They focus on ways in which parents can use selected play materials and books to foster verbal interaction with their children. The home visitor, usually a paraprofessional or trained volunteer, guides the mother in a play session with the child. The purpose is to promote the development of skills in areas of cognitive deficits, such as language use and visual and auditory discrimination. Some programs are a combination of center-based and home-based activities. Many such efforts directed to disadvantaged families have had notable success in increasing the I.Q. and social development of children.[5]

Function of Family Advocacy

The third service component is family advocacy. Family service agencies have traditionally helped families suffering from social problems; in the sixties the need for this effort became more pronounced. The term family advocacy evolved in the family service field to describe a variety of techniques social workers employ to help clients having difficulty in obtaining necessary assistance from community resources.

A family advocacy program is an agency commitment to recognize that its social workers must give the same attention and level of skill to helping clients with social problems as they do to emotional problems. For many agencies, this means taking a further step, to move from case to cause. It requires gathering data to document unjust policies or serious gaps in institutional programs and developing advocacy actions in concert with both the families affected and other resources.

An agency is bound to be overwhelmed by the variety of institutional shortcomings that threaten family life. The selection of issues for advocacy actions must be based substantially on data from an agency's experiences. The extent to which other agencies should be involved or encouraged to assume leadership in coalition efforts must be weighed; at times the task of assembling agencies to develop a joint strategy for advocacy falls appropriately to the family service agency, especially when it can provide the most significant documentation of how the problem undermines families.[6]

Case to Cause

In order to help clients solve problems with social services departments, schools, housing project managers, landlords, the courts or other institutions, it is necessary to understand the facts and make plans to help clients to act on their own behalf, to act together with clients or to act for clients. All these approaches might be used; whatever approach or combination, it should be based on a diagnostic assessment of what promises to be the most effective way to help the client.

The staffing pattern for a family advocacy program can range from a commitment by staff with existing supervisory and administrative staff as a backup and training resource to a separate department with one or more staff members. In most agencies, there is a board committee or board-staff committee and, sometimes, community representatives who act as a planning and advisory group to help select priorities and develop strategies.[7]

Relating Counseling and Family Life Education

The three service components discussed above should be closely integrated to maximize service effectiveness. Counseling is a basic service offered by a family service agency, as well as by most multiservice centers and other settings. Family life education is increasingly available from family service agencies,[8] but generally is not regarded as having the same value as counseling. Not everyone wants counseling, or needs it, or can face the threat it poses when it is needed. Agency programs, however, are frequently not designed for this reality. Family life education activities provide a unique opportunity for group members to learn to listen, to express concerns, to clarify confusions, to give and receive support, and to review options for improving relationships. They put people in touch with other people so they can help each other. This type of service meets a critically important need, is prevention-oriented, and opens the way for many individuals to obtain service who might otherwise not apply.

Family life education and counseling should be viewed as having equal potential for helping families and should also be promoted as part of a continuum in the helping process. Frequently, individuals in counseling can also benefit from a family life education experience that affords the opportunity to compare children, marriages, and responses to life adjustments. The special value of a group is that members discover the universality of human problems and derive substantial support. Counseling and family life education can be mutually reinforcing; the insights and knowledge gained from counseling might be relevant content for the group, and material from the group might be brought to counseling to apply to particular conflicts and adjustment problems. Moreover, the family life education group may help members recognize or accept the fact that their special problems require counseling, and counseling may help clients to realize that there are no easy answers and that the exploration of an educational group can provide a greater appreciation of the human scene.

Case Examples

Mrs. A sought help because she was depressed. Widowed for a year, she was immobilized and unable to make the changes in her life she felt were necessary. She had made some progress through coun-

135

seling, but her loneliness and despair were difficult to overcome. The formation of a widows' group was in progress at the agency and Mrs. A was invited to join it.

The common plight and sharing of deep feelings of anger, fear, and despondency of group members helped Mrs. A to become less defensive and better able to examine her situation. The support and concern of group members and the accounts of courageous efforts to face problems strengthened her, and she came to counseling with a rekindled determination to solve her problems.

A further example is Mrs. G, an Hispanic mother who applied for help because her daughter was having serious problems in school. The family arrived from Central America less than a year ago, and Mrs. G appeared defeated by the problems of adjusting to a new country and by the emotional tensions in her marriage and with her three children. Mrs. G, with limited English, tearfully described her unsuccessful efforts to discuss her daughter's difficulties at school and her humiliation at being scolded by the school principal.

The client was assigned an Hispanic worker who acted as an advocate and together they met with school officials until the situation was resolved; this required the intervention of the school superintendent. Mrs. G was helped to understand better her anxieties and frustrations and how these affected her family. She was subsequently referred to a family life education group of Hispanic parents.

After six months in the group it was difficult to recall the shy and seemingly helpless Mrs. G of the initial contact. She made friends in the group, which ended her sense of isolation; she gained a helpful identification from her increased knowledge of the struggles of other Hispanics, and she learned more about child rearing, cultural conflicts, and community resources, and how to use them, and she learned to advocate for herself when necessary.

Family life education groups are especially effective in reaching out to high-risk groups such as minorities, youth, the poor, and the aged. The contract in recruiting is nonthreatening and can be seen as a social as well as an educational opportunity for target populations who are isolated and feel stigmatized.

Integrating Family Advocacy

Both counseling and family life education should operate in a framework of advocacy, in which workers are given support and guidance to help clients and groups suffering from social problems. It is a mistake to see advocacy simply as an adjunct service; rather, it should represent an essential purpose of the agency. Family service agencies are in a unique position to observe how some programs and procedures of organizations undermine families, and they have a responsibility to help families fight these instances of institutional unresponsiveness and to use the information gathered to change systems. It is necessary then to integrate the three approaches into the basic structure of the agency and, more specifically, into its mission statement and goals.

The three programs can be conceptualized as three possible doors through which a client may enter the agency and then be routed through other doors if necessary. The family advocacy door should be visible; in some agencies it takes the more tangible form of a crisis intervention center. For example, the door symbolizing advocacy at the Family Service Association of Nassau County (FSA) is called CAIR (Client Advocacy, Information and Referral)—it offers a crisis intervention service for a broad range of social problems. So, as well as promoting family advocacy as an integral part of counseling and family life education, the social agency can feature family advocacy as a paramount service of some program units. This spotlighting serves to interpret the basic purpose of the agency and to reach out to disadvantaged groups in dire stress.

Long-Range Planning and Administrative Structure

An especially important place to integrate the three services is in long-range planning. In the design of shifting of program emphasis, the planning structure of board members or board members and staff can strive to develop the three basic services in a suitable mix in response to community needs and to foster their close coordination. In meeting new challenges, if the planning process is not locked into the traditional pattern of considering one program (usually counseling) as its response to an unmet need, but is instead open to the possibility of using counseling, family life education, advocacy, or all three, the chances for imaginative program development are increased.

The administrative structure of the agency offers another vital means of connecting information and decisions about the three services. The staff performing the different services should have access to the planning and policy process. In some settings, generic workers will perform the three services; in others, workers may be more specialized. Whatever the staffing pattern, supervisors or administrators in charge of counseling, family life education, and advocacy should be part of the administrative structure that participates in decisions about program implementation.

137

Parent and Child Training Project: An Example of Integration

The awareness of the value of integrating counseling, family life education, and family advocacy can be especially helpful in designing special projects. The Family Service Association of Nassau County is headquartered in a suburban village plagued by social problems similar to those in urban centers. The task of creating a demonstration program with significant impact led to the Parent and Child Training Project (PACT). Its goal was to reach the most vulnerable groups in the community—families on welfare, those reported for child abuse and neglect, and Hispanic families, isolated and overwhelmed by the demands of their new environment. The vehicles for reaching out were family life education groups that focused on child rearing, helping children in schools and advocacy actions to obtain needed services.

The program, which was located in a storefront, also offered counseling and advocacy assistance. Nine out of ten participants in the parent groups requested counseling and advocacy assistance with crisis problems. Some families initiated their contact with the agency through a request for counseling or help with an advocacy intervention and, eventually, most joined parent groups. The members of one group, outraged by school problems, founded an organization called Parents Involving Parents (PIP) that has played an active role in the community's efforts to improve the school system. The project has also trained thirty mothers to conduct discussion groups of ten-session duration to multiply the effort to reach families at risk.[9]

Mixed Staffing Patterns

In designing programs that use counseling, family life education, and advocacy to reach out to minorities and other target groups, it is important to consider certain factors. The program should be visibly located in the area to be served and employ staff that represent the client group. FSA has developed projects with different staffing patterns: black staff to work with black families, Hispanic staff to work with Hispanic families, a mixed staff of white, black, and Hispanic to work with the three respective populations, and a mixed staff to work in a black community.

The merit of using staff members of the same racial or ethnic background is obvious. This should not, however, preclude the use of workers who have the ability to work with families of different cultural or racial identity. The mixed staffing pattern in the black ghetto program demonstrated the gamut of possibilities. Black workers provided positive role models and special understanding of the problems of the families and the communities. White workers estab-

138

lished effective helping relationships and earned the respect and trust of clients. The close working relationship of black and white workers had significance for the neighborhood and for the broader community. The racial tensions that sometimes erupted among staff and between staff and community were opportunities to clarify the pervasive issues of racism. The black workers thought the white worker did not expect enough from the youth and families; the white workers felt the black workers expected too much. The exchanges of this kind, sometimes painful, led to a deeper understanding of the methods necessary to help families in a seriously depressed community.[10]

So, it is possible to support different views of how to staff a program to serve minorities. The project must weigh the philosophical, political, fiscal, and professional considerations in assembling a staff that can best achieve its objectives. If possible, it is also advisable to involve the community in the decision to hire the project director. In the experience of FSA this has been done on three occasions—twice black candidates were recommended and once a white staff member of the project was endorsed for promotion to the position.

Class and cultural background significantly influence the extent to which families use community resources. It is observed at FSA that middle-class minorities tend to use counseling services more readily in time of stress than low-income minorities. Thus, it is necessary to use outreach approaches to engage minorities, especially those of low income.

Outreach Techniques

Establishing close ties with key staff at appropriate referral agencies is paramount. The PACT project has relied primarily on a legal service program for the poor, hospitals, schools, and Children's Protective Service for referrals. The staff of these resources have been closely linked to the project; they have been invited to activities to share in its spirit and purposes. Mailings and follow-up telephone calls are made to describe parent groups and other services; mailing lists are obtained from referral sources with clients' permission and constitute families known to have serious problems. Posters have been placed in stores, laundromats, and government offices such as social service departments. Door-to-door canvassing, as the next step to a mailing, frequently reaps the best results.

Establishing contact provides an opportunity to invite a mother to visit the storefront for a cup of coffee, attend a holiday party with her children, join a social activity, and learn about the range of services available at the agency and in the community. Some parents move

139

into a relationship with the project cautiously and test out several informal activities before joining a parent group; others respond immediately. Patience, awareness of the reasons for client resistance, determination to meet clients with aggressive concern that stops short of intrusiveness, and meeting the immediate needs of clients all contribute to the successful outreach effort. Here, it is interesting to report a pattern of how low-income Hispanic and black families initiate contact with FSA. Most Hispanics start in counseling and are recruited for family life education groups only after a relationship has been established with the agency. Many more black families, however, are introduced to the agency through a family life education group and then avail themselves of other services.

Another vital requirement for projects designed to involve minorities is transportation. When public transportation is not easily accessible, it is necessary to arrange transportation for clients. This often means children as well, and indicates the need for on-site child care while mothers attend a parent group or other service.

The Need for a Supportive Ambience

The climate of a project is often the key to its success. Low-income and minority families frequently have been intimidated and made to feel inadequate in their dealings with institutions. Many of the families feel isolated and alien from the mainstream of society, wary of involvement with a social agency, and unaware of how services might help them. Thus, the atmosphere at the agency must be informal, supportive, and accepting of the level of client readiness for participation. Impromptu socializing, including the sharing of food at meetings and calling quick get-together parties to celebrate events, is necessary to break through the loneliness and to meet the need for belonging. At PACT, for example, the return of a child to a family from court custody is cause for celebration. It is viewed as a victory and joyfully shared by all the parents and staff. Such poignant events promote a spirit of hopefulness and community support.

A further value of fostering a warm social climate is that many friendships are created and parents find ways of helping each other. As well as the spontaneous development of many mutual help arrangements, the PACT project has developed networks that link stronger families to families in need of help. A graphic example is that of a parent who called one Friday afternoon expressing the fear that she would kill her child. The mother was seen immediately and the child taken by another family for the weekend; she was a white child taken in by a black family. Both families later spoke about the profound nature of the experience.

140

The Community Development Approach

At FSA, projects that pursue a community development approach are encouraged and an attempt is made to involve clients as much as possible in the planning and reshaping of programs. The extent to which this occurs depends on the constraints of funding. The involvement of minorities has been most successful in projects where there was considerable freedom to develop services in response to the emerging needs of clients. PACT, for example, which serves a population of 60 percent black, 25 percent Hispanic, and 15 percent white, exceeded the objectives cited to obtain foundation support by establishing a collection of other activities—educational, cultural, recreational, and social—that were organized and conducted primarily by the parents with staff support. In essence, the parents transformed a prescribed storefront project into a neighborhood center with a broader range of services.

Moreover, the parents stimulated the creation of a cooperative nursery workshop, a program to give overwhelmed parents relief periods from child rearing. An anguished refrain of parents in group meetings is the frustration of never having time for themselves. Parents reported for child abuse and others who were depressed and overwhelmed pointed to the desperate need for a respite from child rearing. The cooperative nursery workshop offers morning and afternoon play sessions for preschoolers and, in return, mothers act as volunteers at play sessions and learn about their children's behavior in the group and child-rearing skills. A social worker is part of the staff and available to counsel parents with problems.

Program Autonomy

A family agency should also be alert to ways in which minorites can control the programs that serve them. This has been done in different ways at FSA. For example, a multiservice project in a black community was helped to become incorporated as a separate agency. The government contract that supports the project was transferred and membership in the United Way eventually obtained. This action followed the development of a local board and a two-year period of training and sharing the responsibility of operating the project before separation.

FSA conducts a Hispanic counseling center under government contract and has established an advisory board of Hispanics. The project director is responsible to both the advisory board and the administration of the agency. In the unlikely event of conflict, the funding

141

source acts as arbiter. As the program is strengthened, the advisory board will entertain the options of remaining a program of FSA or becoming independent.

Another example is the community organization services project, created to help relocate black families on welfare houses in motels. The black staff is encouraged to operate with maximum autonomy.

Summary

It is especially important to note that the projects mentioned as examples of efforts to engage minorities all use various combinations of the three essential services—counseling, family life education, and advocacy.

The integration of these three services increases the effectiveness of efforts to help families with serious problems: Counseling assists individuals and families to resolve conflicts and frees energy for constructive use; family life education builds on the strengths of individuals to extend knowledge of personality development, interpersonal relations, and the influence of environmental factors on behavior; and advocacy helps individuals to negotiate institutional systems and obtain needed services. The three programs pursue strategic paths to help individuals and are inextricably related, just as emotional and environmental factors are bound together in family crises.

Further, the three services are especially relevant in programs designed to reach out to minority communities. It is important in the development of such programs to give consideration to staffing patterns, location, outreach techniques, creating an informal climate of support, and involvement of clients in the planning and establishment of additional services and in the various mechanisms for having the client group influence and control the program.

If this trio of services is to become more available, agencies will have to focus more attention on family life education and advocacy. This will require a greater conviction that families can learn in educational programs and that the agency has a responsiblity to help families suffering from institutional injustices and critical gaps in services.

Notes

1. Stephen M. Drezner and William B. McCurdy, *A Planning Guide for Human Service Delivery Agencies* (New York: Family Service Association of America, 1979).

2. Salvatore Ambrosino, "New Directions for the Family Agency," *Social Casework* 46 (January 1968): 15-21.

3. Peter B. Neubaur, *The Technique of Parent Group Education. Some Basic Concepts* (New York: Child Study Association of America, 1952), p. 12.

4. Aline B. Auerbach, *Parents Learn Through Discussion* (New York: John Wiley, 1968).

5. See Phyllis Levenstein, "Third Grade Effects of the Mother-Child Home Program," *Developmental Continuity Consortium Follow-up Study* 30 (April 1978); and Barbara Goodson and Robert Hess, *The Effects of Parent Training Porgrams on Child Performance and Parent Behavior* (Palo Alto, Calif.: Stanford University, 1976).

6. Robert Sunley, "Family Advocacy: From Case to Cause," *Social Casework* 51 (June 1970): 347-57.

7. Ellen Manser, ed., *Family Advocacy: A Manual for Action* (New York: Family Service Association of America, 1973).

8. See "Family Services: Family Service Agencies," *Encyclopedia of Social Work*, vol. 16 (Washington, D.C.: National Association of Social Workers, 1977), pp. 429-35.

9. See Parent and Child Training Project, "Evaluation Report—September 1976-August 1977." Prepared by Family Service Association of Nassau County, Hempstead, New York, 1978.

10. Salvatore Ambrosino, "A Family Agency Reaches out to Slum Ghetto," *Social Work* 11, no. 4 (October 1966): 17-23.

Counseling from a Black Perspective

Naomi T. Ward

This article identifies some of the issues that are involved in the provision of counseling services to black people, and suggests a framework that responds with a problem-serving methodology undergirded with a theoretical framework and value system. The goals are resolution and prevention of interpersonal and social functioning problems that are encountered by black people, people of African descent and of American nationality. To accomplish such goals suggests that effective helping strategies should be developed from a knowledge base that includes an historical and contemporary perspective on the socioeconomic conditions of black people in America and a familiarity with the meaning of resource control, power, locus of power, and the responses of a colonized people to oppression and unmet needs.

Status of Blacks in America: An Overview

It is essential to recognize continually that the black individual is of Afro-American heritage with origins in an African family. Equally significant is that the black family, the Afro-American family, has experienced cultural changes as a result of being forced to leave Africa, the inhumane system of slavery, and the continued impact of oppression on life experiences in America. Andrew Billingsley identifies three salient facts:

> "First, [black] people came to this country from Africa and not from Europe; second, they came in chains and were consequently uprooted from their cultural and family moorings; and third is that they have been subjected to systematic exclusion from participation and influence in the major institutions of this society even to the present time."[1]

The significance of these facts is that blacks in America are a colonized people subjected to labor and economic strategies that were

144

initially used to advance European political and economic control and, subsequently, an American colonial structure.

Although the status of blacks during slavery was one of powerlessness, emancipation brought double-bind messages of "freedom" with the absence of resources to meet basic survival needs. Since then and throughout all that followed—reconstruction, the civil rights movement, and the affirmative action laws, policies, and programs—the participation of blacks in decision-making positions of power has been limited, as have the goods and services that are important to life satisfaction in this society.

Institutional Racism

Institutional racism permeates the industrial, political, educational, health, justice, and welfare systems in America. The locus of power in these systems, especially the industrial component, is manifested through systematic denial of black access to economic and social resources basic to the development of skills for environmental negotiation. This cyclical power control produces poverty and regulated classes of people resulting in dependency and stress in social functioning. This process is described by Elaine Pinderhughes as an interlocking process of poverty and racism. Further, she cites Louis Knowles and Kenneth Prewitt's elucidation of interrelated barriers that keep blacks in powerless positions:

> The lines that functionally define the black subsectors in the major institutions are effectively linked together. The black man's career in any one subordinate subsector establishes pre-conditions for him to get inferior results from any other sector. Therefore, the actual racial discrimination in a particular institution need not be as great as the differential in its racial outcome, for the other institutional sectors have previously performed much of the discrimination for it.
>
> The ghetto provides the base for the segregated schools. The inferior education in ghetto schools handicaps the black worker in the labor market. Employment discrimination causes low wages and frequent unemployment. Low incomes limit the market choices of black families in housing. Lack of education, low-level occupation and exclusion from ownership or control of large enterprises inhibit the development of political power. The lack of political power prevents black people from changing basic housing, planning and educational programs. Each sector strengthens the racial subordination in the rest of the urban institutions.[2]

Research reports provide more data on the status of blacks in America and have implications for counseling blacks. The National Urban League's research on black families presents such findings:

145

Throughout 1974 and the first half of 1975, Americans suffered significant declines in their purchasing power as well as their standard of living. But black Americans were one of the groups hardest hit by "stagflation"—a combination of stagnation or decline in production with price inflation. By the first quarter of 1975, official black unemployment reached 1.5 million—the largest number of blacks out of work since the Great Depression of the 1930's. And, based on the NUL Hidden Unemployment Index, which incorporates the discouraged workers the actual black unemployed was 3 million or 26 percent of the black labor force during both the first and second quarters of 1975. In inner-city poverty areas, an estimated 50 percent or more of blacks were unemployed—with the unofficial unemployment rate for black teenagers in poverty areas going much higher. And black adult male breadwinners were being laid off at a record setting pace, while discouraged black adult women and teenagers were being forced to drop or stay of the labor market.

Thus, while the rest of the nation was experiencing an acute recession, the black community was being racked by a "depression" of profound dimensions. Indeed, this depression only accelerated the decline in middle-income blacks that had begun as a result of the skyrocketing price inflation of 1973.[3]

These findings and more recent ones indicate that the status of powerlessness is shared by both lower socioeconomic and middle-class black families.[4]

Responses of Blacks to Oppression and Powerlessness

Throughout history, the behavior response to conditions resulting from racism have varied during periods when structural and functional aspects of American communities changed technologically. Although there are variations across class lines, there are commonalities of response that transcend the effects of racism, as well as those that indicate a submission to racism.

The responses that are transcendent in quality result from a value base that has been transmitted through Afro-American culture from generation to generation in the socialization process. In the transcendent response, the socialization process is characterized by a concept of strong ethnic identity, a sense of peoplehood, a resistance to incorporation of materialism and competition as basic values, and the expression of a spiritual connectedness. Living in a pluralistic society where major socialization institutions are controlled by the dominant society, blacks who develop a transcendent response are also influenced by the values and behaviors of the dominant culture. The resulting dual response supports adaptation in wider society institutions and the retention of nurturing family and community relationships.[5] These responses seem to have evolved from a value

146

orientation that is antithetical to the American value system of competition, individualism, independence, and control.[6]

John S. Mbiti states that in African tradition, the individual belongs to the community and that the individual "owes his existence to other people, those of past generations and his contemporaries. The individual is a part of a whole. The community must therefore make, create or produce the individual; the family and community takes precedence in that the individual's existence is predicated on the family and community."[7] Nobles elaborates on this concept of self as a derivative of an African world view of "dynamism, interdependence, variety, and optimism [based on values of] "cooperation, interpersonal connectedness, and collective responsibility."[8] Scholars have observed that "black slaves created unique cultural forms which lightened their burden of oppression, promoted group solidarity, provided ways for verbalizing aggression, sustaining hope, building self-esteem and the social organization of the slave quarters consisted of ethical roles as well as fostered co-operation, mutual assistance and black solidarity."[9] These are descriptive of transcendent responses.

Observable Strengths

During slavery and after emancipation the values of cooperation, interdependence, connectedness, and collective responsibility seemed to have been operative through the black development of churches, schools, fraternal organizations, and mutual aid societies to address group needs. These institutions became the social service delivery system of the ante-bellum period and were symbolic as a source of independence and a vehicle for experiencing decision-making roles from which they were excluded in the wider society.[10] It can be argued that these institutions exhibited many Euro-American characteristics, however, the communal character of this adaptational response to individuals and families is the key to understanding their utility for black people.

Robert B. Hill has identified a number of strengths observed in contemporary black families: strong kinship bonds, strong work orientations, flexibility in family roles, aspirations toward achievement goals, and strong religious orientations.[11] Although these strengths have been noted in low income middle- and upper-class black families, rapid technological changes, escalated competition among countries to obtain and control resources, and continued oppression through rising costs of living and unemployment cause debilitating effects in the black community. Helping agents must be clear in their recognition of the task behaviors and communication patterns that can be

147

utilized in a positive approach to helping black families negotiate the systems of survival and achievement.

Oppressive conditions of poverty limit the chances to function as adequate parents, family members, or heads of households, but Afro-Americans in poor communities demonstrate their resourcefulness in the reciprocal exchanges of goods and services, sharing of households, and the development of kin-friend networks that support stability and growth. Children are viewed in a circular perspective in that they are cared for by a number of different adults in the family network.[12] The flexibility in family roles continues to be a vital element in the coping patterns of the working and nonworking poor as well as middle-class black families. These task behaviors reflect caring, trust, family commitment, and connectedness, highlighting survival skills in the use of scarce resources as well as the transactional behaviors of mutuality.

Frances Welsing has described some of the functional and dysfunctional responses and personalities reflected in the behaviors of oppressed racial minorities.[13] Functional patterns of behavior are seen as "those which produce solutions to problems posed by the total environment. Harmony . . . with or sense of power over the environment is sensed when functional patterns are used. It is characterized by accurate perception, decoding, and responding to the environment. Dysfunctional patterns are those that . . . fail to solve environmental problems giving a sense of disharmony with the environment, sense of frustration, anxiety, despair and experiencing a sense of powerlessness."[14]

Adaptational responses to feelings of powerlessness are highly individualized in the black community, and some of its members are oriented toward goals of autonomy and independence in an attempt to alleviate the effects of racism and oppression. These task behaviors are characterized through self-aggrandizement, distant kinship relationships (except in instances of promoting individual goals), and obtaining needed resources at the expense of others in the family or the community.

Personality Reflections

The submissive personality is characterized as being totally overwhelmed by oppression, lacking self- and group-esteem, and feeling helpless in gathering the resources to combat the negative impact of external systems. Such an individual becomes alienated from his or her own ethnic identity, yields to the larger society value system, and accepts the definition of self and the rewards offered by the oppressor.

The cooperative personality recognizes the destructiveness of institutional racism, but goes along with the process for the economic, social, or educational gains to be had with little regard for the harmful effects that may accrue to family or the community. The emphasis on individualism, "making it," and material success produces estrangement from those in the family or community whose needs may interfere with personal achievement.

There are individuals and families in the black community who understand the operations of oppressive external systems and resist cooptation, compromise, or acquiescence at great expense to their inner resources. Although some relief is obtained through externalizing the problems, the energies expended are debilitating and immobilizing, requiring assistance from helping agents if they are to survive.

An individual committed to intense struggle to eradicate oppression may elect both functional and dysfunctional behavioral responses with little regard for the consequences to his or her life. It is clear that clinicians and organizations must understand the sources of power and the nature of belief systems if they are to assist, advocate, or mediate in the interest of black individuals and families.

Issues and Implications for Counseling

Culturally sensitive helping agents who understand the social conditions in the black community and the adaptive responses that are utilized for survival and achievement are basically equipped for the development of a counseling approach addressed to the resolution and prevention of problems presented by black clients. Given that adaptational responses vary in the capacity to counteract powerlessness resulting from racism, conditions, problem situations, behaviors, and also counseling approaches would be different in character. Whether low income or middle class, the black client's identified problem situation could be reflected through a combination of interpersonal or institutional transactions.

Identifying the interpersonal and social functioning condition and the internal/external systems dynamics requires exploration of transactions and task response behaviors of the personality system and other social systems. This is cited as a crucial issue in counseling blacks because it requires a clinical assessment focus of all components of the interpersonal and social functioning matrix.

Illustrative of the multiple-level assessment approach is the following composite case that highlights a number of issues that may occur in working with black clients.

Todd, a twelve-year-old black child, who lived with his twenty-nine-year-old divorced mother, was referred for counseling by juvenile court to a delinquency prevention program under the auspices of a family agency in a large metropolitan area. The prevention program was located in a low-income black community with high incidences of juvenile delinquency.

The manager of a surburban shopping center drug store had filed a juvenile court petition against Todd alleging theft; Todd was accused of taking candy from the drug store at 11:00 a.m. on a school day. As a first-time offender, Todd was referred for counseling, which also met with his mother's approval. According to Mrs. S, the store manager indicated that Todd was frequently in the store during school hours and he surmised that Todd was a "school dropout like most of the black boys." The manager was suspicious that Todd would "rob him." Mrs. S agreed with his suspions because "children are so bad."

Mrs. S expressed disgust with Todd because he was not to be trusted and because during the past year his teachers had sent notes to her about his disruptive behavior at school. Mrs. S said that she did not know what was wrong with Todd and expected counseling to straighten him out. She worked hard, provided Todd with more than adequate food, clothing, games, and toys. He attended a "good school." Her future expectations were that Todd would get a job and become independent.

Todd, a small-framed, frightened-looking youngster, expressed dislike for school because the teachers "seem like they forget me—they don't call on me," and because the "other children don't play with me." He had no explanation for taking the candy, and admitted frequent visits to the drug store because he did not like school. He feared what would happen at the agency.

Todd's parents divorced when he was seven, about sixteen months after Mr. S returned from Vietnam. Although Mr. S had graduated high school and completed one year of technical school, he experienced twelve months of unsteady employment, and he flunctuated between dejection and anger. Mrs. S saw her dream of owning a house slowly disappearing, which she attributed to her husband's sporadic employment. Mounting tensions in the marriage soon led to divorce. Mr. S moved in with a brother who lived in another state. He secured employment for minimum wage in a garment factory. He visits Todd periodically and Todd visits him during the summer.

Mrs. S had an associate business degree and had worked at a secretarial position with an insurance company for eleven years. She worked primarily with whites and provided on-the-job clerical training for several white women, one of whom became her supervisor at a salary exceeding Mrs. S's own. Two other former trainees' salaries paralleled her salary. Mrs. S was aware of the inequities but rationalized the company's need for more clerical staff; she was proud of her knowledge of the company, her training ability, and her social relationships that extended beyond work.

In 1975, Mrs. S had purchased a house in a white suburban community that had only two other black families. Mrs. S and Todd were the only black family on the street, and Todd attended a predominantly white school.

Todd's teachers were white and he was the only black in his seventh-grade class. Over the telephone, the teachers had discussed with Mrs. S Todd's need for special education because of his "below-level math and reading skills." Also, by telephone and notes, Mrs. S had been advised of Todd's "hyperactive behavior," which she responded to by whipping him. She visited the school twice and verbalized her embarassment over Todd's "bad behavior." She was concerned that Todd did not associate with any of the other boys in the school. Todd was not permitted to ride the school bus after cutting a two-inch slit in a seat.

Todd spent most of his time in the house when at home. This resulted from a neighbor complaining that he had pushed her nine-year-old daughter. Mrs. S's response was a harsh lecture to Todd. Todd always enjoyed visits to his maternal grandmother and eighteen-year-old uncle, who remained in the black community where the S family formerly lived. Mrs. S preferred Todd to have minimum contact with the former community, except for relatives, because of possible negative influences.

The counseling agency's consultation staff, which consisted of a psychiatrist with a psychoanalytic orientation, a clinical psychologist drawn toward behaviorism, two senior social workers, one black and one white, and both of the ego-oriented approach, recommended a casework supportive relationship to increase Todd's self esteem and to clarify the mother-son relationship. Weekly in-agency sessions were recommended, for which Todd would receive tokens, later to be cashed in for a toy or game that he could select based on his improved school attendance and his avoiding the drug store.

Assessment

Although characterological disorders and ego boundaries were a part of the consultation staffing, the following areas were not discussed:

ethnicity, value conflicts, ethnic self-identity or the alienated self of Mrs. S and Todd, racism through exclusionary tactics by the school and community, Mrs. S's responses to her neighbors, the school, and employment, exploration of positives for reconnectedness in the former community, and Todd's father's periodic presence. Further, a juvenile delinquency prevention program in a black community with an individual counseling and token economy system minus involvement of supportive systems of the target community were not addressed relative to Todd or other cases.

This youngster was devalued by his mother through her well-intended desire that he perform and succeed and her materialistic and individualistic values. Mrs. S was devalued economically in her employment. The school system was promoting the isolation of Todd; he then became a high risk for juvenile delinquency through the prevention program.

The concern of the black female counselor for the S family gradually altered the problem-solving plan to that of a systems approach with an educational and advocacy stance. Techniques of support were utilized where appropriate. These were:

1. An educational approach with Mrs. S focused on an examination of her life experiences, cultural matrix, relatives, and the rationale for her personal and family responses to the wider society.
2. Alternative responses to the school, her son, original family and community for Mrs. S to explore.
3. A refocus of ties for Todd in the black community through relatives, recreational activities with a black team, black history games, and supportive extended contact with relatives.
4. Advocacy by the counselor obtaining and interpreting the school system's policy on transportation and children's behaviors, with Mrs. S entering this process.
5. Role playing relative to the classroom setting and white students.
6. The counselor's entry to the elementary school for PTA speaker's forum to address broad issues.

These intervention approaches extended beyond agency sessions for the S family. Each of these plans were undergirded with humanistic values as well as an awareness of the range of consumable and nonconsumable products that are introduced in the black community by legal and illegal means. Mrs. S was attuned to these issues and for this reason thought that a "clean, quiet, middle-class community" would shield her and Todd from such problems; the recognition of the cyclical process that Pinderhughes described served to aid Mrs.

S in recognizing debilitating forces in her environment and evolved into her reordering her support resources.

Ethnic Content in Counseling

Appropriate use of ethnic content in the counseling process broadens the pluralism of service givers, decreases cultural dissonance, and enhances the commitment to humanistic problem resolution and prevention. Content in the human behavior base of counseling, particularly as related to the S case, should include an African perspective that negates the American view of adolescence that "new urges and powers suggest breaking the connectedness and collective attention. The social realities for many black youth compound the struggle and healthy strategies for living can only be gained within the collective family and community. A process of reestablishing ties, rechanneling energy and providing attentiveness, instructing from a structure of community, continuity and connectedness is the only response."[14]

Practitioners who have developed a basic understanding of the social conditions and the variety of adaptational responses that may be observed in the black community should also be aware of the influence their own values and those of the dominant culture have in the assessment process and the outcome of service. The ability to establish an effective helping relationship with Afro-Americans must be undergirded with the knowledge that cultural dissonance may result in misinterpretation and mistrust on the part of the practitioner as well as the individual or family. The helping agent's recognition of his or her own world view regarding the Afro-American family and attention to the sociocultural matrix in which functional as well as dysfunctional behaviors may develop are essential tools for practice.

The inclusion of such content would demand a reordering of the base of counseling, salient redefinition of and utilization of the relationship process, and reexamining how the communication process evolves; also crucial is a reordering of methodological approaches, because parent-child problems are often indicative of wider family and community problems. The issue of collectivism in the counseling process, in which the black individual's family and group goals are screened against the consequences for the global black community, dictates a humanistic process and behaviors based on the counselor having a sense of connectedness.

The final issue and implications of the behavioral response to powerlessness relates to the inappropriateness of traditional treatment models and the development of a quad-level model for counseling. Counseling a group of black single parents in conditions of poverty on parenting skills certainly suggests goals of improved interpersonal relations and social functioning. An examination of the cultural content and the parents' view of the world, however, may reveal the mutual aid and socialization functions of other family members.

Another level of socialization is experienced by a child's attendance in formal day care centers, churches, and schools. These resources have a responsibility to build on ethnic and cultural content and to be aware of the pervasiveness of racism rendering poverty. Counseling may take the role of consulting within recognition that many times parenting skills are in process with the community. The counselor learns from the community and must develop differential use of assessment, communication, relationship, and group facilitation skills from an advocacy stance to counteract the disruptive effects of oppression.

Toward a Quad-Level Systems Framework

The issues involved in counseling black clients lead toward a planned change problem-solving counseling process requiring multilevel intervention.[15] This suggests a social systems approach with focus on roles and behavioral responses of each system as they interact and transact. Although in many black situations counseling may not reach each level by the nature of the problems and the structural and functional roles within an agency or community, identifying the interlocking components of wider society systems, community systems, and family and individual systems from a stance of collectiveness, interdependence, and cooperation is essential to the effectiveness of this approach.

Individual System Assessment

When the individual system is viewed as an integral part of the family and community, the socialization process, value stances, emotional bonding, and feelings of responsibility to family and community are areas for exploration. The impact of the family and black community as well as subsystems of the wider society and the task behavior responses to racism must also be explored for accurate perception of interpersonal relations and social functioning in a pluralistic society.

Family System Assessment

The exploration of family social functioning encompasses the structural and functional roles of each family member in a process of interdependence, collectivism, and cooperation. The black family's concept of self, its individual members, its network, and its relationship and transactions with the black community and subsystems of

154

the wider society are crucial elements in the counseling process. Family values should be assessed for both African and white Euro-American-western perspectives to determine what works best for the family and the community as they negotiate the environmental systems of survival and achievement.

Black Community

Counseling from a black perspective requires an appreciation for the institutions or organizations of the black community that serve as mutual supports and socialization frameworks for black individuals and families. In communities where these institutions and organizations exist, their roles and functions must be understood and used as resources to enhance the development and functioning of black clients.

Subsystems of the Wider Society

Larger society subsystems are established to meet the needs of all citizens, but often they do not function in an equitable way when the element of color is interjected.[16] Black participation in the production, distribution, and consumption of goods and services has been less than desirable to meet basic needs and has implications for the quality of life experienced by black families. Although the family has primary responsibility for the socialization of its members, institutions such as schools, day care centers, churches, and so on transmit knowledge, larger society values, and expected behavior patterns. Given the content and quality of the educational systems addressed to the black population, services to strengthen the role of the black family in the socialization process merit greater attention. In the black community, the church, fraternal organizations, social clubs, and recreational groups are vital mediums of social participation. The connectedness of these social units to other community functions can provide service beyond that of religious and social expression.

Social control is a process through which a group influences the behavior of its members toward conformity with norms. Local, state, and federal governmental systems, the police, and the courts are examples of social control in American communities. Service givers must understand the operations of these systems with regard to racial minorities if they are to serve as advocates for black clients.

Mutual support on the local level is a community function performed by families, relatives, neighborhood groups, friendship groups, and local religious groups. The relevance of these functions in defined communities depends on the dimensions of relatedness of these institutions as they affect the community's autonomy, the

155

psychological identification of the community, and the community's horizontal pattern of structural and functional behavior patterns and systems.[17] Counseling the black American without knowledge of and interplay with the community resources tends to support a continued position of powerlessness.

Summary

Counseling from a black perspective is a problem-solving prevention process necessitating a historical perspective of black Americans' general position of powerlessness, and how this underclass status is circularly maintained through racism and the behavior responses of blacks to oppression.

Counseling must be undergirded with knowledge of black value systems that have an African base, and an understanding of how these values contrast with white (Euro-American-western) value systems. Knowledge of black individuals, family-kinship networks, and black community connectedness in a circular bond and the skills needed to develop that bond are crucial aspects of counseling.

Counseling requires the use of ethnic and black cultural content and a reordering of the concept of relationship and modes of communication, as well as content focus in the process. A theoretical framework of social systems, functional and structural role analysis, and a quad-level orientation to the black individual system, the black family system, black community systems, and the functional units of the larger societal systems would promote greater accuracy in perception of need and design of helping strategies. There is an obvious need for further study on the results of such an approach.

Notes

1. Andrew Billingsley, *Black Families in White America* (Englewood Cliffs, N.J.: Prentice-Hall, 1968), pp. 37-38.

2. Louis L. Knowles and Kenneth Prewitt, quoted in Elaine B. Pinderhughes, "Afro-Americans and Economic Dependency: Implications for the Future," *The Urban and Social Change Review* 12, no. 2 (Summer 1979): 25

3. National Urban League, *Black Families in the 1974-75 Depression: Special Policy Report* (Washington, D.C.: U.S. Government Printing Office, 1975), p. 1.

4. See National Urban League, *The State of Black America 1979* (New York: National Urban League, 1979).

5. Leon W. Chestang, *Character Development in a Hostile Environment,* Occasional Paper, no. 3 (Chicago: University of Chicago, School of Social Service Administration, 1972).

6. Wade W. Nobles, *A Formulative and Empirical Study of Black Families*, Grant no. 90-C-255 (Washington, D.C.: U. S. Government Printing Office, 1976), p. 34.

7. John S. Mbiti, *African Religions and Philosophies* (New York: Doubleday, 1969), p. 141.

8. Nobles, *Formulative and Empirical Study*, p. 176.

9. Andrew Billingsley, *The Evolution of The Black Family* (New York: National Urban League, 1976), p. 9.

10. Gayle J. Alexander, ed., *Social Service Delivery System in the Black Community During the Ante-Bellum Period: 1619-1860* (Atlanta, Ga.: Atlanta University School of Social Work, 1973).

11. Robert B. Hill, *The Strengths of Black Families* (New York: Emerson Hill, 1971), pp. 5-7.

12. Pinderhughes, "Afro Americans and Economic Dependency," p. 26.

13. Frances C. Welsing, "Mental Health: Etiology and Process," in *Mental Health: A Challenge to the Black Community*, ed. Lawrence Gary (Philadelphia: Dorrance, 1978).

14. Ibid., p. 54.

14. Thomas A. Gordon, "The Black Adolescent," in *Mental Health: A Challenge*, ed. Gary, pp. 119-31.

15. Ronald Lippit and Jeanne Walton, *Planned Change: A Comparative Study World of Principles and Techniques* (New York: Harcourt Brace Janovich, 1958).

16. Roland Warren, *The Community in America* (Chicago: Rand McNally, 1972).

17. Ibid., pp. 6-49.

Counseling Puerto Rican Families

Sally L. Romero

Descriptions and generalizations about cultural issues cannot be applied to all Puerto Ricans. Other variables such as sex, class, socioeconomic level, rural or urban origins, education, religion, occupation, racial identification, length of residence on the mainland and other factors affect how an individual Puerto Rican client behaves and the degree of his or her adherence to a particular belief system within the culture. Studies of subcultural and class groups on the island have revealed distinctive and contradictory behaviors, norms, and expectations and varying psychological dynamics, all of which affect the way a particular group of Puerto Ricans raise their children and conduct their own lives as adults. For example, differences abound among mountain farmers in the highlands of Puerto Rico, landless sugarcane workers from coastal areas, coffee and tobacco hacienda workers, small town, middle-class wage earners, urban slum dwellers in San Juan, and migrants from the island to the mainland's inner cities.[1]

There is a danger, therefore, in tagging certain labels or descriptions on to any ethnic group as if they will explain fully or in part the infinite range of adaptations and lifestyles within that culture. Just as many people may erroneously view all Hispanics as a homogeneous whole, so also can we treat all Puerto Rican clients as if they were the same, depending on the description given in the last workshop attended or the journal article or books read about Puerto Ricans. Although the social sciences are currently quite conscious of the concepts of cultural pluralism and ethnic diversity, the substance of what these concepts mean in terms of specific knowledge and curriculum content has only begun to be incorporated into the in-service or graduate training of social workers and other helping professionals. In other words, individualization or seeing each client as a unique individual *in relation* to his or her sociocultural framework is *still* a basic principle for work with minorities and all human beings.

Attitudes Toward Authority

The black experience in America cannot be viewed without its historical connection with slavery; the Puerto Rican experience cannot be viewed without its socioeconomic connection with colonialization under two world powers, and with the American presence on the island. Eduardo Seda, a social anthropologist who conducted two studies in 1957 and 1967 of Puerto Rican attitudes toward civil rights on the island, found that:

> A considerable number of people in Puerto Rico perceive themselves as dependent upon the absolute authority of the government. Since they conceive the state as limitless in its authority, they consider themselves helpless and dependent. In other words, a great segment of Puerto Rican society ignores the principles of how to organize the social processes that lead to a government by consent of the governed, to freedom to express and communicate one's positions in the political community, to tolerance of dissent, and to limitation of the authority of the state by civil rights.[2]

Others refer to this attitudinal stance as the "colonialist mentality or syndrome."[3] This has tremendous implications in terms of the Puerto Rican's attitude towards authority, feelings of dependency and powerlessness, and the application of the social work principle of self-determination to practice with Puerto Rican clients. How this orientation gets played out in the society and in the family structure is an area that is only beginning to be understood.

A Treatment Planning Tool

Some years ago, the author taught a course in Puerto Rican culture and social welfare at the Hunter College School of Social Work and gave the students the following assignment as one final project option: A paper describing your treatment of a Puerto Rican client in your agency. The following outline* was provided for their use as a psychosocial assessment and treatment planning tool:

PSYCHOSOCIAL SUMMARY

Client's Name (alias):
Area of Residence in N.Y.C.:
Agency:

---

*This outline is adapted from one used by social workers at the Puerto Rican Family Institute, New York, New York.

Worker:

1. Identifying Information About the Client

Name, birthdate or age, place of birth, (urban, rural, coastal, or mountain region), religious affiliation, marital status, number of children, age, sex (1st, 2nd, or 3rd generation), school attending, grades, employment history of adult family members in Puerto Rico, educational level, date of arrival in New York City, reasons for migration, length of residence in New York City, present occupation of adult family members, (skills), socioeconomic status (income range), living conditions, (housing, neighborhood), relatives living in New York City, in Puerto Rico, attitudes toward and perceptions of New York City environment, how client views migration as achieving his or her personal and familial goals, English language proficiency.

2. Presenting Problem and Reason for Referral to Agency: Source

3. Client's View of Problem and Motivation for Accepting Agency Services

Was it a self-referral or was client referred? How does your view of client's problem differ from client's perception? Does the client have a choice about accepting agency services. How does this affect his or her use of casework help?

4. Current Functioning of Client

(a) As seen in his or her social functioning in the areas of level of education, vocational choice and employment, relationships with various family members and friends, and recreational or leisure time interest. Primary patterns with which the client deals with life tasks and stresses that arise. Consider and highlight cultural aspects. Illustrate how the above are evidenced in dealing with current stresses, i.e., adjustment to New York City, separation from family and previous environment.

(b) As seen in social work contacts, does he or she verbalize easily or not? What is the quality of the client's characteristic way of relating to you, i.e., helpless, sees you as solving his or her problems; actively engaged, assertive, sees you as helping him or her to solve his problems and able to follow through (keeps appointments); not actively engaged, sees you as frightening authority who has to be avoided or guarded against, overtly hostile, etc. Attitudes toward worker (male or female). How does client's cultural orientation influence attitude toward accepting agency help and use of services being offered? Was language a handicap for client or worker? Language dominance (Spanish dominant or English dominant). Extent of assimilation to mainland values.

5. Pertinent Family Data—Past and Present (if known)

Socioeconomic, housing, employment, cultural, religious, and educational data for family members not covered in section 4, health of each member of client's family. Description of each family member seen by you (physical appearance, color identification). Patterns of family interaction and their affect on the client's problem. How do client and various family members view each other?

160

Lines of communication among family members. Status or role in family, primary identification (island or mainland orientation).

6. Psychosocial Impressions

Evaluate each client's social functioning in each of the areas outlined in section 4. Note manifest and latent problem areas in the client and various family members. Evaluate how the above affect their interpersonal relationships. What external systems are impinging on the client's ability to function in this environment?

7. Evaluation and Prognostic Statement

Client's motivation for using help. Note ego functioning that would enhance or hinder positive use of intervention.

8. Treatment Goal and Plan

State what you and client agreed to work on toward problem solving and how you plan to go about it. Spell out what areas of emotional and concrete help you will work on. Note any activity you plan on behalf of client, e.g., collateral contacts, community resources, and so on. Treatment methods utilized, that is, crisis intervention, group therapy, short-term therapy, family therapy, reality therapy, and so on.

Students were to discuss how the outline differed from the usual content or data gathered in their home agencies and what was their personal evaluation of how the sociocultural data influenced their handling of the case and the client's use of carework help. None of the students who took on this assignment was bilingual or Hispanic. However, in the process of engaging the client in this kind of history taking, the students communicated a kind of personal interest in their clients' background, a consideration of their family as a whole, and a concern for a broader understanding of what was going on in their lives, all of which facilitated the building of "confianza" or trust—and a greater movement toward problem resolution than they had anticipated.

All students pointed out that their agencies were not initially concerned about some of the material elicited, and that the size of their caseloads normally would interfere with their inquiring into such details during the intake process. However, all attested to gains students felt they had made in understanding their client's situation more fully, and in their ability to give more appropriate service.

Social Patterns and Concepts

A number of identifiable concepts and social patterns exist in the Puerto Rican culture that have direct implications for practice with Puerto Rican populations, depending on the particular individual's

161

experiental, psychosocial, and cultural history. As already stated, the conditions and specificity of other possible intervening variables must, however, be borne in mind.

Confianza

"Confianza" refers to rapport and trust. This requires more direct effort by the practitioner in order to establish sincerity of motivation and credibility. It may be acquired by using a more personalized approach, one that is more self-revealing and active than traditional approaches.

Community involvement, home visiting, recognition of the importance of food as a correlate to socialization and the conduct of business, acceptance of the Puerto Rican's hospitality and other more ritualized forms of social behavior will hasten the process of establishing the credibility of one who cares as opposed to one who is just doing a job.

Machismo, Marianismo, and Hembrismo

The concept of male dominance in Puerto Rican culture has been misinterpreted by non-Hispanics to mean a caste system based on sexual exploitation of the female.[4] The missing component of this interpretation, not understood fully by Anglos, is, however, its relationship to protectiveness toward and idealization of women, as personified in the figures of the Virgin Mary and Don Quijote. The dynamics of male superiority are often counterbalanced by the idea of "Marianismo,"[5] or veneration of Mary, through the doctrine of the Catholic Church. Women are thus viewed either as pure, sinless, sexless, sacrificing supermothers or as martyred victims of male ego-centrism.

"Hembrismo" recognizes—covertly if not always overtly—the significant role of women, their centrality and power in the home even when expressed in nondirective, manipulative ways. Although much deference and obeisance is still given in Puerto Rican families to the father as decision-maker and head of the household, this patriarchal role appears to be diminishing and becoming instead an ego-protective, social and public formality rather than a true picture of real authority. Power balances in the family, as in many cultures, have been affected by changing economic roles of women who work outside the home and may be at an advantage as breadwinners in lower-status families, as well as by the negative effects to men's self-concept in a setting where options for self-realization among the poor are limited.

Practitioners need to be sensitive to this by reaching out directly or personally to fathers or male clients in general, meeting them on job sites, if acceptable, or when they are apt to be available in the home, rather than going through their wives or mothers for appointments. By making every effort to include the men in treatment plans that may affect them and their children, we are strengthening their status and respecting their role in the family.

Compadrazco and Extended Family

The kinship network of godparents, or "compadre" and "comadre," to children, roles that transcend class and racial lines, extends mutual aid beyond the responsibilities usually assumed by blood kin. It provides additional substitutes for parenting and supportive roles in addition to family members, such as siblings, aunts, uncles, grandparents, in-laws, and cousins. Home-town clubs are also social groupings that can be useful. The sociolegal system of the United States addresses itself to the nuclear family as implemented in our income tax and social security laws, New York City housing authority regulations in the public service sector, and health insurance policies in the private sector. Dr. Lloyd Rogler Canino at the Fordham University Hispanic Research Center in New York City is conducting a major research project on the help-giving systems utilized by intact Puerto Rican families, which has for two generations aided them in coping with life on the mainland through stressing the positive aspects of these cultural linkages.[6]

We need to redefine the concept of family to include the extended family network and make constructive use of this potential for self-help by reaching out to engage these existing linkages on behalf of individual clients and Puerto Rican community groups. Local social service agencies can work to be incorporated by the Puerto Rican client as his or her "extended family" by replicating those aspects of the model that will help the family ride through their crises successfully, providing technical assistance, client advocacy, consultation when needed, as well as casework services.

Hijos de Crianza or Foster Children and Consensual Marriages

These two relationship patterns are sometimes aligned with each other when common law relationships or legal marriages result in children for whom one or both parents can no longer fulfill their child care responsibilities. Children are highly valued by Puerto Ricans. They are raised experiencing several adults in parenting and supervisory roles, whether individuals are related or not.

Many Puerto Rican mothers on the mainland will resort to sending children to relatives on the island when they fear or experience loss of parental authority and children begin to assert themselves according to Anglo ways or to present management problems in the home, school, or community. Puerto Ricans view this more often as an act of caring rather than of rejection, even though separation from the children becomes very painful. This movement of children and sometimes entire families between the island and the mainland may sometimes result in considerable disruption in children's lives and create more problems than it solves. However, it is viewed by the culture as a more acceptable alternative to placing children in impersonal mainland child care institutions that are not sensitized to their needs.

The notion of child placement has a different connotation for Puerto Rican parents, who, although accustomed to considering a "colegio," a parochial or private boarding school, as a place that will teach a child discipline and provide a safer, more closely supervised environment than they can offer in ghetto living in the inner cities, will balk at the idea of "signing their children away" to a child care institution on the mainland where they may not see them often, bring them home each weekend, or arrange for their discharge at will. Practitioners need to consider the meaning of placement in this environment and again determine whether members of the kinship system on the island or on the mainland can offer any kind of meaningful assistance or child care alternatives in lieu of institutionalization.

Socialization norms for children vary from island to mainland. Prized behaviors in Puerto Rican children consist of teaching them to be submissive and dependent, to have "respeto," respect for authority, tradition, and one's family, and to have "verguenza," regard for one's character and honor. Mainland values for Anglo children stress independence, initiative, assertiveness, less restriction and supervision of the female child, and self-accountability, rather than subordination to the wishes and needs of the family or significant others.

Primary social controls reinforced by many members of a small community exercise a restraining influence on individual behavior. The loss of these familial and societal supports on the mainland constitutes a major shift in the locus of control for children and adults. It becomes a debilitating factor in Puerto Rican parents' ability to maintain control over their children. The use of Puerto Rican children, who may be more fluent in English than their parents, as interpreters places children in a superordinate position over their parents. This practice unintentionally undermines parental authority because children begin to perceive their parents as inadequate to deal with the Anglo world. It is superfluous, perhaps, to point out the consequence of possible distortions in communications that may occur

164

between parent and practitioner when the child becomes the intermediate transmitter of information.

Parental fears and anxiety are particularly marked in terms of the close guardianship of female children, whose purity and virginity must be preserved until marriage. Contact with males must be carefully monitored through individual or group chaperonage, as long as the female remains unmarried. Although these patterns have undergone some change, especially in urban areas and among univerity students who live on campus away from home, females who live at home are expected to accept the protection and vigilance of all the male and female relatives against any possible lapse of controls over sexual behavior and, consequently, their reputation as respectable women. The family's honor and status in the community is also at stake if they do not fulfill these responsibilities as guardians of the female's reputation. You can anticipate what kind of conflict this engenders in urban mainland centers when Puerto Rican youngsters compare the freedoms allowed or taken by their peers from other cultures and what their own parents will permit. The issue of greater independence of children to move about outside the home, particularly the female, must be dealt with very slowly and with appropriate respect for the parents' values, bearing in mind the maturation level of the youngsters involved and their need to learn how to handle gradually increasing amounts of personal responsibility for their behavior.

Personalismo and Humanismo

These are interrelated concepts that address a kind of individualism that focuses on the inner importance of the person, or those inner qualities that constitute the uniqueness of the person and his or her self-worth. It is a traditional concept of quality based on the dignity of individuals in opposition to the increasing tendency in today's world to measure the worth of people by the cost and quantity of their possessions. Herein lies part of the Puerto Rican's idealization of the "jibaro" or mountaineer, a folk hero of island culture who personifies the more humanistic traits of a preindustrial society in Puerto Rico and of Hispanic culture in general.

It has been stated by Joseph P. Fitzpatrick that one of the Puerto Rican's greatest fears is that of relinquishing individuality to conformity to the group.[7] Although this appears to contradict the Puerto Ricans' great concern for conformity to community norms of behavior and accountability to a large circle of evaluators in the persons of peers, relatives, and acquaintances, it is not inconsistent with their heightened sensitivity to the feelings of others and how their personal

165

relationships may be negatively affected by their own behavior. The fact that the Puerto Ricans are constantly surrounded by people in their island community, whether in the home or outside of it, makes personal interactions and preservation of relationships at any cost a matter of serious concern.

Privacy is a luxury that the lower-status Puerto Rican is not accustomed to; it makes the isolation and anonymity of city life a much more stressful situation. One also encounters the difference in attitudes toward confidentiality, when what social workers consider to be confidential material is discussed by clients during a home visit in front of all those who may be present and may constitute their social network—neighbors, friends and so on—without apparent discomfort. Puerto Ricans more easily utilize the social network of their familial environment for aid and advice than the institutional network of counseling agencies on the mainland.

Politeness in conformity with the pattern of graciousness and subordinance to the needs of others, even if it causes personal inconvenience, is the keynote of social relations in Puerto Rican society.[8] Assertiveness and confrontation are avoided although this too is changing as Puerto Ricans raised on the mainland learn that survival often requires that the one whose voice is heard most often is the one who gets the "brass ring." Usually, a Puerto Rican has difficulty in giving a straight-out "no" to anyone. This, of course, has implications for the social worker, who may experience the client as ingratiating and very cooperative on the surface but later encounters resistance in other indirect ways. Although these behaviors can be evaluated in terms of their passive aggressive overtones, one must remember that the value system also mandates certain attitudes toward figures in authority, respect, and care not to offend or damage personal relationships. Therefore, the worker will need to consider this as an alternative motivation rather than conclude that the client is necessarily attempting to manipulate the worker.

Perspectives on Dependence Patterns

Ligia Vasquez Rodriguez points out how various historical governmental and social patterns impinge upon the Puerto Rican client's use of self-determination and reliance on others for problem resolution.[9] The delineation of the Puerto Rican's so-called passivity and dependency in the face of serious social and psychological problems must be viewed from several different perspectives:

1. An underlying fatalistic acceptance nurtured by some Puerto Ricans as part of their particular cultural interpretation of Catholic

166

tradition, which is embodied in two commonly used expressions—"Si Dios quiere" and "Ay bendito"—both of which put control of one's fate in the hands of God or other external forces, and a belief in spiritualism by substantial segments of the population, whereby "bad spirits" possess the body and mind of the one who is afflicted, and the client does not have to sustain personal guilt for behaviors unacceptable to the superego; concurrent use of folk therapies can be a useful tool with clients who believe in psiritualism.

2. The historical development of the island, which includes the effect of colonialization.

3. The history of extreme poverty on the island and its geographic limitations.

4. The nature of the political and economic relationship with the United States since 1898, which places the ultimate seat of power over island affairs in Washington D.C. rather than in the island's Commonwealth government. Puerto Ricans have already formed a pattern of perceiving and responding to Anglos and to American institutions when they migrate from the island to the mainland. Powerful exploitative forces that have historically operated on the island since 1898 have molded the particular pattern of adjustment and accommodation that the Puerto Rican has developed in order to survive.

5. The development of social work as an American transplanted model of service delivery under governmental auspices. This model is experienced by the Puerto Rican as an impersonal bureaucratic structure stamped with paternalistic attitudes.

6. Social work practice as a female-dominated occupation in a society in which a submissive-dependent pattern of behavior is encouraged for the female.

Need for Reeducation

The above factors may partially account for the Puerto Rican client's heavy reliance on the social worker as an authority figure who is expected to intervene directly in problem solving and to give concrete help and advice when requested.[10] The idea of the client assuming an active role in the solution of his or her problem is frightening and may be viewed as rejection or reluctance to help on the part of the social worker.

Lack of confidence and experience in asserting one's wishes and needs places clients at a disadvantage when it comes to the worker's expectations that Puerto Ricans will assume certain responsibilities for dealing with their problems, and even exercise their right to intervene on their own behalf and determine their own future. The more familiar pattern is for Puerto Ricans to rely on someone with greater power than themselves, one who has "pala" or pull.

Unfamiliarity with these special components and frustration with the clients' initial resistances may lead practitioners to make false assessments of the clients' readiness to move forward on casework plans, despite ready acquiescence and verbal commitments made to follow through on certain steps. A reeducative and developmental process must be followed in treatment in order to enable clients to feel confident enough in their own right to self-determination without violating their code of social etiquette.

Issues of Racial Identification

Unlike the American, the Puerto Rican has great difficult in using race as a criterion for identification. Coming from a racially mixed, fairly socially mobile society, the designation of a person as white, "trigueno," mixed, black, or any one of sixteen other semantic differentials of color depends largely on the attitude of the person making the judgment, and notions of class have a stronger bearing on that judgment. Julian H. Steward, a sociologist who has studied various subcultural groups on the island, comments that an individual becomes "whiter" in proportion to wealth or social class membership.[11] Exposure to American attitudes and sensitivities regarding race represents a serious threat to the self-concept of the Puerto Rican and is destructive to the unity of the family and community, particularly because members of the same family may vary considerably in racial characteristics.

Fitzpatrick reports in a paper dealing with the attitudes of Puerto Ricans toward color that, in a study of twenty young Puerto Rican addicts in New York City, all but one were the darkest children in their families.[12] Another medical study of migration and health among eighty Puerto Rican families concluded that anxiety over race and color was definitely related to the health problems of Puerto Rican migrants.[13] Piri Thomas's novel of his life in a New York City barrio poignantly described his struggle over his identity as the darkest son in a Puerto Rican family and his resultant diminished capacity to deal with the outside world, its definitions of race, and other related external realities.[14] Because no intermediate category exists in the mainland frame of reference, Puerto Ricans who fall in the "trigueno" group are the most vulnerable in terms of where they can be categorized on the race continuum. Their refusal to define themselves as black engenders much resentment and hostility by whites and also by black Americans, who perceive that Puerto Ricans are denying their blackness by clinging to their culture, language, and "foreign" ways.

Similar tensions exist in various segments of the black community, for example, between West Indians from the Caribbean, also of culturally and racially mixed backgrounds, and the black and Puerto Rican communities of the inner cities. Therapeutic work with Puerto Ricans must, therefore, deal with these nuances, sources of conflict, and stress, not only when the therapist is white but also when he or she is black.

Implications for Practice

Introspection into one's own attitudes as a practitioner toward poor, rural, racially mixed, culturally and linguistically different clients must be a precursor to work with Puerto Ricans. Although the above description more closely describes the island-born Puerto Rican client, we need to be aware that those living or born on the mainland, now some two and three generations removed from life on the island, are still nurtured by their parents and grandparents within the cultural context described. New forms and adaptations are emerging, as they will with any group of people coping in a different environment, that will call on other kinds of mechanisms than those formerly employed by the same group. These new forms may also sound dissonant to the mainland lifestyles of other groups, seeming to be even more deviant or different than those already described.

This newly created version of the traditional model, called the "Neorican," has become in many ways more alien and foreign to the people on the island and among other Hispanics than to those who have already grown used to them in New York City or other urban centers on the mainland. The reverse migration of Puerto Ricans to the island or any other area that has been taking place over the past few years has created as much disruption and puzzlement over who and what manner of person the Neorican is. Language problems, value conflicts, and behaviors strange and threatening to the islander's way of life make these Puerto Ricans marginal people and, in some instances, outcasts among their own. Young people and others who return or visit for the first time have verbalized this sense of disillusionment and disbelief that the journey to the land of their roots could be so painful.

Similar attitudes have been encountered among middle-class Puerto Rican professionals raised and educated in Puerto Rico who come to the inner cities of the mainland and have difficulty in understanding the lifestyles of Puerto Ricans here, seeing only the new adaptations

169

as perversions of their traditional values. They do not appreciate the fact that many families, whether intact or single-parent, struggle to raise their children amid very difficult circumstances and do a good job. Again, among some mental health professionals of other Hispanic origins, biased attitudes against Puerto Ricans who are poor permeate their professional behavior. Being Hispanic and speaking the language does not necessarily ensure that Puerto Rican clients will be well served. The hiring of bilingual personnel by Anglo agencies serving Puerto Rican clients does not relieve the agency of the responsibility to see that their client population receives competent and sympathetic help.

Engaging a Puerto Rican client in treatment beyond the meeting of his or her basic survival and concrete needs may take a longer period of time because of the many factors that impinge on his or her ego. Once trust is established, however, and the social worker from whatever ethnic or racial background is tuned into the value system of the Puerto Rican and allows himself or herself to enter into a more highly personalized and, perhaps, less formal relationship than that ordinarily prescribed in the established norms of practice, Puerto Rican clients, as any other client group, will respond to other forms of therapeutic intervention if needed.

Notes

1. Francisco Cordasco and Eugene Bucchioni, eds., *The Puerto Rican Experience* (Totowa, N.J.: Littlefield, Adams, 1973).

2. Eduardo Seda Bonilla, "The Normative Patterns of the Puerto Rican Family in Various Situational Contexts" (D.S.W. Diss., Columbia University, 1958), p. 24.

3. See Juan A. Silen, *We, The Puerto Rican People* (New York: Modern Reader, 1971), pp. 36-45; Gordon K. Lewis, *Puerto Rico: Freedom and Power in the Caribbean* (New York: Holt,. Rinehart and Winston, 1969), pp. 1-88; and Manuel Maldonado-Denis, *Puerto Rico: A Socio-Historic Interpretation* (New York: Vintage, 1972), pp. 1-130.

4. Manuel Diaz, Jr., "Who Invented Machismo?" Paper presented at the Puerto Rican Women's Conference, New York, November 1976.

5. Evelyn P. Stevens, "Machismo and Marianismo," *Society* 10 (September-October 1973): 57-63.

6. Lloyd H. Rogler, "Help Patterns in Intergenerational Puerto Rican Families," (Fordham University Hispanic Center, 1980).

7. Joseph P. Fitzpatrick, *Puerto Rican Americans: The Meaning of Migration to the Mainland* (Englewood Cliffs, N.J.: Prentice-Hall, 1971), pp. 26-28.

8. Edward W. Christensen, "Counseling Puerto Ricans: Some Cultural Considerations," *Personnel and Guidance Journal* 53 (January 1975): 349-56.

9. Ligia Vasquez de Rodriguez, "Social Work Practice in Puerto Rico," *Social Work* 18 (March 1973): 32-39.

10. Ibid., p. 38.

11. Julian H. Steward, ed., *The People of Puerto Rico* (Urbana, Ill.: University of Illinois Press, 1956), p. 74.

12. Joseph P. Fitzpatrick, "Attitudes of Puerto Ricans Toward Color." Paper presented at the Twentieth Annual Convention of the American Catholic Sociological Society, University of Notre Dame, Notre Dame, Indiana, 28-30 December 1958.

13. Beatrice B. Berle, *Eighty Puerto Rican Families in New York City: Health and Disease Studied in Context* (New York: Columbia University Press, 1958).

14. Piri Thomas, *Down These Mean Streets* (New York: New American Library, 1967).

171

The Clinician as Advocate: A Puerto Rican Perspective

Julio Morales, Jr.

Advocacy is a critical role for the clinician and has historical precedent. This role is essential whether or not an organization has a formalized advocacy program and staff specialists.

It is easy to document that advocacy has had a long tradition in the history of social welfare.[1] Historically, groups and individuals have championed the causes of specific neglected or vulnerable groups in society. Children, the elderly, and the retarded, for example, have had and continue to have advocates in our society. Many such advocates are affiliated with social services.

Nevertheless, problems facing children, the elderly, and the retarded are still very much with us, as are many of yesterday's problems confronting today's poor and minority groups—unemployment, discrimination, inadequate housing, poor health, poor education, and so on. Social service providers of the past and today continue to be forced to establish priorities regarding treatment or prevention. Inevitably, therefore, many service providers must use their skills, talents, and resources to plead, to defend, or to espouse the causes of their clients: to become advocates.

An Historical Perspective for Advocacy

In the past, advocates were often seen as reformers, and they spent much effort in attempting to solve the problems they faced by modifying societal arrangements; settlement houses typified this response. This reform orientation was always coupled with the perceived need to modify the behavior of the clients. Nevertheless, their advocacy—the reform orientation—led to child labor laws, fights against tuberculosis, struggles for the rights of women to vote, expansion of social

172

service benefits, and more. "Workmen's compensation laws, the White House Conference on Children, child labor laws, the establishment of the Children's Bureau and some of the social experiments of the New Deal can be attributed, in part, to the tradition and spirit of the settlement movement."[2]

From the 1930s to the early 1960s, advocacy and reform through advocacy took a back seat to the "development of rehabilitative technique and concomitant preoccupation with professionalization. Charles Grosser says, for example, "through the glass of self-conscious professionalization based on a methodology for the restoration of damaged individuals, an advocacy stance appeared somewhat inappropriate. Advocacy was not compatible with such professional values as clinical objectivity and neutrality."[3] Advocacy was viewed then, and to some extent is still viewed today, as overidentification with clients. During this time, social work became more of a system-maintaining profession than it had been prior to that. Bureaucratization of social work auspices, as agencies developed, grew and combined with professionalization and shied away from more traditional and accepted advocacy roles of the past. Traditional advocacy was seen more as being political, and counseling, through casework or group work, as more professional.

Advocacy and its reform orientation reappeared in the late 1950s and early 1960s. The civil rights movement, the war on poverty, and many other liberal ideologies and movements of the 1960s created a climate that was conducive to advocacy. However, this type of advocacy came at a time when much of the advocating and reform thrusts of the earlier periods discussed had become realities. Government now dominated the financing of social services. Welfare payments and other social security programs were realities.

The Client as Consumer

Advocacy language changed in the 1960s. Welfare providers started seeing people as clients—as consumers, not recipients. Their clients were entitled to services not as charity, but as benefits or rights that could be demanded through advocacy.

Social service advocates pushed for review procedures and due process for clients, laws that were more clear in terms of entitlements, and enforcement of housing and health codes. Expanded educational benefits were fought for and participation of clients was encouraged and, at times, mandated. Sometimes, advocacy was sanctioned and the powerless were seen as constituents. In 1968, the National Association of Social Workers endorsed advocacy as part of the professional's role. Advocacy, was then, theoretically, "in."

173

New allegiances between social workers and lawyers and progressive teachers were very much in vogue. This was a time of test cases, class actions, and court orders, to assert eligibility for poor people vis-à-vis society.

In addition, conflict with an agency or a colleague was not unusual. On some occasions, as in the community control struggles in New York City, many social workers joined grass-roots organizations and, at times, spearheaded movements to challenge the educational system and the established social service order. The sad part of this history is that despite the fact that conditions were ameliorated for hundreds of thousands of people, for others they remained the same and occasionally worsened. Too often it was the most organized, the most vociferous, those with the most power, those "ready to roll" that benefitted most. Compared with other special interest and more organized groups, Puerto Ricans did not benefit to the extent that others did. At times, advocacy became a way of moving within the system, and at other times, a way of pitting one group against another.

The advocacy of the 1970s was a great deal calmer. It became an institutionalized part of the American way of life. It became more of an intellectual fundraising mechanism, but one that to some extent built on the gains of the 1960s. Again, not having gained much in the 1960s, Puerto Ricans were left behind in the 1970s as well.

Assessment Strategies

Assessment from an historical perspective proves important for obtaining tools and placing situations in context. The specific advocacy techniques used then can be used today to advocate with and for Puerto Ricans and other minorities.

Education as an Advocacy Tool

Much advocacy literature places a tremendous amount of stress on education, thus raising people's consciousness. The logic is that when people learn the truth, when their consciousness changes, they will do more good—be less exploitative or not allow themselves to be exploited. Education is for those in and with authority and power as well as for those without power.

For education to be a truly revolutionary tool, however, depends on what truths are taught, who teaches, and who is truly willing to learn and have their consciousness raised. It also depends on how much energy or priority it receives. The importance of this advocacy mechanism is stressed in the model developed by Emelicia Mizio.[4]

Understanding that Puerto Rico was a colony of Spain and today

174

remains a colony of the United States[5] helps workers to understand the Puerto Rican personality, in terms of the strengths and problems that often characterize colonized people. Issues of passive-agressiveness, child-rearing practices, and so on take on a new dimension if, for example, Paulo Freire's understanding of oppressed people and Frantz Fanon's revelations of colonized people are applied to the Puerto Rican experience.[6]

Explaining the reasons why Puerto Ricans are now living in the United States and educating people to the needs and problems confronting Puerto Ricans in the United States may, again, be seen as using education as an advocacy strategy. Theoretically, the more known about why Puerto Ricans left the island, why they migrated to the United States, the forces that pushed them out of Puerto Rico and pulled them to the United States, the more one can appreciate the Puerto Rican experience. Using a political and economic interpretation of these forces can help in consciousness raising.

Comparisons

Such information must also include comparisons between Puerto Ricans and past European groups. Differences and similarities must be explained. Similarities are obvious; Puerto Ricans have a different culture, a different language, and face discrimination. They play the same role that other immigrants have played in the past and that black Americans still play, that is, one of providing nonskilled, cheap labor. In the past, however, one imigrant ethnic group replaced another in this role. As a new group arrived, it pushed the previous group up the socioeconomic ladder. Puerto Ricans must ask, "Who will push us into more desirable, less demeaning, better paying jobs and secure employment?"

Explaining that Puerto Ricans are not like past Europeans helps to bring attention to the fact that intervention mechanisms of yesterday may be less relevant today. It also places the problems confronted on a social system and not on a culture. Unlike the immigrants from Europe who were noncitizens, Puerto Ricans were made citizens, despite the fact that citizenship was not only not requested, but also argued against in Congress by Puerto Rican spokespersons.[7] Puerto Rico has been a colony of the United States since 1989. Puerto Ricans on the Island and in the United States have been used in the same way that colonized people in third-world countries have been utilized for centuries.

Equally important is the issue of race. The Jews, Italians, and Irish of past immigrations were white. Puerto Ricans are racially mixed, very few are white or black. The racism that exists in American society

175

places Puerto Ricans at a tremendous disadvantage. European immigrants faced discrimination because they were newcomers. Puerto Ricans face, in addition, racism. However, it is the "historical moment" itself that may make the most difference. As in the past, Puerto Ricans and blacks were initially recruited to northern cities after America's immigration restriction laws of the 1920s drastically reduced the incoming work force. They worked in marginal industries that tended to pay very low wages, gave little employment security, and offered few benefits. Historically, the bottom positions in America—work in sweatshops, factories, restaurants, hotels, and farms—have been relegated to the latest arrivals. In the past, as one group replaced the previous one, it automatically pushed its predecessor up the socioeconomic ladder. Immigrants took over the menial work that the group before them had done. Today, in our competitive society, blacks and Puerto Ricans simply lose ground to better organized and more politically powerful white ethnic groups. It should be pointed out that the competition existing today is based not only on race and ethnicity. To the ethnic queueing of the past, we must add the competition of women, the elderly, gays, the physically handicapped, the retarded, and so on.

In many cases, automation in this postindustrial society has made obsolete jobs that enabled past newcomers to begin an upward socioeconomic climb. Willingness to work is not enough. Unions, once identified as allies of the poor, are now more interested and involved in protecting those whose parents were poor in the past, but who are now part of America's middle class. Also, in the past, one could drop out of school and get a job. This is no longer possible, yet schools are not able to hold blacks and Puerto Ricans. Too often the curriculum is aimed at the white middle-class child. The result is another support for the present system.

Specific Strategies

Thus far, macro issues that adversely affect low-income people have been presented. Many of these problems could be alleviated if our society were different, and we must continue to advocate for such societal change. Social workers, however, must often intervene on behalf of specific individuals, and it is here that bilingualism, cultural knowledge, and understanding and acceptance of differences play a vital part in advocacy and service provision. Different child-rearing practices, different ways of looking at racial issues, different value priorities in terms of concepts such as dignity and respect, different orientations to community and family, different ways of looking at

176

the spiritual, and the use of spiritualism and folk medicine in healing are all differences that should be studied and understood.

Agencies must look at themselves and see how they are or are not incorporating this knowledge. Workers must advocate not only for bilingual and bicultural staff, they must also begin advocating for the standards of the model outlined in the *Puerto Rican Task Force Report*.[8] Thus, education can become a strategy for advocacy and an advocacy strategy itself. Accompanying clients through difficult bureaucratic procedures, while providing support and encouraging self-help, self-empowerment, and self-advocacy, is an absolutely essential aspect of education as advocacy.

Other advocacy strategies related to the area of education but directly involved with planning include the use of surveys and studies to document Puerto Rican need. There is so much still unknown about Puerto Rican poverty and need. For example, who are the Puerto Rican elderly? Where are they? Are they dying earlier or later than the elderly of other groups? Are nursing homes making appropriate use of Puerto Rican cultural and dietary lifestyles? Are they attempting to provide services to the Puerto Rican elderly? Results of such studies and surveys should be used to address immediately problems and issues uncovered.

Another frequently used advocacy strategy referred to in the model is the use of consultants to advocate, document, and aid in the better provision of services. Unfortunately, often experts and their testimony are considered of greater importance than the testimony, skills, and suggestions of line workers.

Another advocacy mechanism line workers can use as a strategy is that of intraagency case conferences about programs for Puerto Rican individuals, families, or communities or about problems confronting them. There is a tremendous positive value attached to committee work and to conferences, both within social service agencies and between them. Such mechanisms for advocacy are very possible and need not be threatening to workers or their agencies.

Other similar advocacy stances include research, particularly on underserved Puerto Rican groups such as the elderly previously mentioned. Findings could be utilized to demonstrate human need, identify service gaps, suggest service modification, and the like. Research should also focus on how Puerto Ricans cope with day care needs, health concerns, and so on, by examining the role of natural helping networks. This can be employed to help strengthen indigenous mechanisms for self-help and the development of Puerto Rican leadership. These are important advocacy goals.

Collaborating with lawyers, teachers, and other service providers

177

may be an excellent advocacy tactic, as is attending city, state, or national hearings on issues affecting clients. Testifying on behalf of a client or on behalf or programs and projects that will eradicate or alleviate the problems they confront are also effective advocacy tools.

Summary

Thus, education of clients by helping them to see their own oppression also helps them to understand that many of these problems have been structured and that they are victims. Helping them to see that their culture does clash with the dominant values can be part of any ongoing therapy, counseling, or other casework relationship. Reiterating that they are not disturbed, but need to be able to manipulate their environment is in and of itself a very good example of advocacy.

Other advocacy tools include educating the agency, its board, other personnel, and people in authority about the economic situation Puerto Ricans inherit, as well as the different way Puerto Ricans look at life; support of studies, research, surveys, and planning to aid Puerto Rican individuals, families, and communities; an awareness of planning projects that might hurt and the ability to take an effective stand on issues that affect clients; the use of consultants and expert testimony; and the use of administrative redress or making sure the client system knows about such mechanisms. More direct acts include petitions, demonstrations, letter writing, and entering the political arena. Building coalitions and working to develop demonstration projects are two more possible strategies. Another is working consciously to develop community leadership and keeping such leadership informed of issues that are important in an agency or community. Helping a Puerto Rican get on committees and boards will make advocacy on behalf of this group much easier.

The easiest and perhaps most important advocacy tools, however, are simply those of asking questions—about what is being done, how, why, and who is doing it or not doing it—and helping by pointing out weaknesses and contradictions while also offering suggestions.

These strategies for advocacy on behalf of and with Puerto Ricans are important and must continue to be undertaken. Advocacy must also be developed for a new reality, a new ideology—not one that often pits blacks against Puerto Ricans, Chicanos, the elderly, American Indians, women, gays, or other vulnerable groups; not one that advocates for a new social structure and an order that guarantees more equitable distribution of resources. Grosser suggests putting "political viability behind welfare state reforms."[9] The new ideology,

178

for example, should advocate for socialized medicine, universal education, low-income housing, and a guaranteed income.

Martin Rein, in *Social Policy*, says that caseworkers who come into contact with so many clients can help radicalize our society—perhaps to a much larger extent than many organizers or planners.[10] Caseworkers are in an excellent position to help clients understand their troubles, not solely from the prevalent pathology model, but from one that describes and analyzes present society as greatly contributing to the creation of that pathology. Grier and Cobbs, in *Black Rage*, believe that it is possible for clinicians to be very political. They say, "Let us enter a plea for clinicians who can distinguish unconscious depression from conscious desperation, paranoia from adaptive wariness, and who can tell the difference between a sick mind and a sick nation."[11]

Finally, practitioners must understand that the advocacy they do for blacks, Puerto Ricans, and other exploited groups must be the kind of advocacy that will lead to a nation that is healed. In addition to advocacy for specific client systems, they must also become involved in the broader struggle for human liberation and societal change.

Notes

1. See, for example, Esther Brown, *Social Work as a Profession* (New York: Russell Sage, 1942); Elizabeth Ferguson, *Social Work* (Philadelphia: J.B. Lippincott, 1974); Rufus Harris, *Social Work Education and the Elizabethan Era* (New Orleans: Tulane University, School of Social Work, 1958); Ernest Hollis, *Social Work Education in the United States* (New York: Columbia University Press, 1951); Ralph Kramer and Harry Sprecht, eds., *Readings in Community Organization Practice* (Englewood Cliffs, N.J.: Prentice-Hall, 1969); Martin Rein, *Social Policy* (New York: Random House, 1970); John M. Romanyshyn, *Social Welfare* (New York: Random House, 1971); Marjorie Smith, *Professional Education for Social Work in Britain: An Historical Account* (London: Allen and Unwin, 1965); and Roy Lubove, *The Professional Altruist: The Emergence of Social Work as a Career 1880-1930* (Cambridge, Mass.: Harvard University Press, 1965).

2. Kramer and Sprecht, *Community Organization*, p. 13.

3. Charles Grosser, "A Polemic on Advocacy," mimeographed, p. 5.

4. Emelicia Mizio, ed., *Puerto Rican Task Force Report: Project on Ethnicity* (New York: Family Service Association of America, 1979)

5. Despite its Commonwealth title, Puerto Rico was declared a colony by the United States in November 1978. See José A. Cabranes, "Puerto Rico: Out of the Colonial Closet," *Foreign Policy* 33 (Winter 1978).

6. Paulo Freire, *Pedagogy of the Oppressed* (New York: Herder and Herder, 1970); and Frantz Fanon, *The Wretched of the Earth* (New York: Grove Press, 1965).

7. See Manuel Maldonado-Denis, *Puerto Rico: A Socio-Historic Interpretation* (New York: Random House, 1972); and Cabranes, "Out of the Colonial Closet."

8. Mizio, *Puerto Rican Task Force.*

9. Grosser, "Advocacy."

10. Rein, *Social Policy.*

11. William H. Grier and Price M. Cobbs, *Black Rage* (New York: Bantam, 1969).

The "How-Tos" of Advocacy for the Caseworker

Howard Prunty

This article will concentrate on the "how-tos" of advocacy, but first it is necessary to define advocacy. There was a new advocacy that developed in the 1960s, different from what went on in the 1930s; and there is also something that evolved in the 1970s, a new type of advocacy that is occasionally difficult to understand and to apply to what is going on now. One hears the question "What is advocacy?" but there seem to be no real answers to it. Many workers in the field seek an answer to this question so that they can get out and do something. But what new kind of advocacy will evolve, and how will it be defined? Advocacy needs an operational definition and an elaboration of its major concepts. What should underlay the new intellectual approach to advocacy? What are some of the new theories? Answers will help to convey certain universal things to workers, and offer advice helpful to all of us about how best to advocate, individually as well as collectively.

Search for a Definition

At the first Family Service Association of America national conference on advocacy, held in Zion, Illinois, in June 1979, there were advocates from all over the country. One of the first things they did was to work on an operational definition of advocacy so that they could understand each other. A great deal of time was spent trying to define advocacy, because there were some serious differences about what advocacy meant. This controversy pointed clearly to the necessity of developing an operational definition rather than an intellectual one, but a definition that all could use. This process is still going on.

At this point, it might be helpful to say what advocacy is not. Ad-

181

vocacy is not confrontation, although many seem to feel that it is. Confrontation is certainly an advocacy technique that at some point has to be seriously considered and implemented. Neither should advocacy be perceived as community development, which differs from advocacy in the sense that advocates are not out to organize communities, although they support community development efforts. Advocacy has specific purposes and goals; it is more related to collaboration and coalition building than to community building and development. The latter takes a great deal of time, a lot of energy, and a tremendous amount of resources, and it has not proved very helpful in the past. The problems of the community action programs of the 1960s demonstrated that community building is a long, hard struggle with limited outcomes.

A Leadership Vacuum

Another area in which there is some difficulty is leadership. It is evident that there is a leadership vacuum in this country, from local neighborhoods to federal government. Community leaders can be developed through the process of advocating for specific social changes to eliminate or ameliorate the effect of problems that impinge on the lives of minorities and other oppressed groups. Out of necessity, the potential leaders begin by dealing with very specific kinds of problems, rather than by dealing with broader systemic problems, like changing the allocations of funds and other resources in this country, which is a longer-range problem and, ultimately, must also be dealt with in order for anything to be changed. There needs to be effective national health insurance, universal services, a guaranteed income, a right to employment, and so on.

These long-range problems have been ignored in the past and focus has been placed on specific kinds of issues by leaders, representatives, other politicians, and agencies. A simultaneous dual approach—of dealing with specific issues while keeping in mind the ultimate goal of basic societal change by a reallocation of wealth—is necessary, for workers as individuals and as representatives of agencies.

How to Advocate for a Client

Many front-line workers find themselves in an agency that has no advocacy program, is not primarily interested in it or perhaps gives only lip service to it. However, it is possible for a concerned worker to do something—even alone. It is possible to do things that move beyond theory, conferences, and bringing in consultants to do surveys. One of the first things that can be done is to recognize that there are a number of people coming into agencies who do not have

182

emotional and mental problems. In many agencies, particularly in urban centers, more and more minorities come to agencies for help and assistance; their behavior may seem very strange and erratic and these people can easily be diagnosed as having emotional problems, which may or may not be true.

How workers respond to the people who come for help is essential. It should be recognized that many of these people have serious social system problems and have spent a great deal of time, effort, energy, and resources in trying to cope with them. They have waged a losing battle. As an advocate, an individual social worker must first, therefore, shift the focus, even if it means going to the other extreme of refusing to see any emotional problem at all, and deal specifically with the more reality-oriented problem that they bring. Second, keeping the above differentiation in mind, it can be seen that the individual becomes an advocate on his or her own behalf, regardless how bizarre their behavior may be.

Really sick people do also come to agencies. They may have be depressed, be diagnosed as schizophrenic, and so on. This does not mean, however, that they cannot function and consider ways to change their situation. Here, a major role of the worker is to look at the problem and then discuss options with the client. The role is not to look at the emotional adjustment of the client but at the choices available, and then to help the client select an option.

This approach to advocacy has still just the worker and the client. But this can go a very long way to change the thrust of agencies. If enough workers do these things, then agencies certainly will change, because a different clientele will begin to come to agencies, a clientele with different expectations.

Case to Cause with Individual Clients

Another area of how-to is "case to cause." On a case-to-cause basis, workers will rush to the barricades for an individual client without reservation, but is is possible for an individual worker to do something differently. If a number of clients who come in have a specific kind of problem, it may be wise to get them together, and help them look at the problem, and make some decisions about resolving or ameliorating it.

This response moves caseworkers out of the one-to-one and into another arena, one specifically related to advocacy, because it concerns a given problem that has been identified by a number of clients. Sometimes it is not necessary to discuss this with one's supervisor; sometimes it is. In this process, workers have collected information

183

that can be shared with their supervisor, and this can constitute a mini-survey to support the thesis. Workers thus have an opportunity to educate their supervisors.

An Example of this Approach

The case-to-cause approach can be used with broader issues. It is possible to identify a specific problem with a client and focus on a specific problem as a rallying point. That is, identify a specific cause, a specific problem, define it, determine how best it should be approached (bearing in mind the client's priorities and abilities), and move on it for a specific period of time with the expectation of ending it successfully. For example, a woman living in a housing project with her four children, aged sixteen, fifteen, thirteen, and eight respectively, was having difficulty with them. One of the primary problems was that there were no good recreation facilities for the children. She wanted to try to protect her children from the negative influences in the community, a way of life she worried they might stray into that could lead them to trouble.

The worker, along with the mother, realized what the concerns were and asked, "What are you going to do about it? Are you willing to have a meeting at your house with other mothers in the project who feel the same way? If so, get them together and I'll back you up." The woman, although not well educated or very articulate, and although limited as a result of serious physical and emotional problems, pulled together a group of other mothers and discussed the problem. They decided how to go about finding a solution and identified organizations and individuals in the community who would be helpful to them. Each of them was given an assignment to see these potential helpers and to encourage them to assist the community.

Coalition building began. The worker, who kept in the background, had met with the mother and some of her friends during the course of building a coalition to set up a recreational facility in the community. In the process, the mothers identified six or eight organizations in the community who said they would be willing to do something. One, who said it wanted to do something, but only in its own way, was turned down by the mothers, who said, "If you are going to work with us, you are going to have to do what we want our way, the way we define it; not the way you feel you can be of use to us."

Within a period of six to eight weeks, there were firm plans made about who would be doing what, how a recreation center would be set up, where it would be, who would operate it, what role the mothers would play, what role the organizations would play, and what was the time frame. All of this was done by the client and her friends, with the assistance of the worker on a specific problem only. Individual workers can undertake such short-term advocacy projects that are time-limited and specific, with definite goals in mind. The clients use the worker as a consultant and back-up person who offers encouragement and support, but the clients draw on their own strengths to tackle the task themselves.

Internal Advocacy

Thus far, three methods of advocacy have been covered, without leaving casework. Now this article will consider other activities that grow from caseloads. There are some things that can be done about the problems seen every day. In agencies without an advocacy program, internal advocacy is necessary before a cause can be taken outside. This is where education and influence begin to be very important, as is the recognition that it cannot be done alone.

First, there is the possibility of a coalition in an agency with other minorities, or nonminority group members, if they have the same or similar interests. Working together, some specific areas for action by an agency or group of agencies can be defined. Suggestions can be made for reallocation of resources and pressure toward this goal can be applied. With definitions clarified, proposals can be presented to an agency's executive director. It is up to the executive director to make a decision about reallocating resources in the manner suggested. If it appears that appropriate action will not be taken, there are ways an agency can be urged to do so, and one of them is by going through the board.

Working with the Board

Most agencies assign staff members to staff-board committees. This provides an opportunity to work with board members in order to get an advocacy position across in an educated, informed way. It should be remembered that the purpose of staffing committees in this way is to bring to its attention all points of view. These views will be considered in the development of suggestions presented to the full board. Serving on these committees gives an opportunity to shape policy and to have some input into its development. Workers should volunteer to serve on such committees. It is hard work, but fascinating and informative. Workers learn that there are people in the community who have similar concerns and interests, people who want to do something, but frequently do not know how.

185

This is particularly true of minority group members who serve on boards. They are uncertain about what roles they are playing or should be playing. They need to have an opportunity to work with minority staff members so they can get an idea of what is expected of them and how staff can be helpful in the process of changing an agency. This is still close to casework and client-consumer relationships. In agencies where an individual has been given responsibility for being a part-time advocate, or where there is an advocacy program, what gets fed back into that program by the experience of the individual caseworker involved is vital as information and helpful in determining how the agency's advocacy resources will be used.

This leads to the process of building a coalition around a specific issue. A good deal of time and effort will be spent deciding with whom one should join around what particular issue. The issue involved will in great measure determine the size and number of groups involved. The number of issues that can be tackled will be determined by the nature of the issues and resources available for advocacy use. An agency can be working with four or five different groups simultaneously on four or five different advocacy issues, for example, recreation, housing, day care, and so on.

The Role of the Consultant

Another way of being an advocate is to serve as a consultant. An individual caseworker by serving as a consultant to another agency or by being a case conferee can become an advocate on a given problem. For example, in Massachusetts, during the midst of the coldest winter in recent memory, many poor people ran out of fuel oil and could not afford to buy any more. They used space heaters, stovetop and ovens, and all kinds of things occurred. In one family, a mother of five children died as a result of this. A local family agency became concerned about the family and aroused public sympathy for them. The department of public welfare was asked for $1800 to transport the children and the mother's body back to Puerto Rico. Many people did not understand why they should go back to Puerto Rico, why the woman could not be buried where she lived. The agency, however, understood the cultural orientation of the family and continued to put on pressure to secure the money. The woman's roots were back in Puerto Rico; that is where the family really lived, it was important for her to be buried there. Because this aspect of their cultural orientation was known by one small agency that wanted to help, the battle of getting welfare money was won.

It is this kind of understanding of culture that provides an opportunity to do something specific in the way of advocacy that conveys

186

the beauty of cultural orientation. It makes a point that can lead to a policy change. It does not take much time, energy, or board policy change. It does not take an advocacy program or an advocacy committee, just a little time by the agency to see an issue through, part and parcel of what they do from day to day. This sort of action also gives an agency some credibility with minorities, who appreciate the understanding that cultural differences must be taken into consideration. To some extent, there may be a policy change in a department of public welfare—perhaps an American Indian will benefit, one who has lived in Maine and whose burial ground is in Montana.

Becoming Politically Involved: An Example

In agencies with a lot of resources, it is possible to think about the many kinds of things that may be achieved through the political process. Individually, collectively, and in agencies, workers need to become more politically involved, to become part of the political process through testifying at hearings, holding press conferences, or trying to advocate for needed structural change. In the state of Massachusetts, for example, twenty-three new members were elected to the state assembly, twenty-one as representatives and two senators. Subsequently, Family Service Association of Greater Boston invited them to visit the agency. This was done for two reasons: First, politicians must often make decisions with limited or distorted information, and, second, in order to learn what the ramifications of a bill might be, representatives need to have knowledge and information about them. Too frequently, assembly members must make decisions without informed knowledge. The agency believed that, with its long history and accumulated wisdom, it could be of use in making some of its experience available to the new members of the assembly and, at the same time, convey its interest in legislation, particularly that which might have an impact on the family.

The agency offered itself as a resource, offering opinion about the impact of bills on families in as objective a manner as possible. The agency acknowledged its bias toward the family as an institution and the importance of individual family members. Whether a piece of legislation would be considered supportive of the family or detrimental to it was the basis on which information would be provided to political representatives.

The new representatives came to the agency for breakfast and, a week later, submitted questions about what agency staff thought of a proposed bill. Representatives want to be able to call on resources they can trust when deliberating about certain kinds of bills. Advocates waste an opportunity when they do not make similar kinds of service available to legislators, nor must an advocate be hesitant to be the first to approach political representatives. Expertise and knowledge should be shared with politicians as a means of moving toward more effective advocacy and toward achievement of the kind of systemic changes that are necessary today in this society.

Family Life Education

Elaine Johnson

This article has been developed to assess the applicability of family life education concepts developed by both the Family Service Association Task Force on Family Life Education, Development and Enrichment and the reports of the Family Service Association Project on Ethnicity. These documents are important in that they can be considered to represent guidelines for work in the areas of family life education and services to minorities and are having significant impact on the family service field. Key ideas from both reports are delineated and reviewed within the context of services to minorities.

Family life education ". . . is planned intervention by a skilled leader, applying the dynamic process of group learning to improve the quality of individual and family living."[1] When applying this definition to minorities, two other dimensions are significant. Family life education is not only planned by the leader, but planned in conjunction with members of the target population and representatives. Family life education not only seeks to improve family life, but also to identify the individual and cultural strengths that have created positive family living.

The general goals of family life education are improved self-esteem, development of role competency, and social functioning.[2] For minorities, these goals can be actualized in family life education by allowing participants to gain self-esteem through learning to clarify their roles, rights, and responsibilities, and through learning to make institutions and systems work for them. This type of learning views role competency and social functioning as dependent on both internal and external supports. It is important to note that the goals of family life education as outlined should be the same goals of the family agency in its delivery of services to minorities. The agency's self-esteem (image) with minorities should improve, the role of the agency as a provider of services to families becomes more effective (role competency), and social functioning in the community at large is broadened.

189

Family life education helps group members to understand and to anticipate the normal patterns and stresses of individual, family, and community living.[3] The minority group members focus on the stresses of community living more frequently. They seek to improve and expand their problem: solving capacities related to interpersonal and environmental concerns. The goals of family life education are realistic for minorities, as long as these goals include a recognition of external factors.

External and Internal Factors

Many minority family members often see their experiences as particular to them because they are minorities. They are often relieved that what they are feeling and thinking is shared by others, regardless of their ethnicity and socioeconomic status. For example, a mothers' group of black women were discussing the feeling of dissatisfaction with physical appearance. Their initial statements all indicated that these feelings related to some factor of growing up black, not having what they considered nice clothes, and little money for beauty treatments. However, when I told them that the cosmetic departments in most women's stores had the highest volume of sales, they were surprised. The group then discussed the emphasis on self-improvement and numerous books on diet, cosmetics, and the self as a trend.

The members became aware that these feelings were shared across ethnic-income levels and were not necessarily a result of being from a particular ethnic or income group. This kind of education is crucial for participants. The skilled family life educator must be able to direct the group discussion in order to learn whether the issue, problem, or crisis being experienced is a factor of ethnicity, lack of information in general, or an environmental problem. This skill is important in maintaining the group participation.

If the group leader discusses a topic as if it is individually based, the group members will experience more frustration. Equally as important, the leader must not respond to all concerns as rooted in the external environment. One way to avoid either pitfall is to engage the group in a holistic view and allow the members to give direction to its source. For example, a mother was describing feeling like a failure because her child did not like school and wanted to leave in the middle of the day. His school work was good and there were no other behavior problems. She valued education but was told that she was probably sending some unconscious message to him not to stay in school. When she referred to his teacher during her discussion, the group members suggested she visit his classroom. They all either verbally or nonverbally indicated some negative experiences with this teacher. The parents emphasized that the child's lukewarm attitude about his teacher was an important clue to follow up. School phobia was then discussed with the group, emphasizing the counseling role. This allowed the mother to follow two courses of action and not to assume that the problem was totally based on the family relationship or that it was totally the school's responsibility.

Providing Agency Support

Family life education provides both an intellectual and emotional experience. Family life education often overlaps with the problem-solving approach of family counseling and the action orientation of advocacy.[4] There is no possible way these three components can be operationally separated in delivering family life education to minorities. The saying expressed frequently by minorities, "talk is cheap," reflects their expectation in problem solving. The group members will often want action, either by the agency or another source. The agency must respond as appropriate. This action is addressed in any other family life education group. The difference is that other participants have a wider choice of groups and organizations to address their needs. In the initial design of the New Orleans family life education program, counseling was not offered as a part of the total service package.

When a family is referred to the agency, the probability of follow through is lessened. The family life educator must be able to at least offer an initial brief intervention to support the minority client through the referral period.

Situational Crises

Family life education's theoretical base is found in crises and systems theory. Crisis theory states that individuals go through maturational and situational crises as they go through developmental stages.[5] For minorities, there are often more situational crises. Knowledge of the typical crisis points and stages is necessary in delivering family life education. It gives direction to the groups that might more likely respond to the services. The following is an outline of some situational crises and the corresponding crises that may additionally be experienced by minorities:

1. Birth of the first baby versus birth of every baby.
2. Moving to new neighborhood versus remaining in deteriorating neighborhood.
3. Loss of spouse versus abandonment of spouse.

191

4. Retirement versus lay off.

5. Increased income by returning to work versus decrease in assistance by return (food stamps, day care).

The outline indicates another function of family life education. The group discussion can help minimize the crises impact by helping members plan as many changes as possible and by recognizing their own knowledge base and coping skills. Systems theory offers an additional significance for the group. The group members' experiences will affect others who are not a part of the group.

Value Systems

All areas of family life education are value laden. Values encompass certain ideas, feelings, and ways of acting to which we attribute a high regard of worth. The family life educator must develop an awareness of the values on which he or she operates. Additionally, the worker must help participants to analyze, clarify, and determine their own values.[6] The family life educator's values do not have to be the same as those of the participants. It is important to focus on the group members values as related to a specific subject of interest to them. The members might be asked, "What are you hoping will happen by having this as a value?" "Is it happening?" "Have you achieved your goal in the past?" For example, when applied to a topic such as the importance of the entire family eating nightly at the dinner table, many parents rethink this value. When they all eat together it is often felt to be contrived. Although the value of the family dinner remains important, another value takes precedence—flexibility to meet the needs of all family members. Often members can manage comfortably a weekly meal together.

The following are basic values to family life education that everyone must internalize:

1. Everyone has the freedom and right of his or her own life.
2. Everyone has the innate capacity for growth and development.
3. Uniqueness and individuality must be respected.
4. Marriage and family life may take many forms.
5. Family life education is a preventive process.
6. The group process is a valuable medium for learning and interaction.

Target Participants

An important element in developing a family life education program is the defining of the target participants. In actuality, they should never be a race, ethnic, or class population. The target participants have to be defined around the anticipated or already defined crisis points. Although a few were listed earlier, many can be learned from contacting a broad representation of the target population. For example, a survey of learning needs of Hispanics will give some information, but an understanding of the crisis points of Hispanics will define the target Hispanic participants. This distinction between target population and target participants is necessary for program planning. Contacts with resources that serve minority families, such as schools, hospitals, neighborhood centers, day care centers, and city welfare offices will give some indications for target participants. The more specific participant groups seem to respond more favorably to family life education than groups formed from an open intake-recruitment system.

Because many groups are parents' groups, some additional factors have been identified that determine parent participation. When the child or children of parents are receiving some type of service simultaneously, the participation of the parents will increase. Also, parents who are receiving counseling or another service from the agency will often participate in family life education. The location of the group is important. Although many minority families have difficulty with transportation to needed services, a group may get a more favorable response if it is not located in the facility that houses the neighborhood mental health center, welfare office, or probation department. An educational setting such as a school, day care center, or church might be a better choice. The choice of facility depends on the view of it by potential participants.

Elements for Consideration

The following is a partial list of elements that interplay in the success or failure of a family life education program:
1. Sources need to be educated in order to make appropriate referrals. The worker may have to accept some participants who are not necessarily ideal in this process. This requires the worker to have basic diagnostic skills so that he or she can monitor these participants carefully.
2. Referral sources should be given feedback about the group and specific clients. Client feedback will require written client consent.
3. Because family life education will often identify advocacy issues, a board committee on family life education may need to be established.
4. Always give participants an opportunity to establish some of the contents and evaluation of the group.

193

5. Develop some type of reminder of meetings such as postcards or telephone calls by group members or a group leader.

6. The worker must be available to participate in community activities.

7. The racial and ethnic identification of the worker must not be assumed to make the task easier or more difficult. Minority or white workers who attempt to build their linkage with the target participants on a superficial basis will meet with failure.

8. In establishing a program, the agency should start on a small scale and then build. The worker needs a specific percentage time to develop the program rather than an initial target number of groups to be formed. The number of groups can be realistically established at a later point.

9. Validation of the worth of family life education must be actualized in the agency by modification of traditional evaluations, allocation of management support time, and staff development opportunities.

10. Additional tools needed by the worker are creativity (lots of it), flexibility, sound ego development, ability to share and be open, knowledge of community, and common sense.

Conclusion

Family life education can provide needed skills and information to minorities who want help with child rearing and family problems. Family agencies should provide not only family life education, but counseling and advocacy services in order to respond to the needs of these families.

The basis of a sound family life education program comprises thoughtful planning within the agency and with the target participants. The staff should not only be skilled in family life education, but must also have an understanding of the environment and culture of the participants. The family life educator must have access to counseling and advocacy services when necessary. Therefore, the agency must establish an integrative approach to the delivery of family life education to minorities.

Notes

1. Family Service Association of America, *Overview of Findings of the F.S.A.A. Task Force on Family Life Education, Development, and Enrichment* (New York: Family Service Association of America, 1976), p. 2.

2. Ibid.

3. Ibid.

4. Emelicia Mizio, ed., *Puerto Rican Task Force Report: Project on Ethnicity* (New York: Family Service Association of America, 1979), p. 39.

5. Family Service Association of America, *Overview of Findings*, p. 5.

6. Ibid., p. 10.

Reflections on the Cross-Cultural Racial Relationship

Evelyn W. Robinson

This is a personal statement, written after many years of working with the poor. As the percentage of poor in the community in which I work is higher in the black and Puerto Rican population, my experience has largely been with those particular groups. The seeds of racism in our society have been nurtured and allowed to flourish with devastating results. Consciousness of the extent to which racism has become institutionalized has given rise to new scrutiny of education and practice in the social work field. During the 1960s and 1970s, much was published in professional journals about the client-worker relationship in terms of differences of race or ethnicity. Social workers who were either doing counseling or supervising during those years were inundated by "research" that indicated the ineffectiveness of cross-racial counseling and instilled in many workers such guilt that immobilization often occurred. Anglo workers were accused of paternalism, reactive fear, projection, sexual anxiety, inhibition, excessive sympathy, and so on.

No doubt many workers, raised in a racist society, suffered from one or several of these factors and still do. For some, awareness and self-examination has given rise to further opportunity to study, comprehend, and accept themselves as professionals dealing with clients who are troubled and who bring with them an additional dimension to the problem for which they seek help. Social work has its own unique body of knowledge. When a client comes for counseling, all that knowledge and skill must be brought into play toward attainment of the goal that is mutually decided on by client and worker.

Gaps in Education and Training

Identification of the problem is the first step in counseling. Does one's prejudice and lack of understanding interfere with development of the helping relationship? That relationship, of necessity, is based on respect, knowledge, and trust. In the cross-cultural relation between a white Anglo worker and black or Puerto Rican clients, the worker must have empathy for these persons and their situation—respect as an individual with appreciation of the impact of racism upon him or her. The worker must have an understanding of the background, culture, value system, and the economic and social status of these clients. What is also a must is that workers have full recognizance of racism's impact on themselves—all this if they are to gain the client's trust.

Unfortunately, social work education has offered little preparation for workers dealing with clients whose ethnic or racial backgrounds differ from the norm of middle-class white. In the past few years, black and Hispanic studies have been incorporated into the curriculum, but on an elective basis. There is little to prepare workers to deal with individuals and families who are economically deprived, in poor health, undereducated, lacking job skills, or having little self-esteem. It appears that even now—at least in the school that I know best—casework students are being prepared to work with middle-class clients. Psychodynamic material, universal as a base for understanding human behavior, is taught, but omitting the overlay the effects of class and culture have. More emphasis on the latter is incorporated in some community organization curricula, but should be more widely recognized as vital to solid knowledge of casework.

Historical and Prevailing Problems

Many years ago, as a beginning welfare worker in a public agency, I was appalled by the attitude of the staff. Apparently sanctioned by the administration (a professional administration)—certainly not discouraged by them—workers called clients by their first names, talked down to them, and looked under beds and into refrigerators when visiting their homes—"to check." To the workers, clients were suspect of fraud—the primary focus was less eligibility. Staff was almost always white; the clients were black, white, and Puerto Rican. Client hostility was expressed by passivity, "Uncle Toming," and, occasionally, when these coping mechanisms failed, aggression. Workers used their power to give or withhold financial assistance, which was supported by the administrative staff. Little help or encouragement was given to staff to look at themselves and their interaction with clients. Differential treatment between white and minority clients was obvious. Black workers were in the main as hostile as the white workers toward their black clients, ashamed and angry at those who "shamed them by being inferior."

At that time there were no Puerto Rican social workers in the community. The tobacco growers were importing hundreds of Puerto Ricans to work in the tobacco fields. After the growing season, many of these immigrants chose to remain in the area and, with no skills (except farming) and no education, they had difficulty finding employment. Welfare was the only immediate answer, and successful interviewing in Spanish was problematic. At that time there were no Puerto Rican college graduates (one of the job requirements), but there were Cubans. The basic language was the same, but the culture was different—class certainly was different—and the hostility between client and worker was apparent. Only rarely was an attempt made at working through these feelings.

On the highest administrative level there was no recognition of the work that had to be done to eliminate racism. Instead, there was a rather paternalistic direction to the support that was given.

As a supervisor in that agency I had a young black male M.S.W. worker assigned to me. Punitive and rejecting of all his clients, he could not accept supervision from me. I tried to raise the issue of black male worker versus white female supervisor, but he could not accept this. The administration decided that it was a "personality conflict" and transferred him to a black male M.S.W. supervisor. He could not work through his pervasive hostility and was finally encouraged to leave the agency. Race, in this instance, was not a factor. As supervisors, we must continue to expect the best work from all our staff workers, and to attempt to deal with our own feelings as we do with the feelings of our clients.

The Move toward Comprehensive Staffing

The Institute for the Hispanic Family, where I am presently employed, is a program of Catholic Family Services of Hartford, Connecticut. This agency had, in past years, developed a unit of workers geared to serve black clients and another unit to serve Spanish-speaking clients. Services to the black community were conducted from the parent agency and in housing projects with a high concentration of black families. Black workers saw only black clients. But change is occurring; black workers are now seeing white clients as well as black. Those workers who have M.S.W.'s are often in conflict, wishing to serve their own people, but feel that their training has prepared them

198

to work with others. I would expect that help is available to them to sort out their feelings so that they would be freer to give good service to all their clients.

The Spanish-speaking unit moved away from the parent agency, developing a unit in a area of the city densely populated by Puerto Ricans. The Institute began as a training-educational program for bilingual, bicultural high school graduates, directed toward social services for Hispanic families and individuals. Approximately forty persons have completed the program, earning thirty college credits each. About half of the students have continued their education on a full-time and part-time basis, and almost 90 percent of the total number of graduates are employed in social service and educational settings. Having experience in supervision of staff and students, I was asked to take on responsibility as field work supervisor. I now supervise direct services staff and am the only Anglo involved in supervision of Puerto Rican paraprofessional staff. I have learned much from this experience.

Developing Respect for Each Other

It was crucial for me, as a middle-aged Anglo professional person, to examine my prejudices as I viewed and worked with a variety of students, all of whom had different lifestyles, different political viewpoints, different responses to me as authority, different levels of socialization, different backgrounds (those born in Puerto Rico and those born on the mainland), and different ways of absorbing, keeping, or discarding their cultural heritage and traditions. I struggled with this—with the rejection of me and the acceptance of me—and we all won (my students and I); *respeto* in the Puerto Rican culture is a dominant value and as they saw my respect for them, my willingness to learn and to change, they developed respect for me and they learned.

Although I do not do direct counseling with clients—my Spanish is simply not up to it at present—I am often able to share an interview with one of the paraprofessionals I supervise. Although my words in Spanish are stilted and are sometimes translated by the paraprofessional, apparently the empathy is felt, and the concern is recognized, and *confianza* is built.

Summary

In addition to the cultural and racial relationships in social work there are several other similar issues that might be examined:

1. The Puerto Rican upper middle-class worker working with a Puerto Rican of a lower socioeconomic group often lacks knowledge of many of the problems of the poor.

2. The Puerto Rican worker, newly arrived from Puerto Rico, faces a different kind of racism from that in the island, and the uncertainty in clinical practice that that raises should be addressed.

3. The Puerto Rican client may not want a Puerto Rican worker, thinking that it is in his best interest to have a more powerful white worker who can more easily command resources.

At present, power and clout is with the white Anglo. We must use it to educate, advocate, and abdicate power to those who are presently powerless. I began by saying that this was a personal statement, and I would continue by saying that it is my profound belief that, with a solid background in the body of social work knowledge and practice, with a knowledge of the culture, with understanding and trust, with respect, and with an understanding of one's motivation to work with a different ethnic group, one can effectively work with clients in a cross-cultural racial situation.

Contributors

Salvatore Ambrosino, Executive Director, Family Service Association of Nassau County, Hempstead, New York

Anita J. Delaney, Assistant Director, Ethnicity Project, Family Service Association of America, New York, New York

Melvin Delgado, Ph.D., Associate Professor, Boston University School of Social Work, Boston, Massachusetts

Elaine Johnson, Director of Advocacy Programs, Family Service Society, New Orleans, Louisiana

Samuel O. Miller, Associate Professor, Columbia University School or Social Work, New York, New York

Emelicia Mizio, Director, Ethnicity Project, Family Service Association of America, New York, New York

Julio Morales, Jr., Ph.D., Associate Professor, University of Connecticut School of Social Work, West Hartford, Connecticut

Howard Prunty, Director of Advocacy, Family Service Association of Greater Boston, Boston, Massachusetts

Evelyn Robinson, Field Supervisor, Institute for the Hispanic Family, Hartford, Connecticut

Sally Romero, Ph.D. Candidate, Graduate School of Education, Fordham University, New York, New York

Howard J. Stanback, Ph.D. Assistant Dean, University of Connecticut School of Social Work, West Hartford, Connecticut

Naomi T. Ward, Assistant Professor, Atlanta University School of Social Work, Atlanta, Georgia

Advisory Committee
Family Service Association of America
Ethnicity Project

Leon Chestang, Ph.D., University of Chicago School of Social Service Administration, Chicago, Illinois

Manual Diaz, Jr., Fordham University at Lincoln Center, New York, New York

Geraldine Ellington, University of Detroit Detroit, Michigan
Augustin Gonzales, Puerto Rican Family Institute, New York, New York

Anthony Ishisaka, Ph.D.,University of Washington, Seattle, Washington

Ronald Lewis, D.S.W., University of Wisconsin School of Social Welfare, Milwaukee, Wisconsin

Ernesto Loperena, Aspria of New York, New York, New York

Corneida Lovell, Newark Day Center, Newark, New Jersey

Patrick V. Riley, Family Service Association of Greater Boston, Boston, Massachusetts

Frederico Souffle, Chicano Training Center, Houston, Texas

John Spiegel, M.D., Brandeis University, Waltham, Massachusetts